Domestic Violence

The Northeastern Series on Gender, Crime, and Law
    Editor: Claire Renzetti

For a complete list of books available in this series, please visit www.upne.com

Methodologies
in Dialogue

Domestic
Violence

Edited with commentaries
by Chitra Raghavan
and Shuki J. Cohen

Northeastern University Press   BOSTON

Northeastern University Press

An imprint of University Press of New England

www.upne.com

© 2013 Northeastern University

Manufactured in the United States of America

Typeset in Minion Pro and Optima by Integrated Publishing Solutions

University Press of New England is a member of the Green
Press Initiative. The paper used in this book meets their
minimum requirement for recycled paper.

For permission to reproduce any of the material in this book,
contact Permissions, University Press of New England,
One Court Street, Suite 250, Lebanon, NH 03766; or visit
www.upne.com

Library of Congress Cataloging-in-Publication Data
Domestic violence: methodologies in dialogue / edited with
commentaries by Chitra Raghavan and Shuki J. Cohen.
    pages cm.—(The Northeastern series on gender, crime, and law)
Includes index.
ISBN 978-1-55553-829-3 (cloth: alk. paper)—
ISBN 978-1-55553-830-9 (pbk.: alk. paper)—
ISBN 978-1-55553-831-6 (ebook)
1. Intimate partner violence.   2. Marital violence.
3. Family violence.   I. Raghavan, Chitra.   II. Cohen, Shuki J.
HV6626. D66757   2013
362.82'92—dc23   2013022651

5 4 3 2 1

Cover: Feeling Like a Cockroach, Soraida Martinez, 36″ x 48″, c1995, Verdadism painting, acrylic on canvas. Soraida Martinez is a New York–born artist of Puerto Rican heritage who since 1992 has been known for creating the art of "Verdadism," a contemporary form of the hardedge painting style in which every painting is accompanied by a written social commentary. Soraida's paintings depict her life experiences for the purpose of promoting peace, tolerance, and understanding. Soraida's Verdadism art can be seen at www.soraida.com.

Contents

Introduction

This volume brings together various methodologies of inquiry within the social sciences that expose and sensitize students to research, policy, and substantive issues in domestic abuse or intimate partner violence—issues that have a direct impact on people's lives.* Research in intimate partner violence has—and still is—hotly debated by researchers, policy makers, legislators, and activists. Indeed, many believe that the high stakes involved make any inquiry on this subject matter unavoidably political. Consequently, this volume illustrates not only the methodologies used to study intimate partner violence but also how the methods, results, and interpretative frames can inform current debates and, vice versa, how current debates can affect researchers' agenda and preferences.

This volume is divided into four parts, each of which broadly represents important facets of partner violence research. Within each part, two studies using different methodologies that address a similar research question are presented. Each chapter is preceded by learning objectives that focus on increasing the reader's methodological framework and contextualizing this framework within the broader study of sex and gender. Following each chapter, critical-thinking questions help to stimulate a broader discussion on methods, results, and interpretative frames. The critical-thinking questions are divided into general and advanced, giving flexibility to the instructor to assign more difficult questions to advanced students. Each part also concludes with a commentary, in which we explicitly adopt the stance that no one methodology is superior to the other, with the view to both synthesize and unpack the implicit assumptions, implications, and consequences of the individual chapters' methodological choices. We believe this is important because in real life a method alone is only as relevant

*Abuse against an intimate partner or spouse has been referred to by a variety of related terms, including domestic violence, intimate partner violence, intimate partner abuse, dating violence, and spousal abuse. In this book, authors approach the issue using any or some of these labels, as customary within their field.

as the question it is trying to answer, the question is sometimes constrained by the available methodology, and, all things being equal, the question can have different meanings when posed to different populations. The commentaries and critical-thinking question also emphasize a key theme throughout this text—that all research decisions are tied to some philosophical belief, whether or not we realize it (Slife and Williams, 1995).

The internal structure of the book is intended to facilitate teaching and presenting its main points, both methodologically and conceptually with respect to how one might address partner violence in and of itself as a phenomenon. Accordingly, we introduce the reader to definitions and measurements of partner violence (part 1: What Is Domestic Violence and How Do We Measure It?), various ways to read and interpret claims about gender parity and asymmetry data (part 2: Claims about Gender Parity and Domestic Violence: Six Blind Men and an Elephant), same sex violence (part 3: Dating Violence among Sexual Minorities) and the complex role of the criminal justice system on survivors (part 4: Systemic Revictimization). Further, to broaden the scope of students' exposure to different approaches within the social sciences and more specifically, psychology, clinical psychologists from the United States were matched with forensic psychologists from Brazil in part 1; clinical psychologists with a sociologist/social worker and community psychologists in part 2; a clinical psychologist and social policy analyst in part 3; and a psychoanalyst with the same social worker now writing as an expert forensic evaluator in part 4. The book concludes with a chapter by Keith A. Markus and others that interrogates the separation between quantitative and qualitative methods.

While a primary goal of this book is to expose students to applications of different research methodologies, such a discussion cannot be separated from the substantive concerns regarding partner violence. Thus, while contrasting various methodologies within the field of intimate partner violence research, the chapters of this book also illustrate crucial debates in the field. Among the ever-present debates that permeate this book is whether intimate partner violence is a gendered, culture-bound, or class-based phenomenon or whether it is a relatively universal phenomena that does not vary significantly across different groups. We do not try to comprehensively cover all points in these debates, but rather flesh out the key arguments and explicate them sufficiently to make the newcomers into the field familiar with the larger context and climate in which this research is being conducted today. A general understanding of these debates should enhance the students' sensitivity to the underlying tensions implicit in the literature regarding the gendered and contextual nature of intimate partner violence and thus the implications of both the research methodology and the research question.

The two primary debate positions in partner violence research are as follows. The first view holds that women hit male intimate partners equally or at higher rates than men hit female partners (e.g., Archer, 2002; Straus, 2006), for the same reasons and with the same outcomes (e.g., Dutton, 2006). Data used to support this position are generally quantitative (e.g., Straus 2006), emphasize large-scale survey data, and use data from community and college student populations (e.g., Archer, 2002), although a more recent review includes data from various populations (Langhinrichsen-Rohling et al., 2012). Further, central to this view is the association of discrete physical assault with abuse and a corresponding exclusion of measurements of power, control, and fear (Hayes, 2012; Stark, 2012). These studies may at times even aggregate different degrees of violence (severe and less severe) and by doing so create a generalized construct of physical violence that often evinces greater gender parity than more nuanced and context-rich studies.*

Based on these data, proponents of this view argue that treating partner violence as a gendered phenomenon is incorrect—both men and women can be victims or perpetrators or both. By extension, race, culture, class, gender, and sexual orientation rarely influence formal measurement models. Those who espouse a gender symmetry or parity view are generally referred to as family violence or partner violence researchers, although such labeling is a simplification of the many variations under this umbrella (Winstok, 2011).

A second view acknowledges that both men and women can be physically violent in intimate relationships (e.g., Ansara and Hindin, 2010; DeKeseredy, 2011; DeKeseredy and Dragiewicz, 2007; Dobash and Dobash, 2004; Swan and Snow, 2006; Tanha et al., 2010). But the bidirectionality of violence does not necessarily denote gender parity or symmetry for two main reasons. Broadly speaking, the chapters of this book weave two interrelated arguments against straightforward gender parity. The first argues that both sex and gender affect the motivations (e.g., Hamberger and Guse, 2002; Swan and Snow, 2006), context, and outcomes of intimate partner violence (e.g., Ansara and Hindin, 2011; Dobash and Dobash, 2004). This view is often associated with context-rich psychological studies examining the process, function, and meaning of violence

---

*In scientific discourse, the word "construct" refers to a hypothesized ideal state that is not directly observable. For example, intelligence is a construct, since we have an intuitive idea what it is, but observable measurements can only operationalize and approximate it, while never quite capturing it perfectly.

that uncover the (usually asymmetric) coercive environment in which intimate partner violence occurs. The second, complementary, argument points to the shortcomings of studies that constrain themselves only to physical violence (e.g., Stark, 2012; Tanha et al., 2010; chapter 3, in this volume). Most researchers under this umbrella are referred to as feminist partner violence researchers, although, again, this term is broad and covers a wide range of different theoretical schools.

Depending on whom you ask and what evidence is considered valid, proof for both sides is strong. How can such incompatible views exist? The debates surrounding the topic can be furthered by a brief understanding of philosophical epistemologies and the political interpretation of the epistemologies.* Most partner violence researchers, explicitly or implicitly, are postpositivist. This umbrella of research philosophy views valid research as observable, replicable, and reductionist (summing larger constituents to smaller parts and treating unitary indexes as a reliable marker of the larger part), with the capacity to be interpreted similarly by all observers (Creswell, 2009; Sherratt, 2006). To maintain the observable and replicable aspects of positivism, data are collected the same way, using the same or similar instruments across different populations that measure acts of aggression that can be observed and added to produce numbers that can be used to quantify and describe the populations. The observable and replicable aspects of this method as well as the stated apolitical stance of the researchers are ascribed as protecting impartiality. Furthermore, postpositivist frameworks posit that a few universal laws govern many different conditions. Therefore, data generated alongside postpositivist frameworks seek to generate theories that uncover universal models that predict male-to-female violence and female-to-male violence and, in more recent years, same-sex violence. This data-gathering approach does not allow for multiple interpretations of the same act and encourages reductionism and deemphasizes nuance. Therefore, the numerical finding that men and women are equally likely to use similar amounts of violence is interpreted to mean that men and women use violence equally and for similar reasons with similar outcomes. Therefore, sex differences become irrelevant.

Centrally different from partner violence researchers, feminist researchers draw from a wider array of philosophical models that allow for constructiv-

*Epistemology in the scientific and philosophical discourse concerns the ways in which a certain knowledge has been acquired or arrived at. Epistemology essentially asks, "How do we know what we know about the phenomenon?" rather than "What do we know about the phenomenon?"

ist interpretations that depend on who is affected and who is doing the interpretation—including more postpositivist views (Creswell, 2009; DeKeseredy and Dragiewicz, 2007). Feminist views emphasize that the world is different for everyone and cannot be reduced to a few variables nor captured by a few universal laws. Furthermore, many feminist epistemologies do not support causal deterministic laws but rather more complex interwoven paths that are hard to tease apart and must be understood as a whole. Thus, in contrast to partner-violence researchers, feminist researchers believe that the context and the meaning of the acts define the severity and the outcome. Therefore, data are often gathered in such a way to shed light on the impact of violence as well as the violent intent that goes beyond counting acts. When examining interactions at a nuanced level, sex and gender matter (not to mention race, class, and sexual orientation).

It is our hope that this book will stimulate discussion and function as a teaching tool with students in any social science field regardless of their substantive focus. Students studying graduate and undergraduate research methods or enrolled in general survey courses on victimization and violence, legal studies, and more specialized seminars in intimate partner violence may find some of the issues posed to be relevant. Finally, this book may interest scholars and activists in the field of intimate partner violence who seek to better understand how meaning making and the choice of methods should always be viewed as interdependent.

Chitra Raghavan and Shuki J. Cohen, editors
John Jay College of Criminal Justice,
City University of New York

References

Ansara, D. L., and Hindin, M. J. (2010). Exploring gender differences in the patterns of intimate partner violence in Canada: A latent class approach. *Journal of Epidemiology and Community Health, 64*(10), 849–854. doi:10.1136/jech.2009.095208

Ansara, D. L., and Hindin, M. J. (2011). Psychosocial consequences of intimate partner violence for women and men in Canada. *Journal of Interpersonal Violence, 26*(8), 1628–1645. doi:10.1177/0886260510370600

Archer, J. (2002). Sex differences in physically aggressive acts between heterosexual partners: A meta-analytic review. *Aggression and Violent Behavior, 7*(4), 313–351.

Creswell, J. (2009). *Research design: Qualitative, quantitative, and mixed methods approaches.* (3rd ed.). Thousand Oaks, CA: Sage.

DeKeseredy, W. S. (2011). Feminist contributions to understanding woman abuse: Myths, controversies, and realities. *Aggression and Violent Behavior, 16*(4), 297–302. doi:10.1016/j.avb.2011.04.002

DeKeseredy, W. S., and Dragiewicz, M. (2007). Understanding the complexities of feminist perspectives on woman abuse. *Violence against Women, 13*(8), 874–884.

Dobash, R. P., and Dobash, R. (2004). Women's violence to men in intimate relationships. *British Journal of Criminology, 44*(3), 324–349.

Dutton, D. G. (2006). *Rethinking domestic violence.* Vancouver: UBC Press.

Hamberger, L., and Guse, C. E. (2002). Men's and women's use of intimate partner violence in clinical samples. *Violence against Women, 8*(11), 1301.

Hayes, B. E. (2012). Abusive men's indirect control of their partner during the process of separation. *Journal of Family Violence, 27*(4), 333–344.

Langhinrichsen-Rohling, J., Misra, T. A., Selwyn, C., and Rohling, M. L. (2012). Rates of bidirectional versus unidirectional intimate partner violence across samples, sexual orientations, and race/ethnicities: A comprehensive review. *Partner Abuse, 3*(2), 1–104. doi:10.1891/1946-6560.3.2.e3

Sherratt. Y. (2006). *Continental philosophy of social science: Hermeneutics, genealogy and critical theory from ancient Greece to the twenty-first century.* Cambridge: Cambridge University Press.

Slife, B. D., and Williams, R. N. (1995). *What's behind the research? Discovering hidden assumptions in the behavioral sciences.* Thousand Oaks, CA: Sage.

Stark, E. (2012). Looking beyond domestic violence: Policing coercive control. *Journal of Police Crisis Negotiations, 12*(2), 197–217.

Straus, M. A. (2006). Future research on gender symmetry in physical assaults on partners. *Violence against Women, 12*, 1086–1097.

Swan, S. C., and Snow, D. L. (2006). The development of a theory of women's use of violence in intimate relationships. *Violence against Women, 12*, 1026–1045.

Winstok, Z. (2011). The paradigmatic cleavage on gender differences in partner violence perpetration and victimization. *Aggression and Violent Behavior, 16*(4), 303–311. doi:10.1016/j.avb.2011.04.004

Index of Methodological
Approaches by Chapter

Approaches to understanding intimate partner violence

1 | WHAT IS DOMESTIC VIOLENCE AND HOW DO WE MEASURE IT?

Learning Objectives

1. Understanding what intimate partner violence/domestic violence is.
2. Understanding how we make the decision to measure it.
3. Understanding the role of the expert compared to the role of the layperson in defining domestic violence.

Sarah L. Cook, Georgia State University; Sherry Hamby, Sewanee, the University of the South; Sandra M. Stith, Kansas State University; Eric McCollum, Virginia Polytechnic Institute and State University; and Tasha Mehne, Appalachian State University

1 | Developing a Self-Report to Assess Partner Violence

Methodological Considerations

Intimate partner violence has proven to be a difficult behavior to measure. It often occurs in private settings, and individuals are reluctant to discuss their experiences with anyone, let alone researchers. Furthermore, the behaviors that comprise it are complex and viewed differently by people depending on their age, socioeconomic status, religion, ethnicity, and culture. Similarly, researchers often do not agree on what behaviors intimate partner violence entails. In this chapter, we describe the fundamental considerations associated with the behavioral assessment of partner violence.

In the first part of the chapter, we use a hypothetical approach to illustrate the implications of some of the decisions researchers make when developing instruments. In the second half, we present an empirical example of how social and behavioral scientists build a case for the construct validity of dominance in relationships, a construct associated with the use of intimate partner violence, but with greater nuance and versatility.* We begin with a discussion of constructs, variables, and operational definitions as they pertain to partner violence and argue for why dominance should be considered as an important corelated construct.

---

*Construct validity represents the result of scientific attempts to prove that measurements related to a theorized construct, or abstract concept, indeed have the links and associations hypothesized to be relevant. For example, attempts to validate the "intelligence" construct may examine the correlations between IQ and the individual's highest level of education.

Measuring Intimate Partner Violence and Dominance: Fundamental Considerations

Constructs, Variables, and Operational Definitions

Constructs are theoretical, abstract concepts that social scientists seek to understand. They are the building blocks of theories. Because they are abstract, we need a way to represent them in concrete terms and we do so with *variables*. A construct may be represented by many different variables; thus, a variable is not synonymous with a construct, but it offers one of many ways to measure it. More important, identifying a variable leads to a strategy for measurement, called an *operational definition*, an approximation of a construct that uses only observable and measurable aspects or a specific plan for quantifying a variable. An operationalization is a detailed, practical definition that puts into practice basic ideas of what partner violence means. Once operational definitions are clear, a social scientist can identify a behavior, measure it, and generate hypotheses to test the relations between the behavior and other variables.

Partner violence is an important construct within the social study of violence, and research of this construct may advance our knowledge of it and our ability to design adequate preventive and treatment interventions. Research of this construct may also be of importance to policy makers (for examples, see Hamby and Cook, 2010). Questions of interest to most researchers include the following: How prevalent is partner violence? What causes people to be violent toward someone in their life? What are the consequences of experiencing violence? What factors increase risk for perpetrating it? What factors protect against it? What type of interventions reduces its scope and, better yet, prevents it from ever occurring? To systematically examine these questions, social scientists use defining variables that represent key aspects of this construct.

Variables Associated with Partner Violence and Dominance

Some of the preliminary considerations in our search for variables of relevance to partner violence included definitions of partner and qualifications of the types of relationships that could be considered. Then, we considered potential variables associated with violence and victimization.

Relationship Variables

Partner violence focuses on intimate, romantic relationships, but partners can be married, cohabiting, and dating, as well as in heterosexual or same-sex relationships. Some of these relationships are legally sanctioned while others are not. Interest has also been focused on violence that occurs in divorced or other terminated relationships. A related question is what constitutes a relationship, as definitions of the term vary. The nature of the variables associated with this aspect of the relationship may also vary, depending on the type and length of relationship studied. For example, many couples that live together (married or cohabiting) might encounter problems that lead to the use of violence that dating couples do not encounter, such as who controls finances or how money is budgeted and spent. Other behaviors are unique to same-sex relationships, such as involuntarily or malicious outing someone's sexual orientation. Developmental status might also be considered. For example, not all dating couples, particularly among adolescents, are sexually active, and so relationship variables that include this type of relationship may by definition exclude sexual violence. Adolescent couples also tend to have short relationships compared to older couples, which may influence questions about behavior in a relationship that lasted three months or one year. Finally the type of relationship determines what terms are salient to participants and are therefore appropriate to use in questions, for example, whether "husband" and "wife" are appropriate or even "his" and "her."

Decision 1: Relationship Variables

In the following study we opt to study aggression and dominance in intimate relationships among adults in a committed relationship. In addition, we include both male and female partners rather than querying only one partner.

Implication: This may be an expensive and time-consuming method. It will also exclude couples who have separated or couples where the violent partner refuses to allow the other partner to participate. Thus, the sample will be biased toward couples able to negotiate participation regardless of the violence.

Violence and Dominance Variables

Similar considerations arise in the definition of violence, with researchers restricting themselves to physical or sexual violence. Some researchers restrict the violence variables to pertain only to acts that lead to demonstrable harm or injury, while others seek to study markers of victimization as a proxy to violence.

Physical violence is generally a clear-cut behavior; it is usually straightforward whether one has been hit. Likewise, researchers generally agree on behaviors that constitute physical aggression (Cook and Parrott, 2009; Straus and Gelles, 1990; Straus et al., 1996). On the other hand, what behaviors constitute psychological abuse is far more nebulous. For example, shouting and yelling are not uncommon in relationships, but identifying when raised voices and harsh words turn into psychological abuse is difficult. Researchers have cited a wide range of behaviors that might constitute psychological abuse and do not even agree that the term "psychological abuse" is an appropriate label for this behavior (Cook and Parrott, 2009).

In addition to physical violence, sexual assault is an important and common feature of violence between romantic partners. However, it is also a more sensitive topic to ask about than physical or psychological abuse. Some participants are taken aback when researchers ask about sexual aggression in relationships, particularly marital relationships, perhaps because the stereotypical stranger rape guides ideas of sexual assault. Consequently, some researchers avoid asking questions about sexual violence, fearing that the questions will be distressing to respondents, although little evidence exists to support this fear (Becker-Blease and Freyd, 2006).

Decision 2: Violence and Dominance Variables

We decide to limit our focus to a form of control, that of dominance over the intimate partner.
Implication: We will not be able to detect the range of aggressive behaviors that occur within relationships that may understate the scope of the problem. However, we will be able to focus on a construct that has been neglected in most formal studies of partner violence and that we believe to be an important extension of the construct.

Since only a subset of physical violence between partners leads to injury, limiting questions about violence that results in injury will likely detect only a fraction of the afflicted population. Research so far has shown that men perpetrate violence that leads to injury much more often than women. Less is known about emotional and social injuries. Therefore, asking about general injury may identify the most vulnerable groups, such as women, low-income sectors, or elderly people.

Decision 3: Injury Variables

Decision: Because we are measuring a psychological dynamic, that of dominance, the measurement of injury is not relevant.
Implication: To not underestimate violence, we may detect a broader range of dynamics without requiring the presence of an injury.

Overall, our preliminary consideration of variables resulted in thirty-six different combinations of variables that could be considered.

Summary of Partner Violence and Dominance Measurement Considerations

Each of the four variables (type of relationship, form of violence, presence of injury, and perspective) has two possible levels.

Type of relationship	Form of Violence	Presence of Injury	Perspective
Married	Physical	Yes	Perpetration
Cohabiting or dating	Sexual or Emotional Control	No	Victimization

3 relationship types x 3 forms of violence x 2 presence of injury x 2 perspectives = 36 variables

Any of the thirty-six variables that result from combining answers to these questions are construct-consistent, albeit partial, representations of partner violence.

Measurement of Partner Violence and Dominance

Partner violence research poses a peculiar (although not unique) challenge in how it is operationalized or measured. Because violence is frequently ongoing and contextualized within a certain relational frame, the time frame of interest becomes crucial. Additionally, the research literature shows considerable discrepancies between studies that measure incidence, prevalence, or frequency rates of partner violence. What follows is a summary of the strengths and limits of each approach within the context of measuring relationship dominance as an ecologically valid measure associated with partner violence.

Incidence, Prevalence, and Frequency Rates

Incidence rates describe how many people have experienced an event within a certain time frame. Research of partner violence has customarily used six-month or one-year periods, although some studies have used current or last relationships. For example, an incidence rate for each of these periods would reveal how many people have perpetrated physical aggression at least once with six months, one year, or during their current or last relationship. In contrast, prevalence rates describe how many people have experienced physical aggression within their lifetime or in their life beginning at a particular age. As a preliminary goal was to assess dominance in adult relationships, we set the lifetime prevalence rate to age eighteen and asked participants to consider only experiences that have happened since they were eighteen years old. As such, incidence rates are always lower than prevalence rates. A frequency rate describes not *whether* someone has ever experienced an event but *how often* an experience has occurred within a specific time frame. In the next section, we describe what scales of measurement yield these rates and how to calculate them.

Scales of Measurement

Dichotomous scales. Dichotomous scales of partner violence ask participants to respond to questions about the occurrence of partner violence in their life with one of two possible answers, usually "yes" or "no." The advantage of this approach is its very simplicity—it is easy to understand and may be translated easily into multiple languages for cross-cultural studies. One important disadvantage of a dichotomous response is that someone who has been seriously beaten several times will get the same score as someone who has been hit once. Another disadvantage is that fewer people say "yes" when the choice is just "yes" or "no," at least for some types of partner violence questions (Hamby, Sugarman, and Boney-McCoy, 2006). However, dichotomous data translates readily to incidence and prevalence rates. For example, if 210 individuals responded "yes," we would calculate prevalence as follows: 210/1000 = 21 percent. Using our previous example, this would mean that the adult lifetime prevalence rate of perpetration of physical violence is 21 percent. Stated another way, 21 percent of individuals had perpetrated an act of physical violence against a partner in a relationship since they were eighteen years old.

Frequency scales. Another option is to ask how many times an event that can be considered violent has happened in the context of the relationship. Technically, a frequency rate is a continuous variable with a ratio scale, which means that that the rate has a true zero point and values that represent multipliable quantities (e.g., a frequency rate of four is twice as much as a rate of two). To measure frequency, it might seem that asking "how many times" an event has occurred with an open-ended question would be sufficient. When dealing with partner violence, however, which includes sensitive behavior difficult to admit, researchers have found it useful to provide categories as a guide. For example, the most widely used instrument in the field of partner violence, the Conflict Tactics Scales (Straus and Gelles, 1990; Straus et al., 1996), provides this scaling: zero times, one time, two times, three to five times, six to ten times, eleven to twenty times, and more than twenty times. In coding the responses, researchers select either the explicit value of the category (e.g., one or two) or the categories' midpoint (e.g., the midpoint of three to five times is four) and use values ranging from zero to twenty times. This practice does not yield a true ratio scale, but it does provide continuous data. One advantage of this type of scale is that it desensitizes frequency reports, because simply by including categories such as "more than twenty times," the scale implies that this much violence is within the scope of the report. Thus, those who say they have used physical violence in a relationship once or twice since age eighteen may not perceive their behavior to be aberrant and may be more likely to disclose. A disadvantage is that asking about frequency makes greater demands on memory than asking for a yes or no. Although most people will remember rare or serious events, it is hard to report exactly whether frequent behaviors, such as shouting, occurred ten or eleven times in the course of an adult relationship.

The option of Likert-scale intervals alleviates demands on memory by asking people to report whether some behavior occurred "never," "rarely," "sometimes," or "often" (or other similar categories). This scale distinguishes between less frequent and more frequent violence, but many researchers consider this scale problematic because it does not define what the categories mean. For example, what is "rare" to one person may seem "often" to another. In fact, the most seriously victimized individuals might be more likely to think that victimizations that occur several times a year are "rare," and thus not serious enough to warrant seeking help, while others would call that "often" and judge it in need of intervention.

In practice, researchers utilize more than one type of measure. Often, both frequency and incidence or prevalence rates are calculated by recoding frequency data into categories of zero times equaling "no" and all other categories equaling "yes."

Modes of Measurement

The specific mode, or the technique, of measurement determines *who* are the respondents to the measure and *how* they are to respond. Direct modes of measurement ask people to report on themselves and may include paper and pencil questionnaires, face-to-face interviews, telephone interviews, Internet surveys, and experience sampling. In contrast, indirect modes of measurement ask people to report on someone else's behavior (also known as collateral report). Collaterals may be peers, parents, teachers, and, in our example, partners. Violence research has shown that on confidential surveys, a surprising number of people will disclose perpetrating acts of violence, even severe acts. Estimates from perpetrator reports still greatly exceed what we know from official statistics, such as arrests by police. Perpetrator reports can be useful for many reasons. Information from perpetrators may be all that is available, they can be compared to victim reports, and they are highly correlated with other data on violence.

Studies that have compared perpetrator and victim reports do find some systematic underreporting by perpetrators compared to victims, and some evidence that male perpetrators underreport more than female perpetrators (Schluter, Paterson, and Feehan, 2007; Simpson and Christensen, 2005). One meta-analysis also found that perpetrators' report were correlated with social desirability more than victims' reports, although the correlation was fairly modest even for perpetrator reports (Sugarman, 1997).

Traditionally, the bulk of data on intimate partner violence through the early part of the twenty-first century was collected through these methods. Recently, computer-assisted interviews and automated telephonic data collection systems have emerged as promising, low-cost, and effective methods of data collection. Whether these methods influence reporting, however, is an under-researched question. As a result, researchers should think carefully about potential strengths and limits before selecting a method.

Recent studies illustrate the nature of issues that may emerge from computerized or automated data collection in intimate partner violence. One experimental study comparing reports of partner violence obtained from pencil and paper and computer-assisted formats found few differences (Hamby et al., 2006). In another experiment, disclosure of physical and sexual perpetration and victimization did not differ by four methods: in-person interviews, telephone interviews, paper and pencil questionnaires, and automated telephonic data collection systems (ATDC; Rosenbaum et al., 2006). The telephonic methods, however, produced higher rates of participation. In a follow-up study that used the same design, ATDC produced higher rates of disclosure of sensitive information (e.g., abuse experiences versus study habits). Moreover, participants reported significantly more comfort when answering questions in the ATDC condition than those in the face-to-face interviews, and participants in the telephone interviews reported more care in responding than in the pencil and paper format. Clearly the rate of reporting is not the only important matter to consider when selecting a mode of data collection. Considering the lack of established lore regarding the reliability and validity of automated data collection in the context of intimate partner violence, the study we report makes exclusive use of interview and questionnaire data.

The Role of Culture and Ethnicity in Intimate Partner Dominance and Aggression

Culture and ethnicity create a powerful context around the problem of intimate partner violence. Researchers must carefully consider how culture and ethnicity influence our understanding of constructs, the variables we select to represent them, and operational definitions of those variables. We must also think critically about how culture and ethnicity influence the way in which student participants respond to measurement instruments. A comprehensive discussion of these matters is beyond the scope of this chapter. However, we illustrate one way in which culture influences our understanding of the construct of intimate partner violence and one way in which culture may influence responses to measurement instruments.

The majority of measurement instruments developed to assess some aspect of intimate partner violence emanates from Western cultures (e.g., the United States, Canada, and the United Kingdom). Without exception, all these instruments measure variables that define intimate partner violence as occurring only between two individuals involved in a relationship. Recently, scholars and advocates have described how physical violence against women in Asia frequently involves the husband's family, such as mothers-in-law as perpetrators of physical violence (Dasgupta, 2000; Fernandez, 1997). Thus, existing measurement instruments may underestimate the extent to which women from Asian cultures experience physical violence in their intimate relationships because they ask only about violence at the hands of partners. Recently, researchers identified another form that abuse may take within intimate relationships: immigration abuse. These behaviors focus on harming an individual through interfering with a partner's immigration process or status (Hass, Dutton, and Orloff, 2000). In this case, existing instruments would not characterize immigrating women's experiences outside of physical, sexual, and psychological violence.

Culture also influences the way participants respond to questions and use the scale presented to them. For example, in some cultures, and even in some subcultures within the United States, the concept of consenting to have intercourse is foreign because women are not accorded the power and autonomy to make decisions about sexual activity. In this case, using an instrument to measure forced sexual intercourse (i.e., rape) that uses a question such as "Have you ever had sex without your consent?" would not make sense because consent in this culture is irrelevant.

Researchers have also documented that culture plays a role in the way people use scales, such as Likert scales. Social scientists call these ways response sets, which are systematic ways of answering a question that are not directly related to the question's content but instead reflect a characteristic about the respondent (Oskamp, 1977). Two response styles exist: extreme and acquiescence. The extreme response style describes a tendency to use the extreme categories of a rating scale, whereas acquiescence response styles describe a tendency to agree with a statement regardless of its content. If response styles vary by culture, they pose problems for research that compare rates or mean differences across cultural groups (Cheung and Rensvold, 2000; Clarke, 2000). In the case of intimate partner violence, the extreme response style may be more problematic, because acquiescence response styles are related to the degree to which individuals tend to agree or disagree with statements, and researchers rarely use this agree/disagree type of scales (see Javeline, 1999). In the case of scales commonly used to measure physical violence, the extreme response style may lead to high rates of participants endorsing either zero experiences of violence or the highest number of violence experiences.

Scope of Measurement: Identification of Behaviors
That Signify Aggressive Dominance and Control

In this step we seek to identify behaviors that best capture the intimate partner dominance construct within the context of intimate partner violence. To this aim, we have developed a scale that taps a person's assertion of power and control in an intimate relationship. For creating this Dominance Scale, we proposed queries that would be readily answerable by a diverse group of people within the target population of informants. After consulting the literature, brainstorming with colleagues and professionals who work with victims of physical aggression (in this case, advocates, attorneys, physicians, and clinical psychologists), we amassed a range of physically abusive behaviors (fuller details about this strategy can be found in Goodman et al., 2003). From this broad set of behaviors, we selected the types of behaviors about which to ask with the goal of narrowing the number of behaviors queried to include general as well as specific displays of dominance and control within a relationship. In this stage, more questions were produced than we expected to include in the final instrument.

Unusual from most scales, the Dominance Scale does not measure specific behaviors within a time frame. Instead, the scale includes assertions for which participants denote their agreement level on a Likert scale (1 = strongly disagree, 2 = disagree, 3 = agree, 4 = strongly agree). This array of questions concerning assertions of dominance and control may complement behavioral approaches to measuring physically violence behavior and could potentially be used to validate the more commonly used measures of physical violence in existence. Theoretically, the Dominance Scale items are designed to assess three types of power and control in relationships: authority, restrictiveness, and disparagement. A sample item for authority is "sometimes I have to remind my partner of who's boss"; for restrictiveness, "I insist on knowing where my partner is at all times"; and for disparagement, "My partner often has good ideas (reverse scored). All items are listed in the appendix.

Language. We avoided the use of legal terms such as "aggravated assault," expecting that many informants might not be familiar with the definition of "aggravated" or "assault." We also, in general, avoided emotionally laden terms such as "abuse" or "rape," as many individuals who have been assaulted often hesitate to identify themselves as a victim of such acts or might not be familiar with the statutory definition of rape (i.e., nonconsensual sexual intercourse regardless of relationship to the perpetrator). Many studies have shown, for example, that only about 30 percent of women who report that they have been physically forced to have sex without their consent also describe themselves as a rape victim (Percy and Mayhew, 1997). Thus, we phrased our questions to capture behaviors with words that are descriptive and familiar to the average person, with verbs such as "hit" or "punch" and without labels such as "victim." Questions using language suspect of being obscure were written in multiple phrasing, to be pruned later by a pilot study.

Reporting load. To prevent fatiguing the informants—which could lead to underreporting or reluctance to elaborate—we prioritized our questions and focus as best we could. We aimed at a questionnaire that would ideally take most people no more than ten or fifteen minutes to complete. Past research in the area has shown that a smaller number of items may not necessarily lead to underidentifying behaviors. For example, twelve CTS2 items detected as many men who had ever perpetrated physical aggression as twenty-one items from the Severity of Violence against Women Scales (Cook, 2002).

Piloting the Measure

Using a qualitative pilot study design, we asked people to review the questionnaire in focus groups or in a small number of in-depth interviews, during which we asked people to complete the questionnaire and then discuss the instrument. We complemented this tactic with a quantitative approach, in which we administered the questionnaire in a structured manner to a large group of respondents.

The preliminary data analysis of the pilot included estimation of the variability of the data to determine its viability as a statistically meaningful assessment instrument. We still kept several questions for which we obtained low variability, provided they concerned rare forms of violence, as they were deemed important for identifying the worst cases. In addition to variability checks, we checked the measure for evidence suggesting that people did not understand the question or found it too sensitive. This was done by identifying higher-than-average number of blank answers. Items that passed these tests were then retained in the final version of the measure (see chapter appendix for the complete instrument).

Results

Psychometrics Properties of the Dominance
Scale: Reliability and Validity

Participants. The data we present are from 124 couples who completed a base-line assessment in the Domestic Violence-Focused Couples Treatment (DVFCT) study, plus 58 men and 8 women whose partners did not complete the baseline assessment (Stith et al., 2002, 2004). The study recruited participants through the court or police (21.6 percent), self (20.7 percent) or partner (11.3 percent) referrals from people who became aware of the program from such venues as advertisements in local papers and other sources (45.9 percent), including domestic violence treatment providers, therapists, and lawyers. Husbands averaged 36.3 years of age (SD = 9.6) and wives 34.0 years (SD = 9.8). About half (51.7 percent of husbands, 52.1 percent of wives) were white/European American. Another 28.4 percent of husbands and 23.1 percent of wives were black/African American, 8.6 percent of husbands and 11.1 percent of wives were Hispanic, and the remaining participants were Asian, American Indian, mixed race, or identified as "other." Most husbands (80.5 percent) and just over one half of wives (53.4 percent) were employed full time. The average relationship length was 6.56 years (SD = 7.6), and 88.8 percent were together at baseline assessment.

To be in the study, couples had to have experienced male-to-female physical abuse, both partners had to want to participate in couples counseling, and both had to be able to communicate in English. Couples were excluded if they reported that the female partner needed medical care for injuries sustained in previous violent incidents, had current substance abuse problems, refused to remove firearms from the home and car, or refused to sign a no-violence contract. Most clients were screened through private, confidential telephone interviews (a few were screened face-to-face at a domestic violence treatment provider). Eligible couples completed an in-person two-hour intake interview that included a range of questionnaires. Partners were interviewed separately. Participants were not paid to complete the intake interview or to complete treatment, but treatment and child care were free (for more details, see Stith et al., 2002, 2004).

In addition to assessing power and control, interviews and questionnaires measured the use of tactics of negotiation and physical, emotional, and sexual violence (using the Revised Conflict Tactics Scale; CTS2; Straus et al., 1996), marital satisfaction (using the Kansas Marital Satisfaction Scale; Schumm et al.,

1983), romantic jealously (using White's Jealousy Scale; White, 1981), and three types of beliefs about violence toward wives (i.e., marital violence is justified, wives gain from marital violence, and help should not be given to wives; using the Inventory of Beliefs about Wife Beating: Saunders et al., 1987). All of these measures are widely used and have strong psychometric properties.

Reliability and internal consistency. Reliability refers to whether someone's score on a questionnaire is stable. If researchers measured a trait such as extraversion, for example, they would expect that a person would be similarly extraverted today and a month from today. Internal consistency refers to whether people answer similar questions similarly. For example, extraverted people would be expected to give similar answers to "I enjoy meeting people" and "Meeting new people is fun." All questionnaires benefit from high reliability and high internal consistency. It is the case, however, that questionnaires that focus on behaviors are often less reliable and less internally consistent than questionnaires that focus on attitudes. For example, a person may have punched but not kicked their partner. A response of "yes" to one question and a "no" to the other could produce a lower score on internal consistency, even though everyone would agree the person used physical violence. In contrast, questionnaires that focus on tendencies or aspects of personality, if psychometrically sound, are highly reliable and internally consistent.

The DVFCT study provides data to examine the internal consistency of the three dominance subscales. With continuous data such as that collected with the Dominance Scale, the appropriate indicator of internal consistency is Cronbach's alpha (α), which ranges from 0 to 1, with higher values indicating more internal consistency than low scores. Generally, an alpha of .70 or higher is acceptable. High values of alpha are necessary because, mathematically, the alpha for two variables (or scores) sets a limit on the degree to which the variables can relate to one another. In our example, the alphas for the dominance subscales are all respectable. For men, α = .74, .75, and .79 for authority, restrictiveness, and disparagement, respectively. For women, α = .74, .78, and .69 for the same subscales.

Validity. Construct validity refers to whether a questionnaire really measures what the researcher thinks it measures. A questionnaire on violence should, for example, correctly identify people as victim and nonvictims, or perpetrators and nonperpetrators. Validity is established in a variety of ways. One common method is to compare a new questionnaire with more established questionnaires on similar or related topics. For example, a new violence questionnaire should provide results similar to other violence question-

Table 1.1 The correlation of dominance subscales with related constructs

	Jealousy	Marital satisfaction	IBWB justified	IBWB wives gain	IBWB should not help
Men's reports					
Authority	.07	−.17	.43 ***	.26 **	.30 ***
Restrictiveness	.48 ***	.08	.26 **	.22 *	.16
Disparagement	−.06	−.18	.24 *	.15	.13
Women's reports					
Authority	.04	−.06	.12	.18	.03
Restrictiveness	.57 ***	.13	.07	.12	.16
Disparagement	.17	−.31 ***	.02	.07	.05

Notes: * $p < .05$, ** $p < .01$, *** $p < .0001$

White Jealousy Scale (White, 1981); Kansas Marital Satisfaction Scale (Schumm et al., 1983); Inventory of Beliefs about Wife Beating (Saunders et al., 1987). Three subscales of the IBWB were used: "justified," meaning that marital violence is justified; "wives gain," meaning that wives gain from marital violence; and "should not help," meaning that help should not be given.

naires. Scores on a violence questionnaire should be correlated with other theoretically related measures, such as scores on a trauma symptoms questionnaire or, as with our example, of dominance. Sometimes questionnaire results are compared to other types of data, such as, in the case of violence, arrest records. These are all types of *convergent validity,* which means demonstrating that other measures that should be similar are in fact similar to the new measure.

To establish convergent validity, we explored the extent to which the dominance subscales of authority, restrictiveness, and disparagement were related to beliefs about wife beating, marital satisfaction, and romantic jealousy using correlation coefficients (see table 1.1). The degree to which men endorsed statements about authority (i.e., "traditional" attitudes supporting violence and patriarchy) was positively related to all subscales of beliefs about wife beating. Restrictiveness was positively correlated with the belief that marital violence is justified and that wives gain from marital violence. Disparagement was correlated only with the belief that marital violence is justified. For women, the dominance subscales were not related to any beliefs about wife beating.

Discussion

We hypothesized that restrictiveness (i.e., attempts to limit contact with the opposite sex or others that might take attention away from the partner) would be related strongly to romantic jealousy. The data supported this hypothesis. For women and men jealousy and restrictiveness were strongly and positively related. About a third of the variance in women's restrictiveness overlapped with their jealousy scores, and almost a quarter of variance in men's restrictiveness did. Jealously was not related to authority or disparagement. We hypothesized that dominance would also be negatively associated with marital satisfaction, but this proved true only for women's disparagement (see table 1.1). Women who report using more disparagement also reported less marital satisfaction.

Is Dominance Related to Violence Perpetration and Victimization?

Men's perpetration. The classic dominance model postulates that men's dominant behavior would be associated with their perpetration of violence against their partners, assessed by the perpetrator's or the victim's report. Asking people to report on their own dominance and use of violence is difficult because most people want to present themselves in a positive light, a tendency social scientists call social desirability (Sugarman, 1997). Thus, it is not surprising that men's reports of their own dominance and perpetration were generally uncorrelated (see table 1.2). Negotiation is related to authority and restrictiveness; in both cases the greater levels of the dominance type were associated with lower levels of negotiation.

A better way to evaluate construct validity is to use data from two reporters, which we do have. Here we see a very different pattern (see table 1.2). Men's reports of dominance were related to women's reports of their partner's perpetration. All three forms of dominance were positively correlated with women's reports of CTS2 physical assault by their partners. Likewise, restrictiveness and disparagement were also positively correlated with CTS2 injury. Disparagement was also positively correlated with psychological aggression and inversely correlated with negotiation.

Men's victimization. When men reported on their partner's use of violence against them, physical assault was related to their own use of restrictiveness. When women reported on their use of violence against their partners, injury was related to men's restrictiveness (see table 1.2).

Women's perpetration. Based on women's reports of their own dominance

Table 1.2 Correlations among reports of male dominance and conflict tactics scale subscales

	Negotiation	Psychological aggression	Physical assault	Sexual coercion	Injury
		(a) Perpetration			
Men's report of		Men's self–report of perpetration against partner (I hurt her)			
Authority	−.20*	.11	.08	−.06	.05
Restrictiveness	−.28**	.02	.17	.06	.12
Disparagement	−.13	−.08	−.10	−.15	.03
		Women's self-report of partner's perpetration (he hurt me)			
Authority	−.15	.15	.21*	.05	.17
Restrictiveness	.11	.03	.22*	−.00	.19*
Disparagement	<−.23*	.22 *	.28**	.15	.24**
		(b) Victimization			
		Men's self–report of partner's perpetration (she hurt me)			
Authority	<.02	.06	.11	.02	.04
Restrictiveness	−.05	−.04	.20*	.02	.10
Disparagement	−.17	.08	.03	−.07	.18
		Women's self-report of partner's victimization (I hurt him)			
Authority	−.02	.06	.15	.06	.13
Restrictiveness	−.01	.06	.17	−.04	.19*
Disparagement	−.08	−.01	.06	.10	.13

Notes: * $p < .05$, ** $p < .01$; $n = 119$

and their own violence, we see that as women's restrictiveness increases, so does their own sexually coercive behavior. Likewise, women's authority was positively related to reports of their own psychological aggression against their partners. We note the same caution as before. Women's own reports of dominance and use of violence are vulnerable to threats from social desirability. When using men's reports of wives' violence, only one correlation was significant, and it was in the opposite direction expected (see table 1.3). Higher levels of wives' restrictiveness were correlated with higher levels of negotiation.

Table 1.3 Correlations among reports of female dominance and Conflict Tactics Scale subscales

	Negotiation	Psychological aggression	Physical assault	Sexual coercion	Injury
		(a) Perpetration			
Women's report of		Women's self-report (I hit him)			
Authority	−.15	.24*	.14	−.01	.13
Restrictiveness	.03	.16	.14	.26**	.18
Disparagement	−.08	.08	.09	.11	.13
		Men's self-report of partner's perpetration (she hit me)			
Authority	−.08	−.10	−.05	.10	−.01
Restrictiveness	.21*	.08	.06	.08	.12
Disparagement	−.14	.16	.16	.05	.08
		(b) Victimization			
		Women's self-report (he hit me)			
Authority	.12	−.08	−.08	−.05	−.03
Restrictiveness	.02	.15	.21*	.05	.16
Disparagement	−.38**	.29**	.28**	.14	.26**
		Men's self-report of partner's victimization (I hit her)			
Authority	−.12	−.16	−.05	.11	.00
Restrictiveness	.06	.11	.10	.10	.15
Disparagement	−.11	.07	.11	.05	.02

Notes: $* p < .05$, $** p < .01$; $n = 119$

Women's victimization. Women's reports of victimization by their partners were related to their restrictiveness and disparagement (see table 1.3). In particular, women reported more psychological violence, physical violence, and injury by their partners as their own use of disparagement increased. As their reports of restrictiveness increased, so did their reports of their partner's physical assaults. Women's reports of their partner's use of negotiation decreased as women's use of disparagement decreased. No form of men's use of violence, when reported by men, was related to women's dominance scores.

Patterns of Dominance between Spouses

All three Dominance Scale subscales showed mean differences between partners, using repeated measures analysis of variance (ANOVA) with the couple as the unit of analysis, to analyze the typical pattern in relationships, not simply average scores among men and women. Men's scores on authority and disparagement exceeded women's—for authority, $F(1, 110) = 7.40$, $p < .01$; and for disparagement, $F(1, 110) = 7.50$, $p < .01$—providing further evidence of construct validity. Authority is meant to measure values and behaviors consistent with traditional patriarchal marriages. In contrast, women's scores for restrictiveness exceeded men's: $F(1, 110) = 4.42$, $p < .05$.

External and Differential Validity

It is also important to look at external and differential validity, which are types of validity that focus more on the characteristics of the sample, not the questionnaire. Questionnaires do not work equally well for all groups. There are many different groups to consider, including college students versus the general population, males versus females, dating couples versus married couples, heterosexual couples versus same-sex couples, and members of different racial, ethnic, and cultural groups. Questionnaires with diverse samples should establish the ability to generalize equally well to members of all these groups (or identify which ones *can* be generalized to). This is referred to as *external validity*. If the data can be generalized accurately to some groups but not others, then there is the problem of *differential validity*, which will limit conclusions about differences across groups.

In the DVFCT study, 60 percent of husbands and 35 percent of wives had been arrested at least once for domestic violence and 22.1 percent and 4 percent, respectively, more than once. About a quarter were on probation at the time of intake, and 16.1 percent were under a protective order. Thus, this sample represents couples whose behavior is severe enough to have drawn attention from community institutions but is probably somewhat less severe than a sample from a batterers' program, and more severe than many therapy or community samples.

Summary of Psychometric Data

Overall, data from the DVFCT supports the reliability and validity of the Dominance Scale. The instruments' three subscales have acceptable internal consistency. With only one exception, subscales are related to other variables in expected directions. Men's self-report of dominance was consistently related to their partner's reports of their use of violence and negotiation tactics. Women's self-reports of dominance were not related to their partner's reports of their use of violence; however, women's self-reports of restrictiveness were related to their partners' reports of negotiation, a finding admittedly difficult to interpret. Finally, consistent with dominance theory, men reported higher levels of dominance in relationships, except for restrictiveness. These findings support the theory that societal level constructs can be expressed at the individual level. In other words, a social system such as patriarchy can be expressed at the individual level as attitudes, behaviors, and cognition. For example, Herek (2009) discusses how sexual prejudice, defined as all negative attitudes based on sexual orientation, is expressed through antigay violence. In intimate relationships, power and control are behaviors. When expressed by an individual, they represent the internalization of patriarchy, a system whereby men, by virtue of their gender, are accorded power and privilege, and express that power and privilege through dominance in relationships.

Summary

In this chapter we have illustrated the general steps researchers undertake to develop quantitative instruments to measure intimate partner violence. We then showed how the reliability and validity, including the external of an instrument, is evaluated, using data collected from domestic violence intervention participants. We have highlighted limits in social science or behavioral research, but the approach also has significant strengths. Our ability to assess, or measure, women's experiences of violence has been and will be critical to increasing awareness and understanding of violence against women and, importantly, targeting resources to help heal those who have been hurt and to prevent future harm.

Appendix
The Dominance Scale
Items for Dominance Subscales

Authority

5) Things are easier in my relationship if I am in charge.

6) Sometimes I have to remind my partner of who's boss.

8) If my partner and I can't agree, I should have the final say.

9) My partner needs to remember that I am in charge.

14) I dominate my partner.

Restrictiveness

2) I try to keep my partner from spending time with opposite sex friends.

3) My partner should not keep any secrets from me.

4) I insist on knowing where my partner is at all times.

7) I have a right to know everything my partner does.

15) I have a right to be involved with anything my partner does.

Disparagement

1) My partner often has good ideas. (R)

10) My partner is a talented person. (R)

11) People usually like my partner. (R)

12) My partner can handle most things that happen. (R)

13) My partner is basically a good person. (R)

Administration

Instructions for participants: People have many different ways of relating to one another. The following statements are all different ways of relating to or thinking about your partner. Please read each statement, decide how much you agree with it, and then *circle* your answer.

Scoring

Responses are given from 1 to 4 as follows:

4 = Strongly Agree
3 = Agree
2 = Disagree
1 = Strongly Disagree

(R) indicates item should be reverse-scored. To score, first reverse score items as appropriate and then sum to create a score for each subscale (or use mean if missing data). All of the items can also be added to create a total dominance score.

References

Becker-Blease, K. A., and Freyd, J. J. (2006). Research participants telling the truth about their lives: The ethics of asking and not asking about abuse. *American Psychologist, 61*(3), 218–226.

Cheung, G., and Rensvold, R. (2000). Assessing extreme and acquiescence response sets in cross-cultural research using structural equations modeling. *Journal of Cross-Cultural Psychology, 31*(2), 187–212.

Clarke, I. (2000). Extreme response style in cross-cultural research: An empirical investigation. *Journal of Social Behavior and Personality, 15*(1), 137–152.

Cook, S. L. (2002). Self-reports of sexual, physical, and nonphysical abuse perpetration: A comparison of three measures. *Violence against Women, 8*(5), 541–565.

Cook, S. L., and Parrot, D. J. (2009). Exploring a taxonomy for aggression against women: Can it aid conceptual clarity? *Aggressive Behavior, 35,* 462–476.

Dasgupta, S. D. (2000). Charting the course: An overview of domestic violence in the South Asian community in the United States. *Journal of Social Distress and the Homeless 9*(3), 173–185.

Fernandez, M. (1997). Domestic violence by extended family members in India: Interplay of gender and generation. *Journal of Interpersonal Violence, 12,* 433–455.

Goodman, L., Dutton, M. A., Weinfurt, K. and Cook, S. (2003). The Intimate Partner Violence Strategies Index: Development and application. *Violence against Women, 9,* 163–186.

Hamby, S. L., and Cook, S. L. (2010). Assessing violence against women in practice settings: Processes and tools practitioners can use. In C. Renzetti, R. K. Bergen and J. Edleson (Eds.), *Sourcebook on Violence against Women* (2nd ed.) (49–71). Thousand Oaks, CA: Sage.

Hamby, S., Sugarman, D., and Boney-McCoy, S. (2006). Does questionaire format impact reported partner violence rates? An experimental study. *Violence and Victims, 21*(4), 507–517.

Hass, G. A., Dutton, M. A., and Orloff, L. E. (2000). Lifetime prevalence of violence against Latina immigrants: Legal and policy implications. *International Review of Victimology, 7*(1–3), 93–113.

Herek, G. (2009). Sexual stigma and sexual prejudice in the United States: A conceptual framework. *Contemporary Perspectives on Lesbian, Gay, and Bisexual Identities,* 65–111.

Javeline, D. (1999). Response effects in polite cultures: A test of acquiescence in Kazakhstan. *Public Opinion Quarterly, 63,* 1–28.

Oskamp, S. (1977). *Attitudes and opinions.* Englewood Cliffs, NJ: Prentice Hall.

Percy, A., and Mayhew, P. (1997). Estimating sexual victimization in a national survey: A new approach. *Studies on Crime and Prevention, 6*(2), 125–150.

Rosenbaum, A., Rabenhorst, M. M., Reddy, M. K., Fleming, M. T., and Howells, N. L. (2006). A comparison of methods for collecting self-report data on sensitive topics. *Violence and Victims, 21*(4), 461–471.

Saunders, D. G., Lynch, A. B., Grayson, M., Linz, D. (1987). The inventory of beliefs about wife beating: The construction and initial validation of a measure of beliefs and attitudes. *Violence and Victims, 2,* 39–57.

Schluter, P. J., Paterson, J., and Feehan, M. (2007). Prevalence and concordance of interpersonal violence reports from intimate partners: Findings from the Pacific Islands Families Study. *Journal of Epidemiology and Community Health, 61,* 625–630.

Simpson, L. E., and Christensen, A. (2005). Spousal agreement regarding relationship aggression on the Conflict Tactics Scales-2. *Psychological Assessment, 17,* 423–243.

Stith, S. M., McCollum, E. E., Rosen, K. H., and Locke, L. D. (2002). Multicouple group treatment for domestic violence. In F. Kaslow (Ed.), *Comprehensive textbook of psychotherapy* (Vol. 4, pp. 499–520). New York: Wiley.

Stith, S. M., Rosen, K. H., McCollum, E. E., and Thomsen, C. J. (2004). Treating intimate partner violence within intact couple relationships: Outcomes of multi-couple versus individual couple therapy. *Journal of Marital and Family Therapy, 30*(3), 305–318.

Straus, M. A., and Gelles, R. J. (1990). How violent are American families? Estimates from the National Family Violence Resurvey and other studies. In M. A. Straus and R. J. Gelles (Eds.), *Physical violence in American families: Risk factors and adaptations to violence in 8,145 families* (95–112). New Brunswick, NJ: Transaction.

Straus, M. A., Hamby, S. L., Boney-McCoy, S., and Sugarman, D. B. (1996). The Revised Conflict Tactics Scales: Development and preliminary psychometric data. *Journal of Family Issues, 17*(3), 283–316.

Sugarman, D. B. (1997). Intimate violence and social desirability. *Journal of Interpersonal Violence, 12*(2), 275–290.

White, G. L. (1981). A model of romantic jealously. *Motivation and Emotion, 5,* 295–310.

Antônio de Pádua Serafim, University of Sao
Paolo; and Fabiana Saffi, University of Sao Paolo

2 | Perceptions of Domestic Violence in Brazil

Violence (from Latin, *violentia*), refers to the act of violating natural laws in an abusive way, by coercing a particular person into doing something against his or her will. It is a multicausal phenomenon generally manifest through actions that bear the intent of damaging, demeaning, underestimating, and subjugating others, and thus involve, by definition, a power differential—be it intellectual, physical, economical, political, or social. In addition to causing damage to the biopsychosocial structure (e.g., Anderson and Aviles, 2006), interpersonal violence is one of the most common reasons for serious injury.

While research on domestic violence and violence in general is extensive in the West and in the English-speaking world, there is a paucity of research on the subject in Brazil, and only a few studies have been published on the matter for a Portuguese-speaking audience. Nonetheless, violence is acknowledged as a serious problem by both the Brazilian government and the Brazilian community at large (e.g., Minayo and Souza, 1998). This recognition has culminated in Law 10,778/2003, on the compulsory notification of cases of violence against women in health, and Law 11.340/2006 (Maria da Penha Law) that determined the creation of the National Data and Statistics on the Family and Domestic Violence against Women.

A crucial issue in studying violence across cultures is the need to review the construct and local understanding of violence and its potentially different definitions across cultures. The primary goal of this study is to qualitatively explore notions of violence, and in particular domestic violence, among lay-

Antônio de Pádua Serafim, PhD, is a professor in the postgraduate health psychology program at the Methodist University of São Paulo and in the Psychology Unit of the Faculty of Medicine at the University of São Paulo. Fabiana Saffi, MA, is a professor in the Psychology Unit of the Faculty of Medicine at the University of São Paulo.

persons in Brazil. In 2002 the World Health Organization (WHO) launched the first World Report on Violence and Health, purported to estimate the magnitude and impact of violence throughout the world. The WHO defined violence as "the intentional use of physical force or power, threatened or actual, against oneself, another person, or against a group or community, that either results in or has a high likelihood of resulting in injury, death, psychological harm, maldevelopment or deprivation." The report indicated that more than a million people lose their lives annually due to violence, and an even greater number sustain physical and psychological consequences (Krug et al., 2002). This report, therefore, suggests that interpersonal violence presents a serious universal problem.

Over the past thirty years, the Brazilian government has repeatedly acknowledged that violence is one of the major public health problems, contributing to mortality both directly (e.g., homicides) and in association with accidents (Minayo, 2006). The Pan-American Health Organization (PAHO) states that "violence, due to the number of victims and magnitude of organic and emotional consequences it produces, has achieved an endemic nature and converted into a public health issue in various countries. . . . Within this context, the health care sector constitutes a crossroad where all corollaries of violence flow together, because of the pressure on their victims and urgent care, as well as special attention care, physical and psychological rehabilitation and social work" (quoted in Minayo, 1994).

The reality of violence in Brazil is further troublesome, since it ranks second in the general cause of death and has been the most common cause of death of individuals between the ages of five and forty-nine for the past two decades (Minayo, 1994; Souza and Lima, 2007). According to Deslandes and others (2007), by 2005 violence became the sixth most common cause of hospitalization in Brazil. However, many researchers note that mortality rates are merely the "tip of the iceberg" and the larger consequences of interpersonal violence for society and for health care must also be considered (Souza and Lima, 2007). For example, data from the Mortality Information System (SIM/ Brazilian Ministry of Health) suggests that the number of hospitalizations due to violent causes is approximately six times that of the number of people who died from comparable violent acts (Minayo, 2005).

Not all segments of society, however, are equally vulnerable to violent victimization. In spite of the low precision of the available data, there is a consensus among researchers (Day, 2003; Nunes, 2010; Okasha, 2007; Tangwa, 2009) that the population groups most vulnerable to violence are children and youth up to twenty-four years of age, the elderly, women, and people either physically or mentally handicapped.

In this paper, we follow Castel's (1998) model of vulnerability as a dynamic process that results from a series of aspects that include both individual and collective or contextual factors, interlinked with economical precariousness and relational vulnerability. According to this model, populations that may require social intervention are not only threatened by the insufficiency of their material resources but also vulnerable due to the lability of their relationships.

In the Brazilian context, we conceptualize violence against women as a public health issue. Brazilian data indicates that violence-related mortality rates among women between the ages of fifteen and forty-four have surpassed those caused by cancer, malaria, traffic accidents, and war. Physical, sexual, and emotional abuse; sexual exploitation; and murder of women are more frequently perpetrated by their partners, acquaintances, and family members, though women are also subject to violence caused by strangers (Minayo, 2005). This paper uses the United Nations' definition of violence against women and encompasses any violent act that results in physical, sexual, or mental damage and suffering, including acts of coercion or deprivation of freedom, both in the realm of private and public life (WHO, 2012).

According to Minayo and Souza (1998), the effects of domestic violence against women in Brazil are often protracted. Women who live through violent situations have more health complaints than others and resort more often to emergency services both directly for the treatment of the violent consequences and indirectly for primary care services (Oliveira et al., 2009).

Specifically regarding intimate partner violence in Brazil, WHO (2012) data show that between 15 percent and 71 percent of women have reported physical and/or sexual violence that was committed by their husbands or intimate partners; for many women (24–40 percent) the first sexual experience was not consensual, and 4 to 12 percent report violence while pregnant.

In terms of physical intimate partner violence, men are the offenders most of the time (67.4 percent), usually in their capacity as the victim's partner or ex-partner. There are no explicit studies about the incidence of psychiatric pathologies among intimate partner violent offenders in Brazil; however, anecdotal data suggest that some of them suffer from antisocial personality disorders and other personality disorders characterized by emotional deregulation, in addition to histrionic and paranoid personalities and pathological jealousy. Another aggravating factor in the Brazilian epidemiology of domestic violence is the abuse of alcohol and illicit drugs (Anderson and Aviles, 2006).

Studies suggest that an average of 63 percent of the worldwide victims of domestic violence are women (Brasil, Ministério da Saúde, 2001). Among them, 43.6 percent are between eighteen and twenty-nine years old. In 70 percent of the cases the offender is the woman's husband or partner. In contrast, Brazilian domestic violence data from the city of São Paulo estimated the prevalence of domestic violence at 28.9 percent, predominantly against women (Oliveira et al., 2009).

In the United States, Hegarty and Roberts (1998) found that 5 to 20 percent of women are victims of intimate partner violence. This percentage varies greatly because of the different definitions and measures of the violence construct, which may run the gamut from homicide to forced marriage (Humphreys, 2007). As stated by Hegarty and Roberts (1998), intimate partner violence consists of a complex network of different types of violent behaviors that include psychological, physical, and sexual abuse.

Violence against women is a problem that has prevailed for years, and current interventions have not succeeded in eliminating it. In many societies one cause of partner violence is associated with cultural norms that tolerate men's exertion of power over women evinced through physical and psychological violence (Pick et al., 2006). Men can also be the victims of domestic violence, but the percentage of female victims is consistently much higher worldwide (Humphreys, 2007). Some authors question whether men and women are equally violent in their intimate relations, concluding that this, again, depends to a great extent on the definitions of violence used (Taft et al., 2001).

Blay (2003) examined 623 reports in the General Police Station and the Women's Police Stations, with 964 victims, of whom 669 were women and 294 were men. Among the 669 female victims, 285 were victims of murder and 384 of attempted murder. Other data indicated that in half of the incidents, the offender is unknown. Among those identified, when the victim is female, 90 percent of perpetrators are men. Most of the victims—62 percent—are white women, 7 percent are black, and 30 percent brown. The majority of the victims had primary levels of literacy (74 percent), although 14 percent had secondary education and 3 percent completed university studies.

The age of the victims ranged from twenty-two to thirty years. The socioeconomic and age of offenders is similar to the victims. In terms of serious violence, the results showed that five out of ten homicides are committed by the husband, boyfriend, fiancé, partner, or lover. The author emphasized that although the myth that the home is a safe place pervades Brazilian culture, the reverse appears to be true and family relationships are not peaceful: 12 percent of homicides or attempts are made by the father, mother, son, stepfather, or mother-in-law. In other words, the aggressors are known by 66 percent of female victims. Finally, while multiple weapons were used, including knives, acid, fire, wood, iron, and hands, in seven out of ten cases, guns were used.

In a cross-sectional study in the Multi-Country Study on Women's Health and Domestic Violence against Women, conducted between 2000 and 2003 in ten countries including Brazil, Schraiber and others (2007) selected a representative sample in the city of São Paulo and in fifteen municipalities of the Zona da Mata of Pernambuco. Participants were women whose ages ranged from fifteen to forty-nine years. There were 940 women in São Paulo and 1188 in Pernambuco who had been engaged in a prior affective-sexual partnership. Violence was classified as psychological, physical, and sexual and analyzed in regard to overlaps, recurrence of episodes, and severity and time of occurrence. The main results reveal that women in São Paulo and Pernambuco, respectively, reported at least one incident in their lifetime: psychological (41.8 to 48.9 percent), physical (2 to 33.7 percent), and sexual (10.1 to 14.3 percent). The authors found an overlap when more severe forms of violence were used.

According to the special secretariat for Policies for Women (2008), studies by Brazilian nongovernmental organizations in the area of domestic violence show that approximately 20 percent of women have been victims of some type of domestic violence. This number rises to 43 percent when different forms of aggression are included. A third of the women surveyed also reported assault with a firearm, general assault, or marital rape.

Data from research conducted by the University of São Paulo with the World Health Organization (2001) show that 27 percent of 4,299 women interviewed in and near the city of São Paulo and 34 percent in the Zona da Mata reported some incident of physical violence perpetrated by partners or ex-partners. A full 29 percent of respondents over fifteen years reported having been sexually assaulted by strangers. In research conducted by DataSenado in 2005, 17 percent of women said they had suffered some kind of domestic violence in their lives, and 40 percent reported having witnessed an act of domestic violence against other women; 80 percent of these acts of violence were physical (Brasil, 2005).

Deslandes and others (2007), De Oliveira Gaioli and Rodrigues (2008), and Lazenbatt and Thompson-Cree (2009) note that the issue of violence and its serious repercussions do not always reach health care providers. To face this reality, there is a need for continual education programs for health care professionals to perform in a coherent, technically appropriate, and ethical manner when dealing with victims of violence.

Most previous research of domestic violence in Brazil has used definitions that are translations or adaptations of partner violence from other studies, generally from North America. In this study we investigated how laypersons in Brazil understand violence in general and domestic violence in particular. To this aim, we conducted a qualitative study that collected and cataloged verbalized perceptions of these concepts in focus groups of men and women in the city of São Paulo, Brazil.

Method

Participants

A self-report questionnaire was developed for the purposes of this study. The questionnaire was divided into three sections. In the first section, participants were asked about various demographics such as schooling, age, and gender. The subsequent sections pertained to questions about domestic violence.

The questionnaire was administered to forty-two subjects (eighteen men and twenty-four women, mean age 32.2 ± 1.7) recruited randomly by psychologists and researchers in universities and other public and private institutions in São Paulo. Participants were asked to sign an informed consent. Table 2.1 displays sample demographics.

Table 2.1 Demographics

Demographics	Variables	N	Percentage
Gender	Male	18	47
	Female	24	53
Schooling	Less than eight year	1	2
	Eight years	4	10
	Between eight and eleven years	5	12
	Eleven years	12	29
	Incomplete higher education	14	33
	Higher education	6	14
Civil status	Married	14	33
	Single	21	50
	Living together	2	5
	Widowed	2	5
	Separated	3	7

The sample is heterogeneous. In terms of age, this ranged from nineteen to sixty-one years old. Likewise, the sample encompassed all educational levels of the Brazilian system. About half the sample was married, previously married, widowed, separated, or cohabiting, with the other half reporting single status.

Procedure and Measure

Participants were given the self-report questionnaire and were asked to write their answers directly on the questionnaire. After obtaining basic demographic information, participants were asked to respond to a series of questions pertaining to definitions of violence and domestic violence. In crafting these questions, the common Portuguese word *violência* was used to refer to general violence, and the common Portuguese term *violência de gênero* was used to refer to gender-based violence or domestic violence. Next, participants were also asked what circumstances they thought might exclude or include behaviors and dynamics from being considered as domestic violence. For example participants were presented with the following possibilities:

- The partner is prevented from wearing certain clothes.
- The partner requires the partner to wear certain clothes.
- The woman/man has sexual intercourse with a partner when she/he is not in the mood because he/she insists or pressures her/him.
- The woman/man has sexual intercourse with a partner when she/he is not in the mood because she/he threatened to use physical force.
- The woman/man has sexual intercourse with a partner when she/he is not in the mood because she/he used physical force to compel her/him.

Preliminary Categories and Working Definitions of Domestic Violence

Although many definitions of domestic violence exist, most researchers agree that domestic violence is manifested through physical, sexual, and psychological violence and, less commonly, neglect (Day et al., 2003). This conceptualization broadens the construct to include events that go beyond physical violence and may include emotional abuse, sexually coercive behaviors, and controlling behaviors. Souza and Lima (2007) suggest that, due to the different expressions of this construct in Brazilian Portuguese, on its complexity and polysemy, using the plural "violences" as an umbrella term would be more appropriate in data collection based on questionnaires or interviews. To guide our coding, we applied the following definitions.

(A) Physical violence: Physical violence can range from hitting to beating and homicides.
(B) Sexual violence: Sexual violence can be described as any type of sexual conduct perpetrated without consent. It may involve physical violence, psychological violence, or seduction and can range from vaginal and/or anal penetration to touching genitals or breasts, to forcing the victim to touch the offender, and to oral-genital contact. Sexual abuse encompasses everything from disturbing looks and caresses to extremely violent offenses leading to death.
(C) Psychological violence: Psychological violence is characterized by disrespect, verbal abuse, humiliation, intimidation, cheating, death threats, and emotional and material abandonment that results in mental suffering characterized by fear, humiliation, and hopelessness. It is the most subjective type of violence, although it is very frequently associated with corporal offenses. Psychological abuse has received increased attention as a powerful source of abuse in the Western world (Follingstad and Edmundson, 2010; Fortin et al., 2012; Rogers and Follingstad, 2011).

Responses were subsequently read and coded into initial groups using themes culled from both the theoretical literature and those that emerged from the data. A second coding was performed to finalize themes and codes by physical violence, sexual violence, psychological violence that encompassed verbal violence, moral aggression that comprised dynamics forcing the other to submit to his/her will, and other types of coercion.

Results and Discussion

On the whole, the participants treated the concept of general violence as one related to both physical and verbal acts. This finding corroborates the data found in literature (Krug et al., 2002). In addition, in contrast to most studies published in English-speaking literature, a considerable portion of the participants related to violence as a moral issue associated with the attempts to restrict autonomy, rather than merely a physical or behavioral act (see table 2.2). Overall, the responses reflect a multifaceted and interdependent conceptualization of violence. Thus, many participants considered a lack of respect toward the other

Table 2.2 Respondents' conceptualization of violence

What do you see as violence?
Lack of respect, communion / Hurting the other's dignity /Any act that hurts the other
Verbal and physical offense / Corporal offense / Psychological, verbal, and physical pressure / One person being physically attacked by another / Acting angrily
Any and every notion of an individual attacking another person
All that one is obliged [or forced?] to do against one's will
Any action that causes damage (either moral or physical) to another person or to oneself / physical or moral constraint upon a person to oblige him or her to submit to another person's will
A way to express nervousness

What is domestic violence to you?
Generally provoked by men who have some kind of addiction to narcotics or alcohol, who submit their family members to constraints to satisfy their desire
It happens when physical or moral violence happens in one's own home / Attacking one's intimate partner / Actions that happen among family members and can be physical, moral, or psychological / Violence that takes place within the domestic environment / Offense among relatives
Physical or verbal offense, as well as authoritarian behavior / Physical, verbal, or psychological offense / It happens when a person attacks his partner physically
Any way one uses to try to inhibit another person at home, feeling superior to others
Marriage and mistreating domestic workers and children / Treating domestic workers as slaves

as constituting violence. Interestingly, in some cases, lack of respect toward the self was also seen as an integral component of violence. Additionally, abuser's intolerance to the partner and abusive acts designed to bring about coerced submission to the abuser's desires and power were also among the dominant themes.

A further analysis reveals that participants' definitions and understanding of the term *domestic violence* exhibited further discordance with the formal definition of the term used institutionally and within academia. Despite the fact that this term commonly denotes violence between intimate partners within both the professional and the popular discourse (e.g., media outlets, soap operas) in Brazil, participants' responses did not adhere to this constraint. Two interesting themes emerged both in terms of perpetrators and victims. First, in terms of victims, the notion of domestic violence was applied to any physical violence committed against people who live together or share the same living space, including pets, the self, and domestic workers. Responses reflecting the notion of victims in shared space include "Marriage and mistreatment of maids and children, fights and mistreatment of children, elderly and animals."

The second theme pertained to not whom domestic violence specifically targeted but rather the family it generally affected. For example, respondents said, "Practice acts harmful to the welfare of a family," "When there is physical or moral violence in their own residence," "is everything that happens within a family environment," "aggression in your own home," "those who submit their families to the constraints to meet their wishes," and "physical aggression by their partners, verbal, physical, and moral by parents."

This dual understanding of domestic violence, which transcends the distinction between emotional intimacy and physical proximity or cohabitation primarily distinguished by the romantic and sexual nature of the relationship, was also reported in other studies (Day, 2003; Hegarty, 1998; Taft et al., 2001; Oliveira et al., 2009).

Interestingly, all answers were gender specific and referred to the offender as being male and to the victim—usually his partner or a child—as female. None of the responses entertained the possibility that the offender might be a female. Such responses include "Practiced by men with some sort of addiction to drugs or alcohol" and "When a woman is assaulted in the home, being hurt with injuries on the body." Finally, as illustrated by the first response, some participants also included causal factors (generally, drugs, alcohol, poverty, and stress) in domestic violence as part of their responses.

Next, we examined what sorts of events participants considered as constituting a form of domestic violence. The results were marked with great variability and appeared to be influenced by both prevailing gender norms in Brazil and the gender of the informant. Overall, men and women differed in their opinion as to whether nonviolent coercive and controlling acts are considered domestic violence. However, in response to the scenarios whereby an individual does not let his or her partner wear a particular outfit or when he or she compels the companion to wear certain clothes was not considered as domestic violence by both male and female respondents.

In contrast, both male and female respondents expressed the belief that not letting female partners work in a paid job outside the home is a form of violence. Interestingly, the reverse did not hold true. Female responders did not think that restricting men from working was a form of violence, while male responders considered being restricted as a form of violence.

Female respondents believed that searching the female partner's handbag without her knowledge was a form of violence, but male responders did not agree with this statement. However, neither male nor female respondents considered it a form of violence when women searched their male partners' wallets without their knowledge. Women did not consider withholding telephone messages intended for their male partners as violence. Men, however, considered this act as violence only when it was committed by women and not when men withhold messages intended for their female partners.

A plausible explanation for this gender asymmetry is that a restriction of autonomy perpetrated by an intimate partner is first and foremost judged by cultural, contextual, and gender norms, before its interpersonal violence component is appraised (Stark, 2006). Thus, while women in the United States may consider restrictions to their personal preferences in dressing as coercive and controlling when judged against u.s. cultural norms, both male and female respondents in our sample did not consider the same restrictions as violent, despite their acknowledgment of the frustration inherent in that situation, due to the prevalence of such behavior in Brazilian society. In contrast, economic control and surveillance and pursuit behaviors were generally viewed as violent across the gender lines, although women tended to judge these actions as largely benign, while men generally perceived these actions as benign only when committed by them but not when exhibited by women.

Unexpected gender differences also emerged concerning unwanted sex. About half of the participants, without any discernible gender pattern, considered a male pressuring a female to engage in a sexual act as violence. However, pressuring a man to engage in a sexual act by his female partner was not considered an act of violence. Yet when threats or physical strength were used to force either men or women into having a sexual relationship with their partners against their will, both sexes considered this to constitute violence. Thus, using force is seen as crossing a threshold, whereas pressure is seen as violent only when it is male to female and only by some of the participants.

Taken together, these results suggest three interesting cultural and contextual differences between Brazil and other bodies of research conducted in the United States. One, restriction of freedom by way of clothing, which is widely accepted as coercive and controlling in the United States (e.g., Stark, 2006) (and possibly by middle-class Brazilians) does not carry the same meaning in our sample. However, whereas sexual violence is believed to be undetected and underrecognized in other research contexts (Brousseau et al., 2011; Choudhary et al., 2012; EUA Departamento de Justiça, 2005; Rennison,

2002), both men and women in our sample identified male-to-female pressure as abusive. One reason for these findings may be related to cultural value systems that specify what areas of life (and the body) should be recognized as autonomous and which areas as dynamic and collectivist. Finally, the use of physical abuse or threats to obtain sex, which was seen as abusive by most participants, underscored that domestic violence is associated with physical strength.

The association between physical violence and the identification of domestic violence is further corroborated by participants who defined all physical acts, such as pushing, slapping, or attacking the partner, and intent to injure even if there was no injury as expressions of violence by both sexes. When referring to verbal abuse, women believe that being called or calling the partner "useless" during an argument is a form of violence. Men, however, varied on whether being called "useless" in the course of an argument was a form of violence.

Conclusions

The data presented here are part of a pilot investigation for a broader study to be conducted in the city of São Paulo on men's and women's perceptions in relation to the concept of domestic violence. The responses indicate that the concept of domestic violence represents a wide variety of perpetrators and targets who share a household. When asked to identify what constitutes domestic violence, participants' responses were just as complex. While all participants identified situations of physical offenses as domestic violence, multiple differences arose when considering emotional abuse and coercion. In general, men felt that their coercive actions were rarely violent, whereas women identified similar actions as abusive. Interestingly, the reverse was also true in some cases where women felt that their actions were not abusive, whereas men found the same behaviors to be abusive.

The results of this study are the tip of the iceberg. The understanding of what is viewed as violence is the first step toward prevention and intervention. Rather than basing ongoing educational programs for health care professionals on Western models of domestic violence, more studies such as these can aid in proposing culturally relevant policies and interventions. Ultimately, the goal is to train health care providers to act in a coherent, technically skillful, and ethical manner when helping victims of violence as well as perpetrators, leading to a truly holistic health care system.

References

Anderson T. R., and Aviles, A. M. (2006). Diverse faces of domestic violence. *ABNF J.,* *17*(4), 129–132.

Blay, E. A. (2003). Violência contra a mulher e políticas públicas. *Estud. Av., 17*(49), 87–98.

Brasil. (2005). *Violência doméstica e familiar contra a mulher: Pesquisa de opinião pública nacional.* Senado Federal. Brasília, Brasil: Secretaria Especial de Comunicação Social e Secretaria de Pesquisa e Opinião.

Brasil, Ministério da Saúde. (2001). *Violência intrafamiliar: Orientações para aprática em serviço.* Brasília: Ministério da Saúde.

Brasil, Secretaria Especial de Políticas para as Mulheres. (2008). *Política nacional de enfrentamento à violência contra as mulheres.* Brasília, Brasil: Presidência da República.

Brousseau, M., Bergeron, S., Hébert, M., and McDuff, P. (2011). Sexual coercion victimization and perpetration in heterosexual couples: A dyadic investigation. *Archives of Sexual Behavior, 40*(2), 363–372. doi:10.1007/s10508–010–9617–0

Castel, R. (1998). *As metamorfoses da questão social.* Petropólis: Vozes.

Choudhary, E., Gunzler, D., Tu, X., and Bossarte, R. M. (2012). Epidemiological characteristics of male sexual assault in a criminological database. *Journal of Interpersonal Violence, 27*(3), 523–546. doi:10.1177/0886260511421674

Day, V. P., Telles, L. E., Zoratto de Borba, P. H., D'Azambuja, M. R. F., Machado, D. A., Silveira, M. B., Debiaggi, M. R., Blank, P., et al. (2003). Violência doméstica e suas diferentes manifestações. *Rev. Psiquiatr. Rio Gd. Sul, 25*(supp. 1), 9–21.

De Oliveira Gaioli, C. C. L., and Rodrigues, R. A. P. (2008). Occurrence of domestic elder abuse. *Rev Latino-am Enfermagem, 16*(3), 465–470.

Deslandes, S. F., Souza, E. R., Minayo, M. C. S., Costa C. R., Krempel, M., Cavalcanti, M. L., Moysés, S. J., et al (2007). Caracterização diagnóstica dos serviços que atendem vitimas de acidentes e violências em cinco capitais brasileiras. *Ciência and Saúde Coletiva*, 1(supp.), 1279–1290.

EUA Departamento de Justiça. (2005). Estudo de vitimização nacional crime. Accessed August 15, 2012. http://bjs.ojp.usdoj.gov.

Follingstad, D., and Edmundson, M. (2010). Is psychological abuse reciprocal in intimate relationships? Data from a national sample of American adults. *Journal of Family Violence, 25*(5), 495–508. doi:10.1007/s10896-010-9311-y

Fortin, I., Guay, S., Lavoie, V., Boisvert, J., and Beaudry, M. (2012). Intimate partner violence and psychological distress among young couples: Analysis of the moderating effect of social support. *Journal of Family Violence, 27*(1), 63–73. doi:10.1007/s10896-011-9402-4

Hegarty, K., Hindmarsh, E. D., and Gilles, M. T. (2000). Domestic violence in Australia: Definition, prevalence and nature of presentation in clinical practice. *Medical Journal of Australia, 173,* 363–367.

Hegarty, K., and Roberts, G. (1998). How common is domestic violence against women? The definition of partner abuse in prevalence studies. *Aust NZ J Public Health, 22*(1), 49–54.

Humphreys, C. A. (2007). Health inequalities perspective on violence against women. *Health and Social Care in the Community, 15*(2), 120–127.

Krug, E. G., Dahlberg, L. L., Mercy, J. A., Zwi, A. B., Lozano, R., et al. (2002). *Relatório mundial de violência e saúde.* Genebra: Organização Mundial da Saúde.

Lazenbatt, A., and Thompson-Cree, M. E. (2009). Recognizing the co-occurrence of domestic and child abuse: A comparison of community- and hospital-based midwives. *Health Soc Care Community, 17*(4), 358–370.

Minayo, M. C. (1994). Violência social sob a perspectiva da saúde publica. *Cadernos de Saúde Pública, 10*(supp.1), 7–18.

Minayo, M. C. (2005). Violência: Um problema para a saúde dos brasileiros. In Brasil, Ministério da Saúde, Secretaria de Vigilância em Saúde. (Ed.), *Impacto da violência na saúde dos brasileiros* (9–42). Brasília: Ministério da Saúde, Secretaria de Vigilância em Saúde.

Minayo, M. C. (2006). *The inclusion of violence in the health agenda: Historical trajectory. Ciência e Saúde Coletiva, 1*(2), 375–383.

Minayo, M. C. S., and Souza, E. R. (1998). Violência e saúde como um campo interdisciplinar e de ação coletiva. *Ciência and Saúde Coletiva-Manguinhos, 4*(3), 513–531.

Nunes, A. C. S. (2010). *A violência e a saúde pública: Um estudo bibliográfico de artigos publicados sem Brasil, 1998–2008.* Porto Alegre: Trabalho de Conclusão de Curso, Faculdade de Medicina, Universidade Federal do Rio Grande do Sul.

Okasha, A. A. (2007). Mental health and violence: WPA Cairo declaration; International perspectives for intervention. *International Review of Psychiatry, 19*(3), 193–200.

Oliveira, A. F. P. L., Schraiber, L. B., Hanada, H., and Durand, J. (2009). Atenção integral á saúde de mulheres em situação de violência de gênero: Uma alternativa para atenção primária em saúde. *Ciênca and Saúde Coletiva, 14*(4), 1037–1050.

Pick, S., Contreras, C., and Barker-Aguilar, A. (2006). Violence against women in Mexico: Conceptualizations and program application. *Ann. N.Y. Acad. Sci., 1087,* 261–278.

Rennison, C. M. (2002). Rape and sexual assault: Reporting to police and medical attention, 1992–2000. Washington, DC: u.s. Department of Justice and Bureau of Justice Statistics.

Rogers, M. J., and Follingstad, D. (2011). Gender differences in reporting psychological abuse in a national sample. *Journal of Aggression, Maltreatment and Trauma, 20*(5), 471–502.

Schraiber, L. B., d'Oliveira, A. F. P. L., França, I., Diniz, S., Portella, A. P., Ludermir, A. B., Valença, O., et al. (2007). Prevalência da violência contra a mulher por parceiro íntimo em regiões do Brasil. *Rev. Saúde Pública, 41*(5), 797–807. doi:10.1590/S0034-89102007000500014

Souza, E. R., and Lima, M. L. C. (2007). Panorama da violência urbana no Brasil e suas capitais. *Ciência and Saúde Coletiva, 11*(supp.), 1211–1222.

Taft, A., Hegarty, K., and Flood, M. (2001). Are men and women equally violent to intimate partners? *Aust NZ J Public Health, 25*(6), 498–500.

Tangwa, G. B. (2009). Research with vulnerable human beings. *Acta Tropica, 11*(2), S16–S20. doi:10.1016/j.actatropica.2009.08.021

WHO. (2002). *World report on violence and health.* Geneva: World Health Organization.

WHO. (2012). Violence against women: Intimate partner and sexual violence against women. Fact sheet N°239. Accessed November 20, 2012. www.who.int.

Commentary

Chitra Raghavan and Shuki J. Cohen

What Is Domestic Violence and How Do We Measure It?

We begin the book with one of the most fundamental questions in intimate partner violence (IPV) research: what is partner violence and how do we measure it? Both chapters in this section consider this same question, albeit from very different perspectives. Cook, Hamby, Stith, McCollum, and Mehne present a positivist measure development and psychometric study, whereas Serafim and Saffi obtain qualitative responses to open-ended questions. As such, commensurate with their different stances, both sets of authors differ in their general approaches and interpretive strategies. Cook and others present a thorough chapter that explicates the process of developing a measure to assess an important aspect of intimate partner dominance and aggression. The authors meticulously walk the reader through the various decisions associated with this measure and their rationale and provide a sensitive cost-benefit analysis of these decisions. First, the authors provide a clear definition of the construct of intimate partner dominance, along with its related constructs of intimate partner aggression and violence. They then operationalize their definitions by creating a set of reliable observable behaviors and attitudes.

The emphasis on definitional boundaries and operationalization are the core tenets of positivist approaches to psychological measurement. The positivist approach is a venerable tradition of science as an art of measurement. Emphasizing measurement at every step of the way, the authors then tackle the question of how best to measure the particularly complicated construct of intimate partner dominance and the potential violence associated with it.

Unlike, say, measuring depression, which focuses on the individual self, all measures of partner violence must first consider what constitutes a partnership—a task not as obvious as it seems. Indeed, in some countries one can be considered a partner only if the two individuals are legally married. In other countries a partner may be polyamorous with multiple spouses and of different biological sexes. Dating violence in countries where dating and or cohabiting is taboo or forbidden is, expectedly, an invisible phenomenon—underreported and unacknowledged. In contrast, in the United States, where cohabitation of unmarried partners is acceptable, dating violence has been identified as a significant problem. Thus, at the outset, the researchers must carefully define which aspect of partner violence they will measure. This point reemerges in a different fashion in the data of the twin chapter by Serafim and Saffi, which utilizes a radically different qualitative and nonpositivistic approach.

After creating carefully worded questions, Cook and others determine the setting in which they are going to be delivered (e.g., paper-and-pencil self reports, semistructured questionnaires or open-ended interviews). Along this way, the authors also discuss what they are *not* measuring and what lies at the interface between the construct they want to focus on (e.g., dominance) and its neighboring constructs (e.g., physical and sexual intimate partner violence). Cook and others describe several interesting methodological challenges that arise in measuring dominance. The first pertains to the ubiquity of the topic in the discourse about partner violence, contrasted by almost complete lack of instruments to measure it. Dominance, as the authors state, is difficult to measure because it refers to a wide variety of tactics, attitudes, and behaviors that cannot always be observed directly. The construct is inherently dynamic, dealing with power exchanges, rather than with events in which particular behaviors are being enacted. As such, it has a strong subjective and interpretative quality. The behavioral patterns associated with this construct surface in small and seemingly unimportant events throughout the day and are not always felt when they happen but rather exert their damage through their cumulative effect within the context of a restricting, dominating, and disparaging relationship environment. Because of the seeming normalcy of each individual act, the dominated partners have difficulty identifying them, despite the palpable effect of their total sum.

Cook and others approach these difficulties in two ways. First, they frame the questions they pose to their informants not as acts in a specific reference and time frame, but rather as a general characteristic of the partnership that may manifest in broad areas of the participant's intimate life. Second, by using a combination of hypothetical scenarios and existing research on the subject, the authors arrive at a set of carefully worded items operationally tied to their definition of the dominance construct. The authors also obtain data from both the male and the female partners in the relationship. This practice proves crucial to the ecological validity of the study—a point we take up in the commentaries comparing Tehee, Beck, and Anderson and Stark in part 3.

The resulting measure can be used easily and effectively to obtain responses from participants that can be compared across respondents and interpreted with relatively little error between participant groups. The authors demonstrate the effectiveness of the measure by examining its psychometric properties, namely validity and reliability. Short and effective assessment tools are crucial in settings where these kinds of assessments are routinely performed (such as intervention programs or parole boards) and where the results can be interpreted using the same rules by different people and at different time points. Cook and others' measure proves to have excellent reliability. Further, the good psychometric properties of the measure allowed the authors to compare male and female partner responses, resulting in a rather dramatically different interpretation of results than had the authors obtained data from only one side of the conflicted relationship. Specifically, the authors find that examining the relationship between male self-reported dominance and male self-reported violence suggests that dominance is unrelated to physical violence. However, examining the relationship between male self-reported dominance and female reports of male partner violence reveals substantial correlations between the two constructs. This pattern suggests that when self-reports of violence are being considered, perhaps especially when using structured survey measures that can provide only as much data as the questions ask, reports from women are more accurate. Although reports from both parties may be necessary to gain a full understanding of the phenomenon, this finding reinforces other studies that tell us that men underreport their own use of violence.

In contrast, in Serafim and Saffi's chapter, the issue of intimate partner violence is directly embedded in the larger context of any interpersonal violence. It is also directly embedded within a cross-cultural context. In their approach to exploring the boundaries of intimate partner violence, the authors entertain all forms of interpersonal violence that is proximal to the informant and do not restrict themselves to violence between intimates. Furthermore, rather than assume that women are invariably the victims, Serafim and Saffi ground their essay within a discourse of vulnerability and argue for the examination of any interpersonal violence within a domestic setting. Finally, in breaking away from the customary pathological framework that characterizes most psychological studies of the subject, the authors frame domestic violence as a public health problem rather than an individual-level or dyad-level problem.

Serafim and Saffi open with an exploration of the general concept of violence and the more specific concept of domestic violence from the linguistic, rather than the empirical, perspective. This is not unusual for researchers who attempt to explore the relevance of a well-studied construct to another culture and another language. This linguistic perspective is then integrated to the limited research on violence in general and domestic violence in particular in Brazil. To survey the current state of the construct, the authors draw from the legal and public health studies of the subject in their region and ultimately reach a point where they examine the meanings and definitions of what is rational or not, what is relative, and what is real (e.g., Shweder, 1991, 2) in the Brazilian culture and society vis-à-vis IPV.

The authors then converge on an approach to the subject of domestic violence that strikes a balance between the cultural and the cross-cultural conceptualizations of the construct. In seeking to provide a comparative and global understanding of domestic violence, they emphasize the historical developments that put IPV at the forefront of research and popular consciousness in the United States and contrast it with the Brazilian growing awareness to the underpinning of violence, albeit with less regard to the marital, legal, or intimate status of the partner per se.

Framing IPV as a public health issue represents a subtle point of difference with the framework in which violence is viewed and handled in the United States and other countries that follow U.S. research and policy on this subject. While a large body of scholars and practitioners define IPV as a public health issue, this interpretation is uncommon among U.S. psychologists (and is particularly underrepresented in current forensic psychological circles). Psychological theories mostly view IPV as a result of psychological causes rather than the matrix of circumstantial, economic, and sociological factors that the authors suggest. This is particularly interesting considering the fact that both Serafim and Safi are forensic psychologists by training, and their education and training, like those of many forensic psychologists around the world, were largely influenced by U.S. scholarship that typically limits and defines violence strictly at the individual level, making it compatible with existing criminal-justice and legal frameworks. Interestingly, while the authors placement of domestic violence in a general context of interpersonal violence and public health is rare in psychology, their own (academic) definitions of what comprises domestic violence is more mainstream.

Why do the authors situate the IPV question as one that is best viewed from both a general interpersonal violence lens and a public health problem? Or asked differently, why don't U.S. forensic psychologists situate IPV as a general violence and subsequently a public health problem? One pragmatic possibility is offered by the authors themselves—the prevalence of violence and violence-related mortality in Brazil have led the Brazilian authorities and scholars to treat it as a public health issue with only secondary regard to the identity of the perpetrator. This approach directs the attention to the injuries, burden, and cost to both the victim and the state. Thus, Brazilian state and media emphasize violence as a widespread societal problem rather than an individually constructed dysfunction of dyadic relationships.

A pivotal factor in this approach to domestic violence in Brazil hinges on the interdependent nature of Brazilian kinship systems, which, unlike those in the United States, mostly revolve around the extended family—rather than the nuclear family being the group of reference. Within such a system, domestic violence can happen between any coinhabitants or proximal relations, including second-degree relatives and domestic help (and we see this in the participant responses). Thus, the authors situate interpersonal violence in the Brazilian reality of collective kinship. In doing so, Serafim and Saffi's chapter highlights an important consideration that is too often ignored in psychology—that the epistemology or the body of knowledge that we can draw on to decide whether and how IPV occurs is itself culturally bound. In the United States, psychological theories of IPV presume two individual agents in an isolated intimate relationship who have a violent or abusive exchange between them, although, as the reader will see, this view is vociferously disputed by Stark and further critiqued by Allen and others. In this chapter both the conceptualization and the open-ended responses of the participants are in coherence in defining IPV as continuously existing within the general context of interpersonal violence.

Serafim and Saffi interviewed forty-two participants in a large Brazilian city. Using a semistructured questionnaire, their respondents were asked how they would define domestic violence. These open-ended questions resulted in a variety of response content (and response strategies), conglomerating motivation for domestic violence, intent, actual observable behaviors, and circumstantial attributions of the behavior. This open-ended approach has the distinct advantage of reflecting the subjective understanding of the construct by the affected individuals without the biasing effect of the underlying theories that the social sciences might have imposed on it. These multiple interpretations are not reduced or excluded to fit a strict preexisting definition of the construct. Arguably, these subjective experiences are the most relevant and ecologically valid to the reality of the psychological experience of IPV.

These rich responses to the open-ended questions provide much food for thought and psychological insights. The participants' answers challenge the "equal level of analysis" approach that undergirds most current research methodologies in IPV. The participants provided answers that referred to different patterns of IPV that may occur at different social junctures, using motivations as inextricable from their definition and understanding of IPV, and identified perpetrators and victims who may or may not be involved in romantic relationships. In fact, from a strict postpositivist point of view, their answers may seem messy and irrational when contrasted with paper-and-pencil questionnaire data. How could a participant define domestic violence as an injury to the self? How could another include violent acts toward pets or domestic workers in their response? As the authors predicted in their initial reflection on the construct, the participants focused on vulnerability in their understanding of the experience of IPV and anchored their responses in the identification of the victims (i.e., the elderly, the young, children). Participant responses suggest that the query "what is domestic violence?" is inextricable from the rich narrative that melds together the answers to "who does what, to whom, and why?" From a cultural psychology point of view, such answers are irrational only if we believe that the response to the question "what is IPV?" must necessarily conform to an operational definition of IPV as a largely decontextualized set of violent acts perpetrated within an intimate sexual relationship. However, as the authors note, the point of alignment for the responses appears to be not whether one is in an intimate sexual relationship but whether one shares a similar space and codependencies with the perpetrator.

The authors' implicit definition of domestic violence, as expressed in their questions and the participants' descriptions of that which for them is experienced as domestic violence, paves the way to a rich understanding of the construct. First, the authors used items that would be conventionally recognized as comprising acts of abusive partner violence in the West. Indeed, some of the items Serafim and Saffi ask their participants about are reminiscent of items in Cook and others' Dominance Scale. However, the responses themselves are not always aligned with Western formulation or understanding of domestic violence. Second, as the authors note, the infringement of partner autonomy, regardless of concomitant physical abuse, is considered domestic violence for many of the participants. Thus, restricting someone's movement is frequently considered abuse but telling them what to wear is less clearly so. Volpp (2001) makes just this argument when considering what is important to feminists in the United States compared to elsewhere. While female sexuality is a sacred arena in the United States, it may be less so or simply differently defined elsewhere. In Serafim and Saffi's sample, unlike many u.s. samples, sexual coercion was identified as abusive almost unanimously by women. These two responses suggest different sensitivities and expectations of autonomous sexuality than what is widely held in the United States.

Third, many participants used the term *moral* aggression, a term we wouldn't expect in the West. This finding suggests that a wide array of emotional abuses and coercive practices are seen as an attack to the integrity of the partner's honor or sanctity. However, what *did* constitute moral aggression varied widely across men and women. Despite their fundamentally different approach, their findings of gender differences mirror the pattern that Cook and others report. Specifically, in Cook and others' study, men's report of their own dominance doesn't correlate with abuse. However, women's report of men's dominance does correlate with their reported level of abuse. We see the same pattern—men don't consider many of their coercive acts to be abusive, whereas women do. Fourth, the results suggest both universals and differences in the understanding of domestic violence. The results also caution the researcher that using only identification or recognition formats might potentially misrepresent and bias the experiential definition that participants might give to domestic violence and constrain them to a set of factors that may not represent their reality.

In conclusion, Cook and others' chapter is a thorough summary of the most common practices used to measure domestic violence in the West. As such, it makes full use of an existing system of definitions, operationalizations, and quantitative results that have matured over time to a body of knowledge about the issue. The authors then construct a measure corresponding to a hypothesized and underresearched component of the abuse process and test its relevance using statistical methods for detecting association between putatively related constructs. These modifications to the classical straightforward positivistic practices make it possible for social scientists like Cook and others to measure complex constructs that may bear ecological relevance to intimate partner violence. However, self-reports of operationalized constructs like dominance and aggression run the risk of restricting the representation of the subtle ongoing dynamic and subjective experience of these phenomena.

In contrast, Serafim and Saffi start with minimal definitions, operationalizations, measures, and body of results pertaining to their target population. In recognition of the vast differences in the individual, social, and political characteristics of this target population, they embark on nonpositivistic open-ended interviews that emphasize experiential holistic definitions of domestic violence. This approach evinces a natural trade-off, whereby there is no preexisting standardized definition of the construct and no distinction between observable and unobservable or between behavioral and cognitive or moral aspects of it. There is also little way to validate their results or to test a particular hypothesis. Instead, this line of research enjoys greater ecological validity by staying close to the experience of the participants.

As Adorno (1973) so effectively wrote, knowledge is collected through a series of categorizations and subsequent identification of these categories. But in pursuing this way of ordering our world, we lose some of the reality, perhaps because we have constrained reality artificially or perhaps because (in a fact that is at times mystifying to the social scientist) language cannot always represent reality in its entirety and we must sometimes rely on the fuzziness between the boundaries of categorical identities. For most successful scientific paradigms throughout the history of science, it is the growing complementation and integration of qualitative and quantitative methodologies that confer to the constructs at hand, and to the theories associated with them, their ultimate usefulness for society.

References

Adorno, T. W. (1973) *Negative dialectics*. London: Verso.

Shweder, R. A. (1994). *Thinking through cultures: Expeditions in cultural psychology.* Cambridge, MA: Harvard University Press.

Volpp, L. (2001). Feminism versus multiculturalism. *Columbia Law Review, 101,* 1181–1218.

Critical-Thinking Questions

1. In both studies, measurement of a construct is bound to prior knowledge of the construct. Please explicate what this sentence means.
2. Who is a better judge of what is domestic violence—the experts who study it or the people who have experienced it? Why?
3. Can experts ever really be impartial about their subject matter? What are some conscious and unconscious biases that experts may hold about the construct that they are measuring? How might confirmation bias—the nonconscious tendency to prefer data congruent with our preconceived hypotheses—influence research?
4. What is the advantage of acquiring data from both men and women? What do Cook, Hamby, Stith, and Mehne find that they may not have found if they had included only men or only women?
5. What are the advantages and disadvantages of defining intimate partner violence, as Cook and others do in chapter 1?
6. Serafim and Saffi do not predefine the term *domestic violence* for their participants. Which findings in the study by Serafim and Saffi can be attributed to the fact that the term *domestic violence* was not limited to intimate partner relationships? In your opinion, is this an advantage or disadvantage of the methodology used?
7. To what extent do you think male dominance is universal or culture-bound?
8. Of the results reported by Serafim and Saffi in tables 1 and 2, how many would hold in your cultural reference?
9. Based on your answer to question 7, which measurement method—that used by Cook and others or that used by Serafim and Saffi—would you use and why?

Advanced Questions

1. You ask a group of women who have experienced intimate partner violence to define violence. They identify physical and emotional abuse as forms of violence but disagree that sex between an intimate couple can ever be considered rape, even if she didn't consent. As a researcher, would you omit sexual violence in your measure or include it? Justify your response.

2. How would a public health administrator (whose mandate is to heal communities) differ from a clinical psychologist (whose mandate is to treat individuals) when addressing intimate partner violence?

II CLAIMS ABOUT GENDER PARITY AND DOMESTIC VIOLENCE

Six Blind Men and an Elephant

Learning Objectives

1. Develop an increasingly sophisticated understanding of the types and components of intimate partner abuse.
2. Understand how sex and gender represent different constructs and can be treated differently at individual, group, and societal levels.
3. Understand the differential impact of sex and gender on intimate partner dynamics.

Melissa Tehee, University of Arizona; Connie J. A.
Beck, University of Arizona; and Edward R.
Anderson, University of Texas at Austin

3 | Sex Differences in Intimate Partner Abuse Victimization

This chapter contains two parts and works to tease apart different conceptions of physical aggression and intimate partner abuse (IPA) currently found in the violence literature and then tests a popular typology of IPA in divorcing couples (Kelly and Johnson, 2008). For this chapter, the term IPA was chosen because it encompasses the broadest range of harmful behaviors and is defined as any behavior that causes harm physically, psychologically, or sexually (Ellsberg et al., 2008).

Prior research has often conflated lower-level acts of physical abuse (which occur more frequently) with more severe physical violence (which occur much less frequently) (White et al., 2000). From this research, it is then often concluded that women are as violent toward their partners as are men (Archer, 2000; Felson and Outlaw, 2007; Dutton, Hamel and Aaronson, 2010; Straus, 2006, 2008). Because of the differences in reporting rates in these two forms of physical IPA, we questioned whether these sex differences would remain when looking only at lower levels of physical abuse in a sample of divorcing couples. In part 1 we explore sex differences in reported victimization when focusing on lower-level physical acts of abuse only. Part 2 then explores sex differences in reported victimization when measuring a much broader array of IPA-related behaviors.

In addition to conflating forms of physical abuse and violence, prior research has also often excluded from the analyses important forms of abuse and violence. Many highly cited and influential reviews of IPA studies (Archer, 2000) exclude sexual forms of abuse and violence. This systematically biases the knowledge base on sex differences toward finding no differences because sexual abuse and violence have differential rates of victimization (White et al., 2000). Thus, in part 2 we also explore differential rates of reporting sexual forms of abuse and violence.

Gaining popularity in the literature are couple-level patterns of IPA (Johnson, 2006; Kelly and Johnson, 2008; Stark, 2007). Typologies have been proposed as a way to better understand the patterns of different forms of IPA that occur together. A problem with prior research investigating these typologies is that they are often tested on samples of women and men who are not married to each other (Dutton et al., 2010). In part 2 we explore an interesting aspect of the current study, couple-level data. Data for both parts of this chapter were gathered at the same time, using the same method and procedure. The sample consisted of divorcing couples disputing custody or parenting time of their children and attending court-mandated mediation to attempt to resolve these disputes. This chapter provides an important opportunity to empirically investigate different definitions of IPA and to discuss methodological limitations associated with studies on IPA.

Part 1: Use of Lower-Level Physical Acts of Abuse

Widely used measurement tools, such as the original Conflict Tactics Scale (CTS; Straus, 1979), made it possible to quickly measure the frequency and severity of behaviorally specific, physical acts that took place in a relationship within a certain period. "The CTS was revolutionary because it allowed researchers to quantitatively study events that had often been ignored culturally and typically took place in private" (Langhinrichsen-Rohling, 2005, 109). Using the CTS and similar instruments, researchers surveyed men and women, large high school and college student dating samples (Archer, 2000; Straus, 2008), and sometimes community samples (Felson and Outlaw, 2007; Straus and Gelles, 1990; Straus, Gelles, and Steinmetz, 1980/2006). From these studies, some researchers often then concluded that overall women they studied were just as *aggressive or violent* as men or sometimes even more so (Archer, 2000; Dutton and Nicholls, 2005; Gelles, 2007; Straus and Gelles, 1990; Straus, 2008). It is extremely important to understand what was actually measured in making this determination. Research exploring IPA often conflated lower-level acts of physical abuse (e.g., shoving, pushing, hitting, and scratching) from more severe forms of violence (e.g., choking, strangling, breaking bones) (Archer, 2000). Thus, in our study we hypothesize that there would not be sex differences in the lower-level forms of physical abuse as defined earlier.

To test this view of sex and IPA, the current study explores data on IPA from couples who, at the time, were undergoing divorce proceedings in the local court. These couples were mandated to attend mediation by local court rule

(Arizona Superior Court, 1998) before any court hearings would be scheduled. Thus, this sample is unique in some important ways. First, the couples in this study were currently married to (although divorcing) each other. Therefore, instead of generally comparing women's reports of victimization by acts of physical abuse from men's, we could compare couples' reported acts toward each other within each couple.

Assessing both partners in a couple is rarely done because researchers are concerned that doing so would put victims at increased risk of future violence if the abuser learns what is disclosed. Second, couples samples (whether married or unmarried, with or without children in common) are traditionally not assessed in the violence literature. As noted earlier, often researchers study high school and college student's dating partners (Archer, 2000; Dutton et al., 2010) or nationally representative community samples (Tjaden and Thoennes, 2000; Straus and Gelles, 1990). Additional clinical samples have included women residing in shelters or court referred for services (Graham-Kevan and Archer, 2008; Hardesty and Ganong, 2006). Although the current sample is different from general studies of IPA, this sample is one that is at increased risk of IPA. Decades of research have found that during the period directly after a couple separates, levels of violence and rates of homicide increase substantially (Campbell, 2005; Hardesty, 2002). Thus, participating in a court-mandated dispute resolution process at the very time couples are at increased risk of IPA presents important issues concerning the adequacy of IPA screening.

Succinctly, divorce mediation is based on the assumption that couples can come together in a less adversarial forum than a courtroom and, with the assistance of a neutral third party, negotiate an agreement that is fair and better suited to their family than one ordered by a judge (Beck and Sales, 2001). Over the past three decades, mediation has become extremely popular worldwide as a court-connected process for couples disputing custody or parenting time of their children (Beck, Sales, and Emery, 2004; Maloney et al., 2007; Tondo, Coronel, and Drucker, 2001; J. Walker, 2010). IPA is commonly reported in mediation samples, with a recently documented rate of 52 percent when clients were asked directly about physical violence. Interestingly, in 47 percent of the cases in one mediation study, neither parent discussed IPA in either separate screening interviews or separation sessions before or during mediation (Administrative Office, 2010). This finding could have several different meanings: the respondents did not perceive the IPA as serious enough to bring up; it occurred in the distant past; it was mutually perpetrated; it was not thought to be important enough to disrupt negotiations in mediation; or the victims were so fearful of negative consequences they chose not to disclose it (Kelly and Johnson, 2008). Alternatively, it is possible that the mediator failed to sensitively screen for its presence, thus limiting detection options. Many, although by no means all, mediators conduct some type of screening for IPA (Ballard et al., 2011; Holtzworth-Munroe, Beck, and Applegate, 2010).

Concerns have been raised about the fairness of the mediation process for victims of IPA. For example, is it fair for victims to be required to negotiate directly with an abuser? Given power differences in abusive relationships and the fact that the victim and abuser will remain parents and likely have some contact after the divorce, is a victim truly free to discuss issues without fear of escalating the IPA? Beyond fairness, concerns have been raised about the adequacy of agreements negotiated by victims of IPA. For example, will victims insist that safety precautions (e.g., supervised exchanges of children, supervised visitation, or limits on contact between abuser and victim[s]) be included in the agreements that are negotiated? These issues have been a focus of intense debate (Beck and Sales, 2001). Without careful analysis of IPA in divorcing couple relationships, it is impossible to answer these vital questions.

The current data set gathered information on each parent's reported experience of lower-level acts of physical abuse by the other partner in the last twelve months. Based on the first definition of IPA noted earlier, that women in this sample use at the same rate as men, we hypothesize that the amount of lower-level physical acts of abuse will not be significantly different for fathers and mothers in this sample.

Method for Part 1: Use of Lower-Level
Physical Acts of Abuse

Participants

The sample for this study was drawn from married couples with children, living in a large urban area in the Southwest, who had filed for divorce. Only couples attending mediation for the first time as a couple during a specific twenty-nine-month period were included in the study. This resulted in an initial sample of 1,015 couples (i.e., 2,030 individual participants). Cases not retained in the sample were those returning to mediation predivorce or attending mediation postdivorce and those who did not meet the criteria (never-married couples mediating paternity, custody, or parenting time and grandparents asserting rights to see or raise grandchildren). Additionally, these analyses were limited

Table 3.1 Demographic variables

		Range
Age of father (mean/SD)	37 / 8	19–71
Age of mother (mean/SD)	34 / 7	17–54
First marriage of father	736 (86%)	0–4
First marriage of mother	725 (85%)	0–3
Length of marriage in years (mean/SD)	8.85 / 6.19	.04–38.97
Number of minor children per household (mean/SD)	2 / .94	1–6

Education	Mother	Father	Local area 2000 census (%)*
0–12	98 (11%)	78 (9%)	17
High school graduate	304 (36%)	326 (38%)	23
Some college	259 (30%)	231 (27%)	27
College graduate (AA or higher)	146 (18%)	170 (20%)	34
Not answered	45 (5%)	47 (6%)	

Ethnicity	Mother	Father	Local area 2000 census (%)
Caucasian	506 (59%)	515 (60%)	75
Hispanic	265 (31%)	237 (28%)	29
African American	15 (2%)	24 (3%)	3
Asian American	8 (1%)	6 (1%)	2
Native American	5 (1%)	9 (1%)	3
Other	5 (1%)	7 (1%)	13
Not answered	45 (5%)	54 (6%)	

Employment and income	Mother	Father
Reported employment	667 (77%)	797 (92%)
Reported income (mean/SD)	$12,286	$25,230
Reported income range	$0–$109,200	$0–$215,520

Note: *2000 Census data used because of study period.

to those cases in which both individuals of the couple completed the self-report items in the premediation screening. These limitations resulted in the inclusion of 852 couples (i.e., 1,704 individuals). Participant education, employment, and income demographics are detailed in table 3.1.

Procedure

Couples mandated to attend divorce mediation had a choice to pay for a private mediation service or to attend the court-connected, free mediation service. The data in this study were gathered at the court-connected, free mediation service in one jurisdiction. Variables of interest were abstracted from information contained in the mediation case file. The file included demographic information and premediation screening forms, including measures of IPA.

Measures of IPA

Intimate Partner Abuse within each couple was assessed through the Relationship Behavior Rating Scale (RBRS). The RBRS is a revised version of the Partner Abuse Scales (Attala, Hudson, and McSweeny, 1994). The RBRS shows sturdy validity as compared to the original Partner Abuse Scales (Beck et al., 2009) and as compared to the Conflict Tactics Scales (CTS2; Straus, Hamby, Boney-McCoy, and Sugarman, 1996; Beck, Menke, and Figueredo, 2013). The RBRS contains forty-one items concerning a range of behaviorally specific acts. Each partner was asked to report how often he or she experienced each of the items in the past twelve months. The frequency was measured on a scale of 0–6 (0 = none of the time, 1 = very rarely, 2 = a little of the time, 3 = some of the time, 4 = a lot of the time, 5 = most of the time, 6 = all of the time). Five theoretically derived subscales of types of IPA were compiled, and we discuss the subscale of physical abuse in this analysis. Five items made up the physical abuse scale (e.g., My partner pushed or shoved me around; My partner hit or punched me). The remaining subscales are discussed in part 2.

Results for Part I: Use of Lower-Level Physical Acts of Abuse

Internal consistency was assessed using Cronbach's alpha statistic and showed that the items in this scale have a high internal consistency and measure the unidimensional construct of lower-level physical abuse. The Cronbach's alpha for mothers' reports of lower-level physical abuse was .84; fathers' reports of lower-level physical abuse was .87; combined fathers' and mothers' reports was .85.

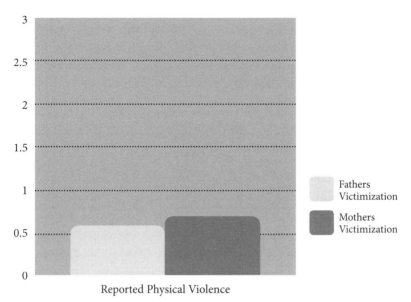

Figure 3.1 Mean reported physical abuse victimization

Mean scores on the subscale were calculated individually for the father and the mother in each couple. A paired samples t-test was used to account for the reports in the context of a couple. This analysis found that divorcing mothers' reporting of her partners' use of lower-level physical abuse (M = .60, S = .88) is not statistically different from fathers' reporting of their partner's use of lower-level physical abuse (M = .57, S = .87) (paired t (837) = .899, p = .37), as shown in figure 3.1.

Discussion of Part I: Use of Lower-Level
Physical Acts of Abuse

Intimate partner abuse has sometimes been defined as acts of physical aggression or lower-level acts of physical abuse. In the current study lower-level physical abuse was measured using a specific subscale of the RBRS. Results of analyses using this subscale showed that there was no significant difference in average (mean) amounts of reported victimization by fathers and mothers in a sample of divorcing couples. This finding supports a limited definition that women are just as likely as men to perpetrate this form of abuse. While this definition is supported in the current data, remember this is an extremely limited definition of IPA. The concept of intimate partner abuse includes many more behaviors than low-level acts of physical abuse. An important question is whether women perpetrate more severe forms of physical violence at the same rate as men. This clear differentiation has not been made in the current literature (Archer, 2000; Dutton and Nicholls, 2005; Felson and Outlaw, 2007).

Part 2: Use of a Range of Intimate Partner Abuse Behaviors

More comprehensive definitions of IPA include a broader list of behaviors, such as psychological abuse and threats of physical violence in addition to lower-level physical abuse, sexual forms of abuse and violence, and what is now termed coercive control (Johnson, 2006; Stark, 2007). Added together, these other elements give a more complete picture of the range of behaviors that occur within the context of IPA. While decades of research have addressed many of these IPA-related behaviors (psychological abuse: O'Leary, 1999; threats and physical violence: Tjaden and Thoennes, 2000; sexual abuse and violence: Bergen, 2004; Koss, Gidycz, and Wisniewski, 1987) coercive control is a concept that is relatively unexplored empirically (Dutton, Goodman, and Schmidt, 2006).

The term *coercive control* was coined to define a pattern of control and manipulation used by one or both spouses to control the other spouse, making him or her subordinate to the abuser. Coercive control is a factor underlying IPA (Kelly and Johnson, 2008; Stark, 2006). There is some consensus concerning this form of IPA once identified as "Culture of Violence" by Fischer, Vidmar, and Ellis (1993) and then as "Intimate Terrorism" by Johnson (2008). The term "Coercive Controlling Violence" was then given to this type of abuse. Coercive controlling violence is a pattern of control and manipulation, in which a person controls their spouse's actions, relationships, and activities. This type of abuse includes surveillance, and victims are often punished when they fail to follow the rules established by the coercive party (Kelly and Johnson, 2008). Unfortunately, since IPV is a relatively new concept, there are not yet established measures of coercive control in studies on IPA. Some researchers further argue for including measures of sexual assault, intimidation, and coercion when comparing use of IPV by men and women, because forced sexual relations is yet another tool used by the abuser to control the victim (DeKeseredy, 2006; Swan and Snow 2006). As noted earlier, an instrument widely used to measure IPV is the Conflict Tactics Scale (CTS). Although the CTS has been recently revised to include sexual abuse (CTS2; Straus et al., 1996), it does not include a measure of coercive control. Therefore, the previous reviews of studies also do not include coercive control (Archer, 2000; Felson and Outlaw, 2007; Straus et al., 1996; Straus and Gelles, 1990).

Assessment of all types of IPA is especially poignant for partners who are divorcing and arguing over custody and parenting time, as the couples in this sample were. It is likely that one partner is no longer acquiescing to coercion, making physical forms of violence more likely, even if there was no prior physical violence in the relationship, but coercive control was high (Beck and Raghavan, 2010). Ellis and Stuckless (2006) found that postseparation, coercive controlling behaviors were highly correlated with serious physical harm. These findings increase the importance of mediators screening for all types of IPA including coercive controlling behaviors and threats, along with past physical forms of violence.

Thus, it is hypothesized that when a broader range of abusive and violent behaviors are considered, a very different picture of the couple-level IPA will emerge, such that mothers will report higher rates of all IPA victimization sub-scales, except for lower-level physical abuse noted earlier, in which there will be no significant difference between fathers' and mothers' reports of victimization.

Another important area emerging in the violence literature is the need to assess couple-level types of IPA. This is particularly important for divorcing couples, as it is the role of the court to determine the living arrangements that are in the "best interests of the child[ren]" as defined by legal statutes (Beck and Sales, 2001). Without a full understanding of IPA within the couple relation-ship, this determination is impossible. While researchers have looked at male abusers' patterns of abuse, far less attention has been paid to female abusers' patterns of abuse, and research concerning both married partners' IPA is nearly nonexistent (Johnson, 2006; Straus, 2006).

When thinking about couple-level patterns of IPA, Johnson (2006) hypoth-esized that there were several patterns. The first pattern, detailed earlier, is co-ercive controlling violence. A second type of IPA is violent resistance (resis-tance to a violent, coercively controlling partner). This type of abuse has been described as the use of IPA in response to a coercively controlling partner. In this context, IPA behaviors are an attempt to stop the violence, defend oneself against an attack, or physically defend others, such as children or pets. Some battered women's advocates and researchers have categorized some female-initiated IPA as this type (female resistance, resistive/reactive violence, self-defense) (Kelly and Johnson, 2008; Pence et al., 2003; L. Walker, 1984; Yllo and Bograd, 1988). This type of violence garners disproportionate media attention, particularly in the most severe cases when women murder their abusive partners (Kelly and Johnson, 2008). Interestingly, in research, few factors differentiated battered women homicide offenders from battered women who did not murder their partners. What did differentiate the battered women who did not kill their partners from the battered women homicide offenders was the nature and type of abusers' behaviors. Abusers who were killed were reported to attack their partners more frequently, attack them with more severe injuries, sexually assault them more often, and make more frequent death threats against them (Browne, 1987; Kelly and Johnson, 2008). And the murders often occurred in the context of separation, when the battered women were attempting to leave the abuser (Kelly and Johnson, 2008).

A third type of IPA is situational couple violence. This type of IPA does not reflect core issues of power and control, and fear is also not characteristic (Johnson and Leone, 2005; Johnson, 1995). Misogynist attitudes are also not characteristic of men involved in this type of IPA, compared to men involved in coercive controlling violence (Holtzworth-Munroe et al., 2000; Kelly and Johnson, 2008). In this type of violence, IPA is contextually the result of situations or arguments between partners that escalate into physical violence. One or both partners are unable to manage their anger or have poor conflict resolution skills. It is thought to occur more frequently than the other types and to involve more minor forms of violence (pushing, shoving, grabbing). When assessed through large population surveys, perpetration by men and women were reported at similar rates (Kelly and Johnson, 2008; Kwong, Bartholomew, and Dutton, 1999). Severe violence and core issues surrounding power and control are nearly always absent from this group.

The fourth type of IPA is separation-instigated violence. This type of IPA occurs upon separation among couples with no prior history of IPA. It is believed to be triggered by traumatic experiences related to the separation. For example, it is triggered when, with no prior warning, a parent comes home from work and finds the family home empty. A prominent professional or political figure is humiliated by being served divorce papers by a process server or comes home and finds the partner with a lover. This type of IPA can include stalking, threats with weapons, destroying cherished property, throwing objects at a partner, sideswiping or ramming a partner's car (Kelly and Johnson, 2008). Perpetrators of this type of IPA generally admit their behaviors, and orders of protection tend to be effective. Nonetheless, it ought to be noted that this form of abuse can be extremely dangerous and potentially lethal (Dutton, 2007; Holtzworth-Munroe et al., 2000; Jacobson and Gottman, 1998; Kelly and Johnson, 2008).

This type of IPA is initiated by both men and women and tends to be uncharacteristic of the parties, as well as unexpected. In a study of high-conflict parents disputing custody, about a fifth of the sample indicated the violence began after separation (Johnston and Campbell, 1993).

The fifth type is mutual violent control. This type of IPA is described as having two coercively controlling and violent partners. By definition it is initiated by both men and women (Johnson, 2006; Hardesty and Ganong, 2006). Kelly and Johnson (2008) found only a few couples who met this criteria, and little is known about its frequency, features, or consequences. This is an important type to investigate in the mediation context in that little is known about this type, and the consequences for children could be severe (Kelly and Johnson, 2008).

One qualitative study assessed divorcing couples in relation to the discussed typology, however, did not find evidence of all five types. This study relied on a sample of women attending a court-mandated education program for all divorcing parents in two counties in the central United States. Results found that women reported one of three patterns of IPA (Hardesty and Ganong, 2006). The first pattern included chronic verbal, emotional, psychological, sexual, and physical abuse, physical violence, and threats of violence accompanied by coercive controlling behaviors, which began early in the relationship and continued throughout the marriage. This type was similar to that of coercive controlling violence noted earlier. The second pattern included episodic physical abuse with coercive controlling behaviors. The central dynamic in this type was control; however, the physical abuse was infrequent and generally not severe. This pattern was not found in the original typology. The third pattern included episodic physical abuse but was not accompanied by a pattern of coercive control. The physical abuse generally occurred in the context of specific arguments often related to money or drug use. This type is similar to that of situational couple violence. It is unclear why the other types of IPA proposed by Johnson (2006) were not found in this sample. It could be that the sample was restricted as all women in the study were screened for experiencing physical abuse and violence prior to or after the divorce.

While these types of IPA have been discussed in the context of mediation samples, they have yet to be investigated empirically with a mediation population. Therefore, it is not yet known if the frequency, severity, context, or type of IPA found in mediation couples resembles that seen in large-scale national surveys of the community (situational couple violence) or the type of violence more commonly found in shelter, agency, hospital, or law enforcement surveys (coercive controlling violence) (Kelly and Johnson, 2008), or whether IPA is more similar to that found in the sample of women attending court-mandated parent education (chronic IPA using all types plus coercive controlling behaviors, episodic physical abuse with coercive controlling behaviors, or physical abuse only; Hartesty and Ganong, 2006). We theorized that the current study sample will more closely resemble those of other help-seeking samples than that of nationally representative samples and would report higher rates of IPA that included higher risk for lethal or near lethal outcomes.

Method for Part 2: Use of a Range of Intimate Partner Abuse Behaviors

A complete explanation of the participants, instrument, and procedure is detailed in the methods section in part 1. As described in part 1, the RBRS assessed five theoretically driven subscales of IPA: lower-level physical abuse; psychological abuse; threats and escalated physical violence; sexual intimidation, coercion, and assault; and coercive controlling behaviors. Seven items made up the psychological harm and degradation scale (e.g., My partner insulted or shamed me in front of others; My partner screamed or yelled at me). The scale for threats or escalated physical abuse consisted of twelve items used to assess threats to life (e.g., My partner threatened me with or used a weapon against me; My partner broke one or more of my bones). Six items made up the scale of sexual abuse (e.g., My partner demanded that I perform sex acts that I did not want to; My partner physically forced me to have sex). The coercive controlling behaviors scale consisted of ten items (e.g., My partner did not want me to have male/female friends; My partner controlled how much money I could have or how I spent it).

Chronbach's alpha reliabilities were high for each subscale overall and for both fathers and mothers separately, with the exception of sexual intimidation, coercion, and assault with fathers as victims. This establishes that the items in each subscale go together well in measuring the unidimensional construct of that category of IPA (see table 3.2).

Mean scores for each subscale were calculated individually for the father and the mother in each couple. Each of the subscales measures different aspects of the latent construct IPA. As expected, the subscales were positively related, such that the possibility of a participant reporting one type of IPA increases the likelihood that the participant may report another type of IPA. Additionally, these correlations are proportioned to leave some variance unexplained, demonstrating that each subscale measures a unique aspect of IPA. Table 3.3 lays out the correlations between the RBRS subscales.

Table 3.2 Cronbach's reliability estimates for RBRS subscales

IPA category	Number of items	Illustrative items	Mothers (α)	Fathers (α)	Fathers and mothers (α)
Physical abuse	5	Pushed or shoved; hit or punched	.84	.87	.85
Psychological abuse	7	Screamed or yelled at me; insulted or shamed me in front of others	.91	.90	.89
Coercive controlling behaviors	10	Did not want me to have male/female friends; controlled how much money I could have or how I spent it	.85	.80	.83
Threats and escalated physical violence	12	Threatened me with or used a weapon against me; broke one or more of my bones	.86	.79	.86
Sexual intimidation or coercion or assault	6	Demanded sex acts I did not want; physically forced sex	.84	.66	.77

Results for Part 2: Use of a Range of Intimate Partner Abuse Behaviors

The broader range of IPA behaviors surrounding a divorcing father's and mother's use of IPA must be further evaluated to gain a more accurate understanding of IPA in the relationship (DeKeseredy, 2006; Kelly and Johnson, 2008; Stark, 2007; Tanha et al., 2010). Mothers reported a wider range of frequency and severity of victimization across the other four IPA categories than did fathers (see table 3.4).

Latent Class Analysis of Patterns of IPA within Couples

Categories of IPA-related behaviors do not occur in isolation. It is therefore important to determine the patterns of IPA-related behaviors from both partners within a couple, particularly in the context of determining the best parenting arrangement for the children postdivorce. To do so we first computed standardized scores separately for men and women for each subscale of the RBRS to be able to more easily make comparisons between partners. Next, we added .5 as

Table 3.3 Correlations of mean scores for RBRS subscales

IPA categories	Psychological abuse	Coercive controlling behaviors	Physical abuse	Threats and escalated physical violence
		Mother victim		
Psychological abuse				
Coercive controlling behaviors	.786			
Physical abuse	.515	.514		
Threats and escalated physical violence	.553	.559	.844	
Sexual intimidation, coercion, and assault	.431	.500	.473	.478
		Father victim		
Psychological abuse				
Coercive controlling behaviors	.755			
Physical abuse	.497	.477		
Threats and escalated physical violence	.501	.435	.723	
Sexual intimidation, coercion, and assault	.337	.380	.379	.333

Note: N = 863. All correlations significant at p < .001.

the constant value and log-transformed the data to account for the skewness of the subscales for physical abuse, threats and escalated violence, and sexual intimidation, coercion, and assault. Using the entire sample of 852 couples, the number of latent classes was increased until deterioration of fit was experienced (Nylund, Asparouhov, and Muthen, 2007), which gave us five latent classes. Next, we randomly split the sample in half to test the robustness of the model. We then tested the five latent class model on both split samples, in which the model was replicated and reliability held steady.

The latent class model of couple-level patterns of IPA are shown with the standardized means in table 3.5 and means in table 3.6 for comparison to previous means (Beck and Anderson, 2011).

Five patterns of couple-level IPA behaviors emerged from the data: (1) mutually

Table 3.4 Means, standard deviations, and frequencies of IPA categories

IPA categories	Mean	Standard deviation	Range
Mother victim			
Psychological abuse	3.01	1.51	0–6
Coercive controlling behaviors	2.35	1.37	0–6
Physical abuse	0.60	0.88	0–6
Threats and escalated physical violence	0.42	0.64	0–5.83
Sexual intimidation, coercion, and assault	0.61	0.92	0–6
Father victim			
Psychological abuse	2.51	1.41	0–6
Coercive controlling behaviors	1.92	1.12	0–5.7
Physical abuse	0.57	0.87	0–6
Threats and escalated physical violence	0.20	0.37	0–3.75
Sexual intimidation, coercion, and assault	0.17	0.41	0–3

Note: Paired sample t-tests confirmed that mothers reported statistically significantly higher levels of IPA on each of the other four subscales: psychological abuse paired t (842) = 8.68, p < .001, Cohen's d =.35; threats and escalated physical violence paired t (833) = 8.42, p < .001, Cohen's d =.35; coercive controlling behaviors paired t (778) = 7.50, p < .001, Cohen's d =.35; sexual intimidation, coercion, and assault paired t (816) = 13.23, p < .001, Cohen's d =.65 (see figures 3.2–3.5).

low: both partners below mean; (2) lower-level coercive controlling violence: male perpetrator; (3) coercive controlling violence (CCV): male perpetrator; (4) lower-level coercive controlling violence: female perpetrator; and (5) mutually high levels of coercive controlling violence (CCV). See figure 3.6 for visual representation of each of these patterns based on standardized scores.

Mutually low: Both partners below mean. Both partners reported victimization below the mean for the combined mothers' and fathers' standardized scores of couples in the sample. This class represented 36 percent of the sample.

Lower-level coercive controlling violence: Male perpetrator. Mothers in this class reported coercive controlling behaviors and psychological abuse victimization well above the combined mothers' and fathers' mean of the standardized scores for each subscale. Scores for the subscales of threats and escalated physical violence and sexual intimidation, coercion, and assault were slightly above the mothers' and fathers' combined mean for the standardized scores.

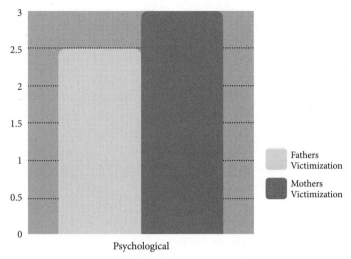

Figure 3.2 Mean reported psychological abuse victimization

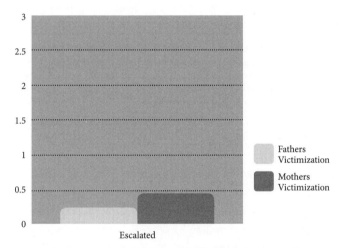

Figure 3.3 Mean reported threats and escalated physical violence victimization

Fathers in this class reported victimization below the standardized combined mean for all subscales. This class represented 30 percent of the sample.

Coercive controlling violence: Male perpetrator (either severe CCV *or lower-level* CCV*).* Mothers in this class reported levels of victimization one and one-half to two standard deviations above the combined mothers' and fathers' mean of the standardized mean score on all RBRS subscales. Fathers in this class reported physical abuse victimization as one-half a standard deviation

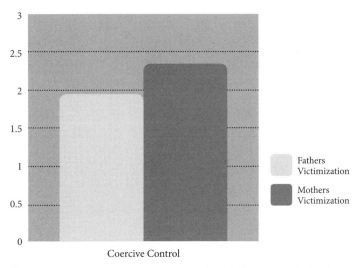

Figure 3.4 Mean reported coercive controlling behaviors victimization

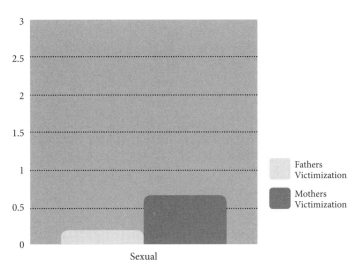

Figure 3.5 Mean reported sexual intimidation, coercion, and assault victimization

higher than the combined mothers' and fathers' mean standardized scores of the sample. This class represented 13 percent of the sample.

Lower-level coercive controlling violence: Female perpetrator. Fathers reported victimization on all subscales except the sexual intimidation, coercion, and assault at one-half to one standard deviations above the combined mothers' and fathers' mean of the standardized scores. Mothers reported scores on all

Table 3.5 Standardized means (standard errors) of domestic violence variables for each latent class: Couple–level data

		Latent class				
Type of violence or abuse	Sex of victim reporter	Mutually low: Both below mean	Lower level CCV: Father perpetrator	CCV: Father perpetrator	CCV: Mother perpetrator	Mutually high levels of CCV
Coercive control	Female	−.77 (.11)	.64 (.14)	1.52 (.09)	.05 (.12)	1.29 (.14)
	Male	−.52 (.06)	−.42 (.10)	.09 (.09)	.49 (.09)	1.27 (.14)
Psychological abuse	Female	−.70 (.12)	.61 (.10)	1.40 (.07)	.07 (.13)	1.21 (.12)
	Male	−.68 (.07)	−.33 (.09)	.19 (.10)	.57 (.12)	1.35 (.10)
Physical abuse	Female	−.69 (.03)	−.04 (.15)	1.57 (.09)	.08 (.12)	1.41 (.16)
	Male	−.59 (.04)	−.41 (.11)	.51 (.11)	.97 (.11)	2.18 (.16)
Threats and escalated physical violence	Female	−.61 (.02)	.23 (.17)	2.04 (.12)	.09 (.11)	1.65 (.22)
	Male	−.62 (.02)	−.54 (.05)	.04 (.08)	.57 (.17)	2.11 (.15)
Sexual coercion, intimidation, and assault	Female	−.29 (.07)	.39 (.10)	1.80 (.14)	.08 (.11)	1.16 (.22)
	Male	−.49 (.03)	−.49 (.04)	−.19 (.07)	−.03 (.09)	1.03 (.25)
Proportions based on estimated model		.36	.30	.13	.17	.04
Class counts based on estimated model		310.9	252.27	113.6	141.0	34.2
Classification based on most likely class membership		312	248	112	146	34

Table 3.6 Raw means (standard deviations) of domestic violence variables for each latent class: Couple-level data

		Latent class				
Type of IPA	Sex of victim reporter	Mutually low: Both below mean	Lower-level CCV: Father perpetrator	CCV: Father perpetrator	CCV: Mother perpetrator	Levels of CCV
Coercive control	Female	1.14[a] (.73)	3.02[b] (.90)	4.14[c] (.96)	2.22[d] (.99)	3.83[c] (1.0)
	Male	1.48[a] (.96)	1.60[a] (.90)	2.26[b] (1.0)	2.80[c] (.98)	3.83[d] (1.0)
Psychological abuse	Female	1.70[a] (1.0)	3.74[b] (.91)	4.85[c] (.82)	2.89[d] (1.2)	4.57[c] (.98)
	Male	1.77[a] (1.1)	2.26[b] (1.1)	3.05[c] (1.25)	3.62[d] (1.2)	4.79[e] (.81)
Physical abuse	Female	0.08[a] (.17)	0.47[b] (.50)	2.06[c] (.97)	0.53[b] (.53)	1.95[c] (1.4)
	Male	0.14[a] (.29)	0.22[a] (.33)	0.90[b] (.74)	1.28[c] (.86)	3.22[d] (1.3)
Threats and escalated physical violence	Female	0.05[a] (.11)	0.36[b] (.34)	1.51[c] (.80)	0.30[b] (.31)	1.34[d] (1.2)
	Male	0.04[a] (.08)	0.06[a] (.12)	0.26[b] (.24)	0.49[c] (.34)	1.54[d] (.89)
Sexual coercion, intimidation, and assault	Female	0.20[a] (.45)	0.58[b] (.70)	1.98[c] (1.4)	0.39[d] (.55)	1.26[e] (1.1)
	Male	0.08[a] (.24)	0.07[a] (.21)	0.21[a] (.35)	0.33[c] (.51)	1.22[d] (1.2)
N		312	248	112	146	34

Note: Means with matching superscripts are not significantly different.

Patterns of Domestic Violence in Couples

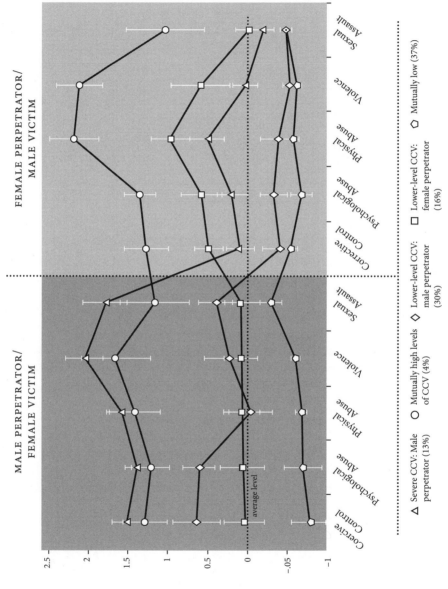

Figure 3.6 Standardized latent class patterns of IPA in couples

subscales at only slightly above the combined mothers' and fathers' mean standardized score of the sample. This class represented 17 percent of the sample.

Mutually high levels of coercive controlling violence. Both men and women reported victimization levels of at least one standard deviation higher than the combined mothers' and fathers' mean of the standardized scores on all subscales. Male abusers were significantly higher than female abusers for physical abuse and threats and escalated physical abuse. The mutually abusive and violent class represented 4 percent of the sample of divorcing couples.

General Discussion

In the violence literature IPA is defined in various ways, and researchers ascribing to each definition often use different samples to assess these concepts. Researchers then often generalize the results to definitions not assessed and to populations never included in the studies. Thus, before making sweeping generalizations concerning sex differences in IPA victimization, it is very important that consumers of research on IPA are informed and carefully assess the research methods used in all IPA scholarship.

In assessing couple pairs, when looking only at lower-level acts of physical abuse, fathers and mothers report similar rates of victimization of type of abuse. This picture changes dramatically when other forms of abuse and violence are assessed. Mothers report victimization at statistically significantly higher rates when including measures of threats and escalated physical violence; sexual intimidation, coercion, and violence; coercive controlling behaviors; and psychological abuse. These results emphasize the need to carefully consider what is being measured when reading the violence literature.

There are several additional important issues to consider in reviewing scholarship on IPA. One issue is how validly and reliably do the instruments used to assess IPA actually measure the construct? Is it a well-validated instrument or is it one question? If it is an instrument, did the researchers use *all* of the subscales of the instrument or did they pick and choose only certain subscales for analysis? Another significant issue highlighted by the current research is that the different types of IPA were positively related such that the possibility of a parent reporting one type of IPA increased the likelihood that the same parent would report other forms of IPA. Therefore, assessing individual types of IPA in isolation does not provide an accurate picture of a parent's lived experience of IPA. It is extremely important to then assess multiple types of IPA at the same time for both parents in a relationship.

In this study, we were able to identify five patterns of IPA in divorcing couple relationships. We decided to pursue a data-driven approach using latent class analysis to test if a theoretically derived typology held for this sample (Kelly and Johnson, 2008). Because the data in this study was existing archival court records, there were two theoretically driven patterns that could not be adequately assessed. The category of violent resistance could not be assessed because the data did not allow a determination of who initiated the violent interaction, as the data indicated only if the behaviors occurred. In addition, the category of separation-instigated violence was not able to be adequately assessed because the data did not allow a determination of when the IPA began in relation to when the separation occurred. With those limitations in mind, we conducted a latent class analysis of the forty-one-item, behaviorally specific questionnaire data using a combined mother and father standardized mean (based on sex-specific means) so that unit weights were equivalent across parents.

This analysis produced five patterns of IPA. An important finding is that there are a tremendous number of couples experiencing IPA in this sample. A full 64 percent of the sample reported some pattern of IPA in the relationship, and of those couples reporting IPA, there is a clear victim and perpetrator. None of the patterns represented the most common found in general community samples: situational couple violence, when both parents perpetrate at equal rates lower-level acts of physical abuse, with no other type elevated. None of the patterns from the current sample fit neatly into that theorized pattern. If, however, the analysis of this data would have considered only lower levels of physically abusive acts as detailed in part 1, an erroneous conclusion could have been drawn that mothers and fathers are victimized at equal rates.

Assessment of IPA patterns in couples is particularly important in the context of negotiating long-term legal agreements regarding custody and parenting time of children. This type of assessment can provide invaluable information concerning precautions that may need to be included in any divorce decrees and parenting agreements. For example, in couples reporting severe coercive controlling violence with the father as perpetrator, lower-level coercive controlling violence with the mother as perpetrator, and mutually high levels of coercive controlling violence, to keep the violence from continuing postdivorce, parenting agreements may need additional requirements. For example, supervised exchanges of the children, supervised parenting time, restrictions on contact between the parents, additional parenting classes, or referrals for family members to treatment programs (domestic violence, individual or family therapy) might be necessary. Without a detailed analysis of behaviorally specific questions and the history of IPA in the couple's relationship over time, it is impossible to determine how best to protect children in the context of divorce.

References

Administrative Office of the Courts. (2010). *Snapshot study 2008: Summary findings.* San Francisco: Administrative Office of the Courts, Judicial Council of California.

Archer, J. (2000). Sex differences in aggression between heterosexual partners: A meta-analytic review. *Psychological Bulletin, 126,* 651–680.

Arizona Superior Court in Pima County. (1998). Local Rules of Practice. Article 8, Section 8.7. Accessed July 3, 2011, from www.sc.pima.gov/Default.aspx?tabid=237.

Attala, J. M., Hudson, W. W., and McSweeny, M. (1994). A partial validation of two short form partner abuse scales. *Women and Health, 21,* 125–139.

Ballard, R. H., Holtzworth-Munroe, A., Applegate, A. G., and Beck, C. J. A. (2011). Detecting intimate partner violence in family and divorce mediation: A randomized trial of intimate partner violence screening. *Psychology, Public Policy, and Law, 17,* 241–263.

Beck, C. J. A., and Anderson, E. G. (2011). Divorce mediation parenting time: A focus on types of intimate partner violence and abuse. Presented at the Association of Family and Conciliation Courts Forty-Eighth Annual Conference in Orlando, Florida, June 1–4.

Beck, C .J. A., Menke, M., and Figueredo, A. J. (2013). Validation of a measure of intimate partner abuse (Relationship Behavior Rating Scale–Revised) using Item Response Theory. *Journal of Divorce and Remarriage, 54*(1), 58–77.

Beck, C .J. A., Menke, M., O'Hara, K. and Figueredo, A. J. (2009). The Relationship Behavior Rating Scale: Validation and expansion. *Journal of Divorce and Remarriage, 50,* 295–308.

Beck, C. J. A., and Raghavan, C. (2010). Intimate partner violence screening in custody mediation: The importance of assessing coercive control. *Family Court Review, 48,* 555–565.

Beck, C. J. A., and Sales, B. D. (2001). *Family mediation: Facts, myths, and future prospects.* Washington, DC: American Psychological Association.

Beck, C. J. A., Sales, B. D., and Emery, R. E. (2004). Research on the impact of family mediation. In J. Folberg, A. L. Milne, and P. Salem (Eds.), *Divorce and family mediation: Models, techniques, and applications* (447–482). New York: Guilford.

Bergen, R. (2004). Studying wife rape: Reflections on the past, present, and future. *Violence against Women, 10,* 1407–1416.

Browne, A. (1987). *When battered women kill.* New York: Free Press.

Campbell, J. (2005). Assessing dangerousness in domestic violence cases: History, challenges and opportunities. *Criminology and Public Policy, 4,* 653–672.

DeKeseredy, W. S. (2006). Future directions. *Violence against Women, 12,* 1078–1085.

Dutton, D. G. (2007). *The abusive personality: Violence and control in intimate relationships* (2nd ed.). New York: Guilford.

Dutton, D. G., Hamel, J., and Aaronson, J. (2010). The gender paradigm in family court processes: Re-balancing the scales of justice from biased social science. *Journal of Child Custody, 7,* 1–31.

Dutton, D. G., and Nicholls, T. L. (2005). The gender paradigm in domestic violence research and theory. Part 1: The conflict of theory and data. *Aggression and Violent Behavior, 10,* 680–714.

Dutton, M., Goodman, L., and Schmidt, R. (2006). *Development and validation of a coercive control measure for intimate partner violence: Final technical report* (NIJ Grant No. 2001-WT-BX-0503). Washington, DC: National Institute of Justice.

Ellis, D., and Stuckless, N. (2006). Separation, domestic violence, and divorce mediation. *Conflict Resolution Quarterly, 23,* 485–561.

Ellsberg, M., Jansen, H. A., Heise L., Watts C. H., Garcia-Moreno C., on behalf of the WHO Multi-Country Study on Women's Health and Domestic Violence against Women Study Team (2008). Intimate partner violence and women's physical and mental health in the WHO multi-country study on women's health and domestic violence: An observational study. *Lancet, 371,* 1165–1172.

Felson, R. B., and Outlaw, M. C. (2007). The control motive and marital behavior. *Violence and Victims, 22,* 387–407.

Fischer, K., Vidmar, N., and Ellis, R. (1993). The culture of battering and the role of mediation in domestic violence cases. *Southern Methodist University Law Review, 46,* 2117–2174.

Gelles, R. J. (1997). *Intimate violence in families* (3rd ed.). Thousand Oaks, CA: Sage.

Graham-Kevan, N., and Archer, J. (2008). Does controlling behavior predict physical aggression and violence to partners? *Journal of Family Violence, 23,* 539–548.

Hardesty, J. L. (2002). Separation assault in the context of post-divorce parenting: An integrative review of the literature. *Violence against Women, 8,* 597–625.

Hardesty, J. L., and Ganong, L. H. (2006). How women make custody decisions and manage co-parenting with abusive former husbands. *Journal of Social and Personal Relationships, 23,* 543–563.

Holtzworth-Munroe, A., Beck, C. J. A., and Applegate, A. G. (2010). The Mediator's Assessment of Safety Issues and Concerns (MASIC): A screening interview for intimate partner violence and abuse available in the public domain. *Family Court Review, 48,* 646–652.

Holtzworth-Munroe, A., Meehan, J. C., Herron, K., Rehman, U., and Stuart, G. L. (2000). Testing the Holtzworth-Munroe and Stuart (1994) batterer typology. *Journal of Consulting and Clinical Psychology, 68,* 1000–1019.

Jacobson, N., and Gottman, J. (1998). *When men batter women: New insights into ending abusive relationships.* New York: Simon and Schuster.

Johnson, M. P. (1995). Patriarchal terrorism and common couple violence: Two forms of violence against women. *Journal of Marriage and the Family, 57,* 283–294.

Johnson, M. P. (2006). Conflict and control: Gender symmetry and asymmetry in domestic violence. *Violence against Women, 12,* 1003–1018.

Johnson, M. P. (2008). *A typology of domestic violence: Intimate terrorism, violent resistance, and situational couple violence.* Boston: Northeastern University Press.

Johnson, M. P., and Leone, J. M. (2005). The differential effects of intimate terrorism and situational couple violence: Findings from the National Violence against Women Survey. *Journal of Family Issues, 26,* 322–349.

Johnston, J. R., and Campbell, L. E. (1993). A clinical typology of interparental violence in disputed custody divorces. *American Journal of Orthopsychiatry, 63,* 190–199.

Kelly, J. B., and Johnson, M. P. (2008). Differentiation among types of intimate partner violence: Research update and implications for interventions. *Family Court Review, 46,* 476–499.

Koss, M., Gidycz, C., and Wisniewski, N. (1987). The scope of rape: Incidence and prevalence of sexual aggression and victimization in a national sample of higher education students. *Journal of Consulting and Clinical Psychology, 55,* 162–170.

Kwong, M. J., Bartholomew, K., and Dutton, D. G. (1999). Gender differences in patterns of relationship violence in Alberta. *Canadian Journal of Behavioural Science, 31,* 150–160.

Langhinrichsen-Rohling, J. (2005). Top 10 greatest "hits": Important findings and future directions for intimate partner violence research. *Journal of Interpersonal Violence, 20,* 108–118.

Maloney, L., Smyth, B., Weston, R., Richardson, N., Qu, L., and Gray, M. (2007). *Allegations of family violence and child abuse in family law children's proceedings: A pre-reform exploratory study.* Melbourne: Australian Institute of Family Studies.

Nylund, K. L., Asparouhov, T., and Muthen, B. O. (2007). Deciding on the number of classes in latent class analysis and growth mixture modeling: A Monte Carlo simulation study. *Structural Equation Modeling: A Multidisciplinary Journal, 14,* 535–569.

O'Leary, K. D. (1999). Psychological abuse: A variable deserving critical attention in domestic violence. *Violence and Victims, 14,* 3–23.

Pence, E., Dasgupta, S. D., Taylor, T., and Praxis International (2003). *Building safety for battered women and their children into the child protection system.* Duluth, MN: Praxis International.

Stark, E. (2006). Commentary on Johnson's "Conflict and control: Gender symmetry and asymmetry in domestic violence." *Violence against Women, 12,* 1019–1025.

Stark, E. (2007). *Coercive control: The entrapment of women in personal life.* New York: Oxford University Press.

Straus, M. A. (1979). Measuring intrafamily conflict and violence: The Conflict Tactics (CT) Scales. *Journal of Marriage and Family, 41,* 75–88.

Straus, M. A. (2006). Future research on gender symmetry in physical assaults on partners. *Violence against Women, 12,* 1086–1097.

Straus, M. A. (2008). Dominance and symmetry in partner violence by male and female university students in 32 countries. *Children and Youth Services Review, 30,* 252–275.

Straus, M. A., and Gelles, R. J. (1990). Societal change and change in family violence from 1975 to 1985 as revealed by two national surveys. In M. A. Straus and R. J. Gelles (Eds.), *Physical violence in American families* (113–132). New Brunswick, NJ: Transaction.

Straus, M. A., Gelles, R. J., and Steinmetz, S. K. (1980/2006). *Behind closed doors: Violence in the American family* New York: Doubleday/Anchor Books (reissued Transaction Publications, 2006).

Straus, M. A., Hamby, S. L., Boney-McCoy, S., and Sugarman, D. B. (1996). The Revised Conflict Tactics Scale (CTS2). *Journal of Family Issues, 17,* 283–316.

Swan, S. C., and Snow, D. L. (2006). The development of a theory of women's use of violence in intimate relationships. *Violence against Women, 12,* 1026–1045.

Tanha, M., Beck, C. J. A., Figueredo, A. J., and Raghavan, C. (2010). Sex differences in intimate partner violence and the use of coercive control as a motivational factor for intimate partner violence. *Journal of Interpersonal Violence, 25*(10), 1836–1854.

Tjaden, P., and Thoennes, N. (2000). *Extant, nature, and consequences of intimate partner violence: Findings from the National Violence against Women Survey.* Washington, DC: National Institute of Justice.

Tondo, C. A., Coronel, R., and Drucker, B. (2001). *Mediation trends: A survey of the states. Family Court Review, 39,* 431–453.

Walker, J. (2010). Family mediation: The rhetoric, the reality and the evidence. *Tidsskrift for Norsk Psykologforening, Journal of the Norwegian Psychological Association, 47,* 676–687.

Walker, L. E. (1984). *The battered woman syndrome.* New York: Springer.

White, J. W., Hall Smith, P., Koss, M. P., and Figueredo, A. J. (2000). Intimate partner aggression: What have we learned? Comment on Archer (2000). *Psychological Bulletin, 126,* 690–696.

Evan Stark, Rutgers University

4 | Do Violent Acts Equal Abuse?
Resolving the Gender Parity and Asymmetry Dilemma

This chapter concerns two issues that have become increasingly contentious in the United States and parts of Europe, whether gender matters to the understanding of partner abuse and *how* it matters. Behind these questions lie two seemingly contradictory findings—that male and female partners appear to use violence in equal numbers and that women make up the vast majority of those who seek outside assistance because of abuse.*

Most of the world takes for granted that violence in relationships is a pervasive expression of male violence against women and that our major challenge is to identify and win government support for the optimum combination of protection and support for victimized women and the punishment and rehabilitation of perpetrators. From this vantage point, it seems both intellectually and politically absurd to debate whether a significant population of men are physically abused by their wives or other female partners. In the United States and United Kingdom, this question has been put on the policy agenda as part of a major backlash against women's attempts to extend their substantive gains in law, economics, and politics into personal life. The triumph of the Conservatives in the United Kingdom and the rise of the Tea Party and its allies on the Religious Right in the United States have resulted in a push to dismantle or render ineffectual a range of reforms that supported women's rights, including legislation focused on the plight of female victims of male violence. One facet of this effort is often associated with the campaign to debunk the gendered asym-

---

*It is currently fashionable in the United States to refer to "gender violence" when describing partner abuse. Ironically, this term was adapted in response to right-wing criticism of the emphasis on violence against women. In other words, the term "gender violence" is used to mean that violence is not gendered.

metry of abuse by organizations that tout fighting for fathers' rights or men's rights, supported by a small group of psychologists and sociologists.

The prevailing assumption, that partner violence is largely committed by men against women, is based on massive anecdotal evidence and crime surveys as well as data from police, courts, hospitals, child welfare agencies, and other sites where abused persons seek assistance. For example, by the early 1980s male violence against women had been shown to be a more common cause of police calls than all other serious crimes combined (Parnas, 1967) and the most common source of women's injury visits to hospitals (Stark and Flitcraft, 1996). Starting in the 1970s a parallel set of studies documented that all family members, including wives, in the United States commonly used violence to address conflicts. Since the implications of this work for our understanding of abuse seemed counterintuitive—almost none of those surveyed sought outside assistance, for instance—little attention was paid to it until it was embraced by self-proclaimed "conservative feminists" opposing the Violence against Women Act (VAWA) in the United States and groups hoping to neutralize the growing propensity for family courts to consider partner abuse in awarding child custody and child support.*

Initially, debate about how seriously to take women's violence against men focused on methodological issues, with each side seeking to discredit the research methods used to reach their opponents' conclusions (Dutton, 2005; Johnson, 2005). More recently, however, attention has focused on how to reconcile the fairly consistent finding that similar proportions of men and women use violence in relationships with the fact that female victims make up the overwhelming majority of those who seek outside assistance for abuse. The only credible explanation for the discrepant findings is that the types of behavior recorded by surveys and at helping sites are as different as the heart disease presented at emergency rooms and the heartburn endured in the privacy of one's home.

The most widely disseminated typology of partner violence was developed by sociologist Michael Johnson (2006, 2008), who distinguished the "common couple violence" recorded by surveys from the "intimate terrorism" that

*The background for the domestic violence revolution was the unprecedented economic and political gains women in the United States and United Kingdom have made since the 1960s and the increasing indispensability of working-class and professional women to the service economy in these countries. Because of this, the disproportionate impact on women from the current recession, rather than the work of the right-wing backlash, has manifested itself with relatively larger and more widespread cuts in victim services.

prompts most help seeking. Johnson argued that intimate terrorism involved a combination of violence and "control" as well as more frequent and severe violence than common couple violence. Seeking to adapt Johnson's typology to the cases in my forensic social work practice, I subdivided "common couple violence" into "fights"—when family members or couples use violence to resolve disagreements—and the "partner assaults" anticipated by current domestic violence laws (Stark, 2007). To complement Johnson's concept of "intimate terrorism" and shift the emphasis from violence to the broad range of oppressive tactics reported by my forensic clients, I drew on a model of abuse as "coercive control" first introduced in the 1970s by feminist psychologists working from a human rights perspective (Singer, 1979; Morgan, 1982; Okun, 1986). This model is often depicted (at times graphically) as the Power and Control Wheel, which is discussed later in the chapter. This pattern of tactics designed and deployed to install dominance directly through a combination of violence, intimidation, degradation, isolation, and control is the most common form of abuse for which women seek outside assistance. Like Johnson, I recognized that coercive control often involved severe, even life-threatening assaults. But I argued that the violent infrastructure of coercive control was typified by low-level assaults that often became routine. I accepted the evidence that women are frequently violent in relationships and had no quarrel with calling attention to the need to find alternative means to address conflicts in relationships. What I challenged was the assertion that the pattern of dominance and subordination that characterized coercive control could be equated with violent acts or that the latter required the same level of societal response.

The oppressive behaviors that make up coercive control extend far beyond physical violence, and the harms it inflicts extend to the most fundamental conditions of personhood and citizenship. While perpetrators of coercive control usually employ physical and sexual violence, they also isolate partners from means of support, degrade them, exploit their resources and capacities, deprive them of such basic necessities as money or transport, and micromanage the activities of everyday living through a combination of more or less explicit rules and regulations, particularly those activities identified with women's default roles as sexual partners, mothers, and homemakers. Later I sketch the technology, dynamics, and consequences of coercive control, but suffice it to say here that coercive control results from a structural rearrangement of the power and authority in relationships that places partners in a position of heightened vulnerability, dependence, and subordination vis-à-vis the dominant partner that is independent of the personalities involved or their family histories. In this situation of vulnerability, dependence, and subordination—which I refer to as *entrapment*—authority is nonreciprocal because the oppressive means deployed undermine, disable, or remove the victim's capacity for self-directed, self-interested decision making. Advocates for battered women have long recognized that men use domestic violence to establish "power and control." But a growing body of evidence suggests that the reverse is at least as true, namely that the regime of intimidation, isolation, degradation, and control often precedes and sets the stage for subsequent violence by undermining women's capacity to resist or escape abuse. As a result, the presence of control predicts fatality in abuse cases independently of violence and even where violence has been minimal or nonexistent prior to the imposition of control (Beck and Raghavan, 2010; Glass, Mangello, and Campbell, 2004).

Much of the debate about the significance of gender in explaining abuse has concerned the nature, frequency, and severity of the violence reported. For example, the same surveys showing sex parity in the use of violence also show that male abusers are far more likely than women to use the most serious types of violence, including sexual assaults, to use them more frequently, and to injure their victims (Archer, 2000). But both those who argue in favor and against the gender parity thesis work from within the "violence paradigm" that dominates our field. This paradigm equates abuse with discrete assaults and then applies a calculus of physical harms to assess the severity of these assaults. Here, gender is little more than a sociobiological fact defined by the sex of partners and their choice of a mate. Data collection and analysis supporting or opposing the gender argument is limited to individual victim and offender relationships. Even researchers who reference sexual inequality have little to say about how systemic inequalities enter, constrain, or shape how men and women do masculinities and femininities in relationships. Thus, the only issues on the table involve what level of violence makes it abusive and how often this level of violence is used proactively by men or women.

In the following sections, I argue that the major differences between male and female abuse reflected in asymmetrical outcomes and help seeking are explained by the fact that males are far more prone than women to coercively control their partners and not, as is commonly assumed, by the differences in the frequency, severity, or contexts in which men and women use violence. The coercive control model of abuse identifies a broader range of abusive behaviors than the violence model and so more closely approximates what abusers do and what abused women and their children experience. However, an even more fundamental contribution of this model is to shift the level at which we understand and explain abuse from individuals and relationships to the ways in which power dynamics in relationships are shaped by and in turn shape structural inequalities in the larger society. From this perspective, men's greater propensity for coercive control derives from the sex-linked privileges they inherit from persistent sexual inequalities simply because they are men and not from their individual personalities, background, proclivities, or pathologies. Conversely, women's vulnerability to coercive control is as much a function of their social location in a matrix of persistent inequalities as it is of personal vulnerabilities or the dynamics in a particular relationship.

To be sure, the different psychological, material, and social resources individuals bring to the table influence the relative shares of power they exercise in a given relationship and how. But the selection and deployment of means of coercion and control are ultimately constrained by the fact that men cannot be unequal to women in the same way and at the same time as women are unequal to them. Even when men and women use ostensibly identical abusive tactics and are similarly motivated by a desire for "power and control," male partner abuse has a different social meaning, follows a different dynamic, and elicits different consequences because of its link to sexual inequality. I've highlighted the fact that male perpetrators of coercive control typically regulate women's sexual performance as well as how they do housework, family maintenance, and child care. Women do not chose their responsibilities in these arenas in each relationship. They inherit them by default with their sexual identity. While motherhood, sexual performance, and even domesticity can be personally fulfilling and socially rewarding, their default assignment to women functions to free men to enact their purposes in the world, including caring for children if they wish, in ways that women are not free. When men micromanage how women enact these roles, they are building on these preexisting inequalities.

Of course, men's choices are also constrained by cultural images of masculinity to some extent, though stereotypic male roles (such as provider or protector) carry monetary and status rewards women's do not and so are as often vehicles for privilege as they are of oppression. My point is not that men's roles are better or less constrained than women's roles, but simply that the dominant and subordinate relationships enforced through coercive control play off and reinforce a preexisting sexual hierarchy that shapes the distribution and substance of the relative shares of power in relationships. On the one side, men would not "need" coercive control unless women's attainment of autonomy and equality threatened the composite of privilege and entitlement identified with masculinity. On the other side, neither the extent nor the form of men's coercive control of women is conceivable apart from the sex-based privileges they derive from inequality. Because of its link to inequality, men's abuse of women comprises what the legal philosopher Michele Dempsey (2009) terms "domestic violence in the strong sense" and so requires a more vigorous and comprehensive response than random violence in relationships or simple assaults of partners by women or men, or "domestic violence in the weak sense."

The Gender Parity Challenge

Starting with the National Family Violence Surveys (NFVS) conducted in the late 1970s and 1980s (Straus and Gelles, 1990; Straus, 1995), women consistently reported that they used violence against partners as often as men and, in some samples of younger women, even more often (Archer, 2000; Swan et al., 2009). Dozens of similar surveys have shown that many of these women initiate the use of force, employ injurious levels of violence, stalk or sexually coerce their partners, and insult or humiliate them ("psychological aggression") (Archer, 2000; Tjaden and Thoennes, 2000; Graham-Kevan and Archer, 2008; Swan et al., 2009).* A larger proportion of women than men identified their violent acts as retaliatory (though not necessarily defensive). But like men, women often reported being motivated by jealousy or a desire to punish or control their partners (Swan et al., 2009; Archer, 2000; Felson, 1996; Tjaden and Thoennes, 2000). There is some evidence that women emotionally abuse their partners as often as men and use many of the same control tactics (Graham-Kevin and Archer, 2009). For example, women arrested for domestic violence reported they threatened or used violence at least sometimes to make their partner do things they wanted him to do (38 percent) and these threats were sometimes effective (53 percent) to "get control" of their partner (22 percent) or to make their partner "agree" with them (17 percent) (Swan et al., 2009). One important difference is that women arrested for partner violence are far more likely than the men who are arrested for the same reason to report being victimized by the male partner they assaulted, with the proportion reporting victimization ranging from a low of 64 percent in the National Family Violence Survey (NFVS; Magdol et al., 1997; Straus and Gelles, 1990) to a high of 92 percent (Swan et al., 2009).

*While many of the surveys documenting women's violence against men has been conducted by researchers critical of the "feminist" approach to domestic violence (but cf. Tjaden and Thoennes, 2000), much of the substantive and ecological work has been conducted by feminists (Swan et al., 2009).

The researchers who conducted the NFVS set out to map the use of force in families because they were morally opposed to any use of force to resolve conflicts and believed violence observed would be enacted in subsequent generations (Gelles, 1995; Gelles and Straus, 1988). Since they also believed that millions of Americans were acculturated to use violence in problem solving, they ignored the possibility that the couples reporting violence might not find it problematic. Even so, they initially distinguished the commonplace violent tactics they identified from the forms of woman abuse or "battering" with which the advocacy movement would be concerned. For example, almost none of the respondents to the NFVS had called police or used other resources for abuse. Of those who did, almost all were women. Gelles (1995) termed the belief that men and women are equal perpetrators of domestic violence a "myth" and Straus (as cited by Ellis and Stuckless, 1996) termed the equation of the violent acts they identified with battering "ridiculous" and "unethical." These distinctions are ignored in fathers' rights' propaganda.

Gender Asymmetry in Abuse

Not all the evidence from the NFVS supports gender parity. For example, the surveys reported that both the proportion of injurious assaults by men and their frequency were roughly six to eight times greater than those committed by women (Straus and Gelles, 1988), though the absolute numbers in both cases were small. Nor do all population surveys show gender parity. In a widely cited meta-analysis of these surveys, Archer (2000) concluded that women perpetrated slightly more than 50 percent of reported partner violence and inflicted 35 percent of domestic violence injuries on men. But Archer excluded the National Violence against Women Survey (NVAWS) from his overview, the largest population survey to date, presumably because the numbers involved would have skewed his results. He also excluded studies of sexual assault and sexual coercion, which are committed almost exclusively by men. Importantly, the NVAWS looked at abuse over the adult life course and included male and female rates of being stalked and sexually assaulted alongside rates of domestic violence.

According to the NVAWS, with the marked exception of knives, which women and men used equally, men used every other means of serious assault much more often than women, including kicking, biting, choking, trying to drown, hitting with an object, "beating up," and threatening with a knife and a gun, with ratios extending from 2:1 (for kicking and biting) to more than 14:1

(for beating up) (Tjaden and Thonnes, 1998, exhibit 11, p. 28). Perhaps the most relevant finding for my purpose here is the large gender differences in victimization that emerged when attention shifted from reported violent acts during the study year (where the male-to-female ratio was only 1.4:1, to partner assault over the life course, where the ratio was more than 3:1 (22.1 percent versus 7.4 percent) (Tjaden and Thoennes, 2000). Gender differences in sexual abuse and stalking were considerably larger.*

There are only a few clinical studies that have compared the abuse experiences of males and females. Although these studies use relatively small samples, like the surveys, they find that a substantial proportion of women report using violence, even among women in shelters, and that the modal pattern is for both partners to report violence. It is misleading, however, to consider this violence mutual or bidirectional. For instance, Phelan and others (2002) compared men and women presenting complaints of injury at a level one trauma center for emergency medical services and who reported being in a currently violent or abusive relationship. Men reported significantly higher rates of violence initiation than did women, with 100 percent of the men reporting initiating violence between 50 and 100 percent of the time. In contrast, 91 percent of the women reported initiating violence between zero and 20 percent of the time.

The vast majority of point-of-service studies assessed only the experiences of female victims either because only women utilized the service (as with shelters) or because researchers believed abuse was largely a problem for women, but not for men. Proponents of the gender parity argument reject evidence from "clinical" samples because of the selection bias involved. They insist that battered men are more reticent than women to report abuse; that women's higher rates of injury reflect sex differences in strength rather than in abuse; and that the predominance of female victims at service sites reflects the feminist "bias" in the provision of and funding for services (Langhinrichsen-Rohling, 2010). While I cannot generalize from my professional clientele, it is commonplace for the men with whom I have worked as a psychotherapist or forensic evaluator or who I have encountered in court to complain about any manner of mistreat-

---

*Proponents of the parity argument dismissed the NVAWS because respondents were asked to report only violent acts that made them feel unsafe. By focusing on violence that threatened personal security, the NVAWS excluded the range of "fights" and other violent acts—covered by the NFVS—that neither party considered threatening, including a significant proportion (but not all) of violent acts self-reported by women. However, this very emphasis is arguably what made the NVAWS more relevant for an understanding of "abuse."

ment by their female partners, including physical abuse. Moreover, while males are more likely than female partners to inflict injury, possibly as a result of their greater physical prowess, well over 95 percent of reported abuse is noninjurious, involving slaps, pushes, shoves, and the like, including the abuse reported to police, emergency rooms, and the military (Stark, 2007). Thus, skewed evidence on help seeking cannot be explained by men's greater propensity to cause injury. Finally, few abused men have surfaced even when they have been offered services and even when there is no bias in servicer delivery. Police arrest the same proportion of female offenders in response to calls from men as they do men in response to calls from women (Buzawa, Buzawa, and Stark, 2011). Yet 75 to 80 percent of police calls are from female victims. This ratio is approximately the same as the female/male ratio of abuse experiences reported to the National Crime Victim Survey (8.6:2.5) and the NVAWS. Calls to hotlines, requests for protection orders, emergency room visits, or use of child welfare or sexual assault services are even more skewed, with the female/male ratios ranging from 15:1 to 20:1 (Stark, 2007).

There may have been gender parity in the use of lethal violence in abusive relationships forty years ago. In the mid-1970s male and female partners were equally likely to be killed in a violent confrontation (Stark, 2007). But lethal violence by female partners has declined dramatically in the United States since then, almost certainly because of the availability of shelter and mandatory arrest policies. Since 1976 the number of men killed by women in intimate relationships has dropped 71 percent, and by 80 percent among African Americans, much more than the overall drop in homicides in this period. By contrast, the number of women killed by male intimates has dropped only 26 percent since 1976, far less than the overall drop in homicide. Thus, from relative parity, the ratio of male/female partner homicide has gone to 3:1. (U.S. Department of Justice, 2006). Since women tend to kill abusive partners when they believe they have no options, the shelters, arrest policies, and protection orders have significantly reduced the risk to men. By contrast, men typically kill female partners when women threaten to leave or actually do so. Continued high rates of woman killing by male perpetrators suggest that current options offer women only temporary respite.

The Problem of the Definition

So long as we restrict our attention to violent acts in relationships, there seems to be little question that a shift is required that would allot a greater proportion of domestic violence resources to male victims, as some of the more moderate critics of the current approach advocate (Langhinrichsen-Rohling, 2010). As I have already suggested, however, this conclusion makes sense only if we accept the popular equation of abuse with violent acts.

Everything starts from the definition. Summarizing the dominant view in the domestic violence field, Gelles (1997) defined violence as an "act carried out with the intention or perceived intention of causing physical pain or injury to another person" (14). From here, identifying domestic violence should have been a simple matter of determining whether partners or former partners are responsible for assaults. So why has it proved almost impossible to consistently apply this definition to the type of domestic violence that prompts millions of victims to seek help annually?

Over ten thousand monographs on domestic violence have been published since the mid-1970s, the vast majority using a variant of this definition. Yet there is still no consensus on the prevalence of domestic violence, who commits it, its principal causes and dynamics, and what types of assistance are required or effective. To illustrate, surveys using this definition have generated estimates of the annual prevalence of partner violence against women that vary by a factor of twenty, depending on whether respondents were asked about "conflicts" (136/1,000), "safety" concerns (15/1,000), or "crime" (7/1,000) (Straus, 1995; Tjaden and Thoennes, 2000; Schafer, Caetano, and Clark, 1998). Without a consensus on the baseline we are working from, service planning and evaluation remain scattershot.

Drawn from the criminal-justice understanding of assault, the definition contains three core assumptions: that abuse can be equated with violence, that violence consists of discrete acts or incidents, and that the severity of abuse can be determined by applying a calculus of physical injury and psychological trauma. These assumptions underlie virtually all the population surveys on domestic violence, including those showing abuse to be a far greater problem for women than men. Modeled after the criminal-justice understanding of assault, the population surveys ask respondents about whether they have engaged in or been the target of specific violent acts during the study year or "ever." Safety planning, protection orders, counseling for batterers, and other intervention strategies are predicated on the assumption that perpetrators and victims exercise sufficient decisional autonomy between episodes to end the abuse, what is called "time to violence" in the treatment literature. Even though the presence of injury is typically not a formal prerequisite to access criminal-justice, shelter, medical, or other services, as a practical matter decisions regarding intervention are often based on a calculus of relative physical and psychological harm (Buzawa et al., 2012; Berk and Loeseke, 1980–81).

The Failure of the Violence Definition

The actual experience of abuse victims contradicts the assumptions in the violence definition. Data from a range of sources and study sites (Stark and Flitcraft, 1996; Stark, 2007; Maxwell, Robinson, and Klein, 2009; Tjaden and Thonnes, 1998, 2000) consistently show that the hallmark of women's physical abuse is frequent, but predominantly minor, assault extending over a considerable period (5.5–7.2 years on average) and with a cumulative impact on women's health unparalleled among other classes of assault victims. Over a third of abused women surveyed report "serial" abuse (once a week or more) (Teske and Parker, 1983; Klaus and Rand, 1984; Mooney, 1993; Stark and Flitcraft, 1996) with some classes of abuse victims reporting abuse daily. Conversely, even 95–97 percent of assaults reported to the emergency medical service or to police are noninjurious (Stark and Flitcraft, 1996; Stark, 2007). These data suggest that abuse is typically a chronic rather than an acute problem, the reason why so many victims describe their predicament as "ongoing."

There is also incontrovertible evidence that, in a majority of cases where women seek outside assistance for abuse, coercion is accompanied by a range of other oppressive acts designed to isolate, intimidate, exploit, degrade, and control a partner (Buzawa and Hotaling, 2001; Tolman, 1989; Rees, Agnew-Davies, and Barkham, 2006; Stark, 2007). In one well-designed study, for instance, six out of ten of the men arrested for domestic violence reported they had taken their partner's money as well as assaulted them and had restricted their partners in three or more additional ways (Buzawa et al., 1999) that include, in a majority of cases, being timed or otherwise monitored, kept from going to work or leaving the house, being routinely humiliated and degraded, and being denied access to necessities such as food, transportation, or medical care. While injury or death is an all too frequent outcome of abuse, coercive control affects a victim's dignity, autonomy, and liberty as much as their physical integrity or security. An injury-based calculus offers an inadequate measure of these harms.

When shelters, police, courts, or health and mental health providers interpolate male partner abuse through the prism of the violent-incident definition, the oppression battered women experience is disaggregated, trivialized, normalized, or rendered invisible, with interventions actually becoming more perfunctory as abuse becomes more comprehensive over time (Stark and Flitcraft, 1996; Stark, 2007). This has tragic consequences for victims. Since the vast majority of violent episodes are minor, for instance, when criminal justice bases its assessment of the severity of abuse on these incidents, domestic violence is reduced to a second-class misdemeanor for which few are sanctioned (Stark, 2007). Believing they are facing "repeaters" who "exaggerate," social workers fall back on pseudo-psychiatric labels that imply the victim is the problem to be managed, not the abuse or its perpetrator (Stark and Flitcraft, 1996). Even when proponents of the domestic violence paradigm recognize the frequency of assaults against women, instead of broadening the definition to include this reality, they attribute this to a subtype of batterer who is prone to "recidivism" (Jacobson and Gottman, 1998; Gondolf, 1988). Ironically, as abuse continues and a victim's entrapment becomes more comprehensive, the service response often becomes more perfunctory, a process I term "normalization" because even sympathetic providers conclude it is inevitable that this "type" of woman will continue to be abused.

The police response in the United Kingdom illustrates the tragic consequences of applying the narrow violence model. Research teams from the University of Bristol and the Home Office followed 692 offenders arrested between 2004 and 2005 in Northumbria (Hester, 2006; Hester and Westmarland, 2006). The ratio of arrests to calls was quite high (91 percent). But because the incidents were taken out of their historical context, arrests were primarily for breach of the peace and perpetrators were charged and convicted in only 120 (5 percent) of 2,402 incidents of domestic violence reported, indicating an attrition rate from report to conviction of 95 percent. Even in the few cases of conviction, the most common penalty was a fine. Abuse in these relationships was chronic, an indication of its severity. Exactly half of the offenders were rearrested for domestic abuse crimes within the three-year period covered by the study (2002–2004) and many were arrested multiple times. Unsurprisingly, given the episode-specific response, there was no correlation between the likelihood that an perpetrator would be arrested and the number of his domestic violence offenses or even whether he was judged "high risk." To assess the risk, police classified the target incident rather than the assailant. As a result, the same offender classified as "high risk" when he punched his wife on Monday is judged "low risk" a week later, when he slapped her. Neither the likelihood that offenders would be punished nor the punishment itself were related to previous offenses. Interviews confirmed that the absence of sanctions sent a clear message to the arrested men that their domestic assaults would not be taken seriously.

A New Paradigm: Domestic
Violence as Coercive Control

The gender parity and asymmetry dilemma cannot be satisfactorily resolved so long as we abstract violent acts from their historical and experiential context and assign them meaning based on their physical valence. From this vantage point—but only from this vantage point—the parity in violent acts appears to reflect a relative symmetry in abuse, making it appear that the gender asymmetry in outcomes and help seeking is an anomaly that arises from individual differences, a bias toward women in the provision of services or a related factor that leads women to get assistance but not men.

Crafting an alternative model that accounts for the sexual asymmetry in help seeking begins with three elements research shows to be typical of woman abuse, that it is *ongoing* rather than incident-specific, consists of a range of oppressive tactics in addition to physical assault and inflicts a cumulative burden on victims. While the violence involved in coercive control is often severe, the typical pattern consists of low-level assaults whose significance derives from their frequency over time rather than their severity and their relationship to concurrent coercive and controlling tactics. The alternative model shifts attention from physical injury and psychological trauma as the major harms caused by partner abuse to *entrapment*, the term used to describe the victim's structural subordination due to coercive control.

Severity can now be assessed by the nature and degree of a victim's subordination, not by applying a calculus of physical and psychological harms to her predicament or by dividing so-called "normal" (or low-level) violence from "real" abuse. Indeed, coercive control is most devastating when low-level violence becomes part of the routine of dominance. Although this alternative model has been available at least since the mid-1970s and is widely used by advocates in one variant or another, it has remained marginal to research and intervention in the field.

First, we distinguish violent acts from "abuse." At present, the term "abuse" is used to describe the illegitimate use of power by someone like a parent, family member, or guardian who has formal responsibility for protecting and caring for persons who are dependent because of their age or physical or cognitive status, such as children or the frail elderly. Adult partners are formal equals, however. Thus, in the absence of any marked and legally recognized disability, any structural condition that allows one partner to constrain the independent and self-interested decision making by the other is illegitimate by definition. From this vantage point, we can define adult partner abuse as the nonvoluntary establishment of unreciprocated authority by one party over the other and the resulting reallocation of resources and opportunities in ways that benefit the dominant party (Young, 1990).* An important facet of this definition is the implied distinction between a pattern of subjugation and the widespread propensity for individuals or couples to use violence when they fight; express jealousy, frustration, or anger; settle conflicts; or negotiate power differences. Note too, that a relationship between formal equals is considered abusive not because of the tactics one partner or both deploy, but because the context and consequence of these tactics is a structure of dominance and subordination, in which one partner is constrained to follow a rule of obedience to the other that is nonreciprocal and nonvoluntary.

This definition excludes situations in which both parties use violence but neither is subordinated and in which one party assaults the other but does not establish a regime of dominance. So-called fights and assaults are excluded from the category of abuse not because I believe they are inconsequential or acceptable, but because from a juridical and moral standpoint violence is a different type of wrong and causes a different type of harm than the wrong of subordination. Since dominance and equality are incompatible, this definition of abuse highlights harms to equal personhood within and outside of relationships. It is because this harm violates a central tenet of the liberty at the base of our democracy that it merits special attention in ways that simple assaults do not.

This understanding of abuse as the illegitimate exercise of dominance among equals was already implied when feminist advocates adapted the term from the child maltreatment field in the 1970s. Shortly after the first shelters opened in the United States, advocates advanced a definition of abusive violence as the means used to exercise "power and control" in relationships (Schechter, 1982; Adams, 1988; Jones and Schechter, 1992) rather than simply to hurt or injure a partner. This work built on a picture of what psychologists had called "coercive control" or "conjugal terrorism," terms they borrowed from the brainwashing and hostage literature to apply to the range of tactics abusers used over time to break down a victim's will, constrain their decision-making power, exploit their resources, and entrap them (Singer, 1979; Serum, 1979; Morgan, 1982). In the first definitive chapter on coercive control, Okun (1986) drew an extended analogy between the techniques of "coerced persuasion" the Chinese had used on u.s. prisoners of war, the experience of women being conditioned to prosti-

*I am referring here to the expectation by one partner that the other will follow a rule of obedience to them "or else," even when doing so is contrary to their interest and will. I am not referring to situational power, where one or another partner cedes decision making on particular matters to the other.

tution by pimps, and the experiences recounted to him in his counseling work with abusive men and battered women. A similar model of domestic violence as "control" provided the foundation for Emerge in Boston, one of the first programs for abusive men (Adams, 1988), as well as for the Power and Control Wheel developed by Ellen Pence at the Domestic Abuse Intervention Project in Duluth, Minnesota. With "power and control" as its hub and surrounded by a rim of physical and sexual violence, the spokes of the wheel were subdivided into economic abuse; coercion and threats; intimidation; emotional abuse; isolation; minimizing, denying, and blaming; using children; and abusing male privilege. Jones and Schechter (1992) added "control through decision-making" to the list of abusive tactics and focused particular attention on the abuser's micromanagement of a victim's everyday life, including "picking out your clothes," "telling you what to wear," and "forbidding you to shop."

In *Coercive Control* (Stark, 2007), I built on this rich body of work to classify the dimensions of abuse into four tactical groups: violence, intimidation, isolation, and control. I initially classified the varied forms of sexual degradation that accompany these tactics as facets of intimidation. But subsequent experience has demonstrated that they merit an independent role in a typology of coercive control because they violate a basic right to respect and elicit harms to a victim's sense of personhood that can be distinguished from fear. Under control, I included the range of tactics abusers use to constrain victim access to basic survival resources (such as money or transportation); exploit their resources (by taking their money or redeploying their work time for their own benefit); and regulate how they go about their everyday lives by imposing explicit or implicit rules for living that may extend from basic activities such as toileting or sexual performance to the most trivial facets of how they cook, clean, talk on the phone, watch TV, and so on. Unlike psychological abuse, I consider this patterned form of subjugation structural because it affects dependence directly and without regard to the psychological, economic, or social status of its victims or their gender or whether a person is injured or traumatized as well as deprived of independence.

Based on the limited empirical data available on the prevalence of intimidation, isolation, and control tactics in abusive relationships, we can estimate that 60 to 80 percent of the women who seek outside assistance for abuse in the United States are victims of coercive control rather than of partner assault or simple domestic violence. Since the assaults identified by the NFVS and other population surveys are generally low level and since low-level assaults are typical in simple domestic violence and coercive control as well as in fights where neither party considers themselves victimized, there is simply no way to know how to categorize these incidents on the continuum of abuse. The primary significance of the NFVS and other early surveys is in demonstrating that the use of force is commonplace in U.S. homes. But the fact that almost none of those surveyed by the NFVS called the police or attempted to access other forms of outside assistance suggests these may not have abuse cases at all.

Two other elements of the coercive control model are relevant to the current discussion about gender. First, case descriptions and some surveys have identified the fact that how women enact the default roles they inherit simply because they are females is the primary target of the regulation deployed in coercive control. Although the activities men seek to micromanage in these cases are wide-ranging, rules almost always dictate how women dress, do housework, care for children, and perform as wives. In other words, men use control tactics not merely to establish domination or power over partners in the abstract but to enforce specific gender stereotypes that conform to how they believe women *should* be. Second, the alternate model replaces the current theory of harms with an understanding of coercive control as a "liberty crime" that violates women's basic rights to autonomy, independence, and dignity as well as to physical safety and psychological security. Because the domestic roles targeted by coercive control are already devalued by their default consignment to women, the micromanagement of daily activities that accompanies coercive control is "invisible in plain sight."

Women's Use of Violence

Starting from a coercive control framework allows us to reclassify women's use of violence as well as men's. Women appear to use violence in fights in similar numbers and with many of the same motives as men. They may also assault men in similar numbers, even if their assaults are not as frequent and are less injurious. Many of the violent women with whom I work in my forensic practice expect a quid pro quo from their male partners that includes financial commitment and fidelity in exchange for their deference and loyalty. These women feel entitled to punish male partners who fail in these roles, and they are no less possessive or prone to jealous rages than are men. As we've seen earlier, the sparse data we have on abusive violence in couples suggests that, where both partners use force, women's violence is more likely to be retaliatory and defensive than men's. Finally, in an important subset of cases, women engage in what Johnson terms "violent resistance," where they use violence in response to coercive control. Here, their aim in using force is less to protect themselves physically than to protect their rights to enjoy autonomy, security, independence, and dignity. These rights are recognized as worthy of a vigorous defense in an international context and in public settings such as the workplace, but not in personal life. Persons are widely recognized as justified if they kill or otherwise harm persons who have entrapped them as hostages or as prisoners of war. Moreover, it is a common tenet of street lore that men are justified if they respond violently to being humiliated (or even disrespected) or threatened with harm or constrained, a principle often applied informally in criminal cases involving male offenders. But women similarly entrapped in personal life are as yet accorded no such right and must present proofs of physical harm or profound psychological trauma to justify their defense of rights.

The Role of Sexual Inequality

The aim of feminist activism is to work backward from the fact of gender inequality to identify its means and remove them. Despite the failure of the Equal Rights Amendment in the United States, women have largely achieved formal (i.e., legal) equality and, whether measured by the proportion in the labor market, college graduations, or the right to vote, are rapidly approaching substantive or "real" equality with men. These changes extend to married women. Where only 5 percent of married women were in the labor market in 1900, by 2000 over half of mothers with children under one were working and four out of five mothers with children ages six to seventeen were in the workforce. These gains have been accompanied by a major erosion of cultural barriers to women's equality, including gender stereotypes that justified treating them as second-class citizens in the wider world by portraying their social achievements as mere complements to their default responsibilities for homemaking and child care.

A major challenge in the 1970s was how to extend gains in women's equality into personal life, perhaps the single major preserve of male privilege. So long as women are constrained to serve one master in society and another at home, they cannot fully develop or commit their personal resources as workers or citizens, a fact that exacerbates and justifies persistent sexual inequalities in the larger world. At the same time, persistent inequalities disadvantage women as a class, rationalizing the preservation of male privilege and skewing the distribution of power and control in families and relationships, including the power and control exercised through abuse.

The women's movement in the 1970s selectively targeted rape and woman battering as the most dramatic expressions of the coercion needed to sustain sex-based privilege against the diffusion of sexual equality into personal life. But the politics of antiviolence activism was built around a contradiction. Protecting women from rape and battering required alliances with the state and other parties and institutions whose legitimacy derived to a major extent from their recognition and support for sex-based privilege. The achievements of the domestic violence revolution were unprecedented. But one cost of these achievements was the gradual substitution of "ending violence" in relationships for combating the use of coercion as one among many means deployed to sustain male privilege in personal life and sexual inequality in the larger society.

With sexual inequality taken off the table, the only plausible rationale for focusing on violence against women rather than other common forms of relationship violence is empirical, the claim that women merit special attention because they are more likely than men to be victims of violence. Evidence of gender parity in the use of force in relationships exposed the weakness of this line of argument. As we have seen, embracing the violence model of abuse has also been a disaster for victims. Conversely, the singular focus on violent acts is a conceptual dead end because it forces us to account for the well-documented asymmetry in the experience of abuse by highlighting individual differences rather than the interplay of structural inequalities, the enactment of gender roles, the formation of personhood, and the relational dynamics that mediate these levels of experience in abusive relationships.

By treating abuse as a course of conduct with cumulative effects and focusing on the multiple tactics abusive men use to subordinate female partners, the coercive control model takes a major step toward closing the gap between the mode of oppression that drives most abuse victims to seek outside assistance and the violent acts that are the current focus of research, debate, and intervention. Moreover, by identifying the enforcement of gender stereotypes as a major focus of control tactics, the model offers substantive evidence that coercive control is a means men use to "do" gender, to paraphrase Connell (e.g., 1985). At a minimum, adapting the model implies building interventions that address women's isolation, humiliation, and subordination as well as their physical safety and implementing these along the broad spectrum of activities where women are oppressed, including the workplace. Everything changes when we approach abuse as an ongoing or chronic problem rather than as episodic. A doctor who views each complaint of chest pain as separate may become frustrated by multiple visits with identical complaints, as many police, physicians, mental health practitioners, judges, and advocates are when abused women return repeatedly for help or remain in abusive relationships. However, if physicians recognize the particular complaints as symptoms of heart disease, a chronic problem, they become proactive, view repeated use of their services as appropriate and even desirable and take steps to ensure long-term risk reduction.

Whatever its advantages as a description of abuse, as a model of how gender operates in abuse, the coercive control model is susceptible to many of the same challenges as the violence model so long as analysis limits itself to individuals or relationships. Some of the same researchers whose work supports the argument for parity in violent acts are moving toward similar assertions about acts of intimidation, isolation, humiliation, and control. The full significance of reframing domestic violence as coercive control emerges only if we restore the focus on sexual inequality as the principal wrong we hope to counter with antiabuse policies and programs.

The central claim of coercive control is that the asymmetry in the dynamics and outcomes of abuse reflected in the data drawn from points of service reflect the asymmetry in the social position of men and women. Whether a particular partner will be abusive and how a victim will respond are shaped by individual differences; social standing; a range of cultural, familial, and psychological factors; and the relative power in material and other resources contending parties bring to the table in relationships. But these individual differences cannot change the basic fact that structural inequality endows men with an incremental advantage in relationships reflected in the peculiar cast of coercive control.

As Langhinrichsen-Rohling (2010) has argued, incorporating a full understanding of women's violence into our picture of women's oppression will facilitate a shift away from the patronizing and victim-blaming practices commonplace at many of the sites where battered women seek help. A full appreciation of women's violence also entails embracing a broader view of what is at stake in abusive relationships, understanding that it is liberty and personhood and the larger rights of women as fully entitled citizens that require defense, not merely their physical integrity.

There can no longer be a serious debate about whether women often use violence to hurt and abuse other women as well as male partners. Even if future research were to establish that women are as physically assaultive as men, injure them as often, and are similarly motivated by control, this would not change the fact that woman battering is distinctive in its dynamics, consequences, and social significance. This is not because men are more violent or inherently more prone to control than women, but because men's abuse and coercive control of women occurs in the context of sexual inequality, further subjugating a class of persons already devalued and disadvantaged. Because it builds on and exacerbates sexual inequality, coercive control jeopardizes the social foundation of a free society and so raises social justice concerns that forms of abuse that leave the status quo intact do not.

References

Adams, D. (1988). Treatment models of men who batter: A pro-feminist analysis. In K. Yllo and M. Bograd (Eds.), *Feminist perspectives on wife abuse* (176–199). Newbury Park, CA: Sage.

Archer, J. (2000). Sex differences in aggression between heterosexual partners: A meta-analytic review. *Psychological Bulletin, 126,* 651–680.

Bancroft, L. (2002). *Why does he do that?* Putnam: New York.

Beck, C. J. A., and Raghavan, C. (2010). Intimate partner abuse screening in custody mediation: The importance of assessing coercive control. *Family Court Review* 48(3), 555–565.

Berk, S., and Loseke, D. (1980). "Handling" family violence: Situational determinants of police arrests in domestic disturbances. *Law and Society Review, 15,* 317–346.

Buzawa, E., Buzawa, C., and Stark, E. (2012). *Responding to domestic violence: The integration of criminal justice and human services* (4th ed.). Newbury Park, CA: Sage.

Buzawa, E., and Hotaling, G. (2001, June). *An examination of assaults within the jurisdiction of Orange District Court: Final report.* Washington, DC: National Institute of Justice.

Buzawa, E., Hotaling, G., Klein, A., and Byrne, J. (1999, July). *Response to domestic violence in a pro-active court setting: Final report.* Washington, DC: National Institute of Justice.

Caliber Associates. (2002). *Symposium on DV prevention research.* Washington, DC: Department of Defense.

Campbell, J., Rose, L., Kub, J., and Nedd, D. (1998). Voices of strength and resistance: A contextual and longitudinal analysis of women's responses to battering. *Journal of Interpersonal Violence, 14,* 743–762.

Connell, R. W. (1985). Theorizing gender. *Sociology, 19,* 260–272.

Dempsey, M. M. (2009). *Prosecuting domestic violence: A philosophical analysis.* New York: Oxford University Press.

Dutton, D. G. (2005). On comparing apples with apples deemed nonexistent: A reply to Johnson. *Journal of Child Custody, 2*(4), 53–64.

Ellis, D., and Stuckless, N. (1996). *Mediating and negotiating marital conflict.* Thousand Oaks, CA: Sage.

Felson, R. B. (1996). Big people hit little people: Sex differences in physical power and interpersonal violence. *Criminology, 34,* 433–452.

Gelles, R. J. (1995). Domestic violence not an even playing field. Safety Zone (formerly Serve.com). Accessed February 17, 2007. http://thesafetyzone.org/everyone/gelles .html.

Gelles, R. J. (1997). *Intimate violence in families* (3rd ed.). Thousand Oaks, CA: Sage.

Gelles, R. J., and Straus, M. A. (1988). *Intimate violence: The causes and consequences of abuse in the American family.* New York: Simon and Schuster.

Glass, N., Manganello, J., and Campbell, J. C. (2004). Risk for intimate partner femicide in violent relationships. *DV Report, 9*(2), 1, 2, 30–33.

Graham-Kevan, N., and Archer, J. (2008). Does controlling behavior predict physical aggression and violence to partners? *Journal of Family Violence, 23,* 539–548.

Graham-Kevan, N., and Archer, J. (2009). Control tactics and partner violence in heterosexual relationships. *Evolution and Human Behavior, 30,* 445–452.

Hester, M. (2006). Making it through the criminal justice system: Attrition and domestic violence. *Social Policy and Society, 5*(1), 1–12.

Hester, M., and Westmarland, N. (2006). Domestic violence perpetrators. *Criminal Justice Matters, 66*(1), 34–35.

Jacobson, N., and Gottman, J. (1998). *When men batter women: New insights into ending abusive relationships.* New York: Simon and Schuster.

Johnson, M. P. (2005) Apples and oranges in child custody disputes: Intimate terrorism vs. situational couple violence. *Journal of Child Custody, 2*(4), 43–52.

Johnson, M. P. (2006). Conflict and control: Gender symmetry and asymmetry in domestic violence. *Violence against Women, 12,* 1–16.

Johnson, M. P. (2008). *A typology of domestic violence: Intimate terrorism, violent resistance and situational couple violence.* Hanover, NH: Northeastern University Press.

Jones, A., and Schechter, S. (1992). *When love goes wrong.* New York: Harper Collins.

Klaus, P., and Rand, M. (1984). *Family violence. Special report.* Washington, DC: Bureau of Justice Statistics.

Klein, A. (2009). Offenders and the criminal justice system. In E. Stark and E. Buzawa (Eds.), *Violence against women in families and relationships* (Vol. 3, pp. 115–133). New York: Praeger.

Langhinrichsen-Rohling, J. (2010). Controversies involving gender and intimate partner violence in the United States. *Sex Roles, 62*(3), 179–193.

Macmillan, R., and Kruttdschnitt, C. (2005). *Patterns of violence and women: Risk factors and consequences.* Report No. 2002-IJ-CX-0011, NCJ 208346. Washington, DC: Department of Justice, National Institute of Justice.

Magdol, L., Moffitt, T. E., Caspi, A., Newman, D. L., Fagan, J., and Silva, P. A. (1997). Gender differences in partner violence in a birth cohort of 21-year-olds: Bridging the gap between clinical and epidemiological approaches. *Journal of Consulting and Clinical Psychology, 65*(1), 68–78.

Maxwell, C. D., Robinson, A. L., and Klein, A. R. (2009). The prosecution of domestic violence across time. In E. Stark and E. S. Buzawa (Eds.), *Violence against women in families and relationships* (Vol. 3, pp. 91–113). Santa Barbara, CA: Praeger.

Mooney, J. (1993). *Domestic violence in North London.* Middlesex: Middlesex University, Centre for Criminology.

Morgan, S. (1982). *Conjugal terrorism: A psychology and community treatment model of wife abuse.* Palo Alto, CA. RandE Research Associates.

Okun, D. (1986). *Woman abuse: Facts replacing myths.* Albany: State University of New York Press.

Parnas, R. (1967). The police response to the domestic disturbance. *Wisconsin Law Review, 2,* 914–960

Phelan, M. B., Hamberger, L. K., Hare, S., and Edwards. (2000, August). The impact of partner violence on male and female emergency department patients. Paper presented at the meeting of the American Psychological Association, Chicago, Illinois.

Rees, A., Agnew-Davies, R., and Barkham, M. (2006, June). Outcomes for women escaping domestic violence at refuge. Paper presented at the Society for Psychotherapy Research Annual Conference, Edinburgh, Scotland.

Schafer, J., Caetana, R., and Clark, C. L. (1998). Rates of intimate partner violence in the United States. *American Journal of Public Health, 88,* 1702–1704.

Singer, M. (1979, December). The nature of coercive control. Paper presented to the Michigan Coalition against Domestic Violence. Ann Arbor, Michigan.

Stark, E. (2007). *Coercive control: How men entrap women in personal life.* New York: Oxford University Press.

Stark, E., and Flitcraft, A. (1996). *Women at risk: Domestic violence and women's health.* Thousand Oaks, CA: Sage.

Straus, M. (1995). Trends in cultural norms and rates of partner violence: An update to 1992. In M. A. Straus and S. M. Stith (Eds.), *Understanding causes, consequences and solutions* (30–33) Minneapolis: National Council on Family Relations.

Straus, M. A., and Gelles, R. J. (1990). How violent are American families? Estimates from the National Family Violence resurvey and other studies. In M. A. Straus and R. J. Gelles (Eds.), *Physical violence in American families: Risk factors and adaptations to violence in 8,145 families* (95–112). New Brunswick, NJ: Transaction.

Swan, S. C., Caldwell, J., Sullivan, T. and Snow, D. L. (2009). Women's use of violence with male intimate partners. In E. Stark and E. Buzawa (Eds.), *Violence against women in families and relationships.* (Vol. 3, pp. 48–67). New York: Praeger.

Swan, S. C., and Snow, D. L. (2002). A typology of women's use of violence in intimate relationships. *Violence against Women, 8,* 286–319.

Teske, R. H., and Parker, M. L. (1983). *Spouse abuse in Texas: A study of women's attitudes and experiences.* Huntsville, TX: Sam Houston State University, Criminal Justice Center.

Tjaden, P., and Thoennes, N. (1998). *Prevalence, incidence and consequences of violence against women: Findings from the National Violence against Women Survey.* Washington, DC: National Institute of Justice Centers for Disease Control and Prevention.

Tjaden, P., and Thoennes, N. (2000). Prevalence and consequences of male-to-female and female-to-male intimate partner violence as measured by the National Violence against Women Survey. *Violence against Women, 6,* 142–167

Tolman, R. (1989). The development of a measure of psychological maltreatment of women by their male partners, *Violence and Victims, 4*(3), 159–177.

U.S. Department of Justice, Bureau of Justice Statistics. (2006). *Homicide trends in the United States.* Washington, DC: U.S. Department of Justice. Accessed October 15, 2009. htttp://www.ojp.usdoj.gov/bjs/homicide/homtrnd.htm.

Young, I. (1990). *Justice and the politics of difference.* Princeton, NJ: Princeton University Press.

Nicole E. Allen, Shara Davis, Shabnam Javdani,
and Amy Lehrner, University of Illinois Urbana
Champaign

5 | Gender as Ecology

One Understanding of Men's Use of Violence against Women

Understanding and responding to men's violence against women has posed significant conceptual and methodological challenges for both researchers and practitioners. Competing explanations for such violence range from theories about individual pathology (e.g., men and women's psychopathology) to theories about the role of cultural norms and social structures (e.g., men's dominant social position in many societies). Some theorists have attempted to integrate the vast literature and theoretical perspectives on violence against women by applying multiple levels of analysis. Such comprehensive models suggest that individual, familial, social, and cultural factors contribute to the expression of violence against women (e.g., Heise, 1998) and aim for more complex understandings of violence against women. Still, examining each level of analysis in turn adds to our knowledge of how factors at one level or another are important and how they work together to perpetuate violence against women and girls.

The current chapter aims to explore the specific role of gender in the expression and maintenance of men's violence against women. Importantly, the approach we are taking in this chapter is to consider gender as an ecological variable, one that helps us understand the social context in which men and women live and how gender shapes men's and women's experiences (Wasco and Bond, 2010). This approach is distinct from viewing gender as an individual attribute or characteristic (i.e., as an individual demographic category) and emphasizes how gender norms and expectations and their expression within particular contexts can contribute to men's perpetration of violence against

Authorship was determined alphabetically.

women. Focusing on gender as an ecological variable may be particularly useful in light of research on intimate partner violence asserting that women are as violent, if not more violent, than men (i.e., the "gender symmetry" argument; Archer, 2000; Kimmel, 2002). Some interpret these findings as evidence that gender is therefore no longer relevant as an explanatory factor in men's use of violence against women (Dutton and Nicholls, 2005; Ehrensaft, Moffitt, and Caspi, 2004). This position reflects an individualist view of gender, see Anderson, 2005; Lehrner, 2008). While we do not assert that gender is the only relevant construct in understanding men's violence against women, we argue that gender remains a critical social category and helps explain the pervasiveness of men's violence against women and the negative consequences of such violence for women.

Further, we view centralizing gender as particularly important in light of research that suggests that a gendered analysis has been largely absent from the public discourse on how to respond to violence against women (Garske, 1993) and that even some of those working in the field of domestic violence, in particular, may be losing a connection to gendered theories of violence (Hammons, 2004; Lehrner and Allen, 2008, 2009). Thus, centralizing gender as one critical explanatory variable for men's use of violence against women provides a critical window for not only how we come to understand and explain such violence but also how we craft an effective response.

It is important to note that this chapter focuses on men's use of violence against women. Understanding women's use of violence against intimate partners is also important, and while not the focus of this chapter, a gender-sensitive analysis of the contexts of women's use of violence is also essential for any meaningful understanding and response to this phenomenon (e.g., Dobash and Dobash, 2004; Lehrner, 2008). The phrase "male violence against women" can encompass multiple forms of violence against women (e.g., psychological, physical, sexual), but the current chapter emphasizes empirical and theoretical examples of such violence in the context of heterosexual intimate relationships (e.g., as opposed to male violence against women perpetrated by strangers). The current chapter explores gender as a social, or ecological, variable. First, a brief overview is provided of the social construction of gender. Second, we distinguish between gender as an ecological, versus individual-level, variable. Third, the intersection of gender with other social factors (specifically, race and class) in shaping men's violence against women is briefly reviewed. Finally, attention is given to the peer context to illustrate the expression of gendered violence.

The Social Construction of Gender

In this chapter, we take the now relatively common view that gender is a social construction (e.g., Lorber, 1994; West and Zimmerman, 1987). This means that gender is not simply the result of biological differences but of social processes that shape gender identity. The construction of a person's gender begins at birth, when they are given a sex category, male or female, and continues throughout the lifetime. The social construction of gender implies that gender identity is shaped by the social environment through interactions with other people and social structures. This view of gender stands in contrast to an understanding of gender as solely an internal, individual attribute (e.g., a continuum from "masculine" to "feminine"). The individual-level understanding of gender assumes that gender (and gender-specific behaviors, attitudes, preferences, etc.) resides within and emerges from individuals and their biological makeup. As an alternative and complement to the individualist view, one can analyze gender as an ecological variable that shapes the context in which people organize their lives, such that gender-related behaviors are influenced by forces outside the individual, including gendered spaces (e.g., fraternities) and social norms.

Indeed, ecological influences emerge over the course of gender development. Children begin to demonstrate clear gender roles as young as three years old. One notable difference in how children learn gender is that girls tend to imitate gender roles modeled by women, whereas boys imitate men and avoid anything feminine. This difference is illustrated by girls' ability to cross over into masculine activities with fewer consequences compared to boys who participate in feminine activities (Thorne, 1993). This gender difference suggests that masculinity may be more rigidly constructed than femininity (Kimmel, 2000). Additionally, it is possible that the gender construction of masculinity is more precarious than femininity in that manhood must be "earned" and "can be lost" (Vandello et al., 2008). Understanding hegemonic (i.e., culturally dominant) norms and expectations for masculinity may be particularly important in understanding men's use of violence.

An Ecological Approach to Gender and Men's Violence against Women

An important review of the literature on gender and intimate partner violence, Anderson (2005) distinguishes between interactionist and structuralist conceptualizations of gender, both of which are relevant for taking an ecological approach. The interactionist approach views "gender as a characteristic of social interactions rather than of individual persons" (856). For example, social norms and expectations offer a set of rules for how people should behave according to their gender. These expectations are reinforced by religion, laws, and social values and may vary in different settings (for example, there may be different rules for how men should behave with friends versus with their children). Yet despite these social constraints, individuals actively negotiate such expectations. In this way, gender is actively created rather than being ascribed from social categories or simply an expression of one's essential sex category. In this sense, it has been argued that gender is something a person *does,* rather than something one *has* (Kimmel, 2000; Lorber, 1994; West and Zimmerman, 1987). Thus, gender is achieved and enacted through social interactions with others and social structures (education, occupation, marital status, etc.).

This approach opens up the possibility of understanding men's violence against women as an expression or "performance" of masculinity, which may be particularly urgent when masculinity is threatened. For example, one study (Totten, 2003) examined how the construction of masculinity influenced teenage boys' use of violence with their girlfriends. Ninety youth between the ages of thirteen and seventeen were screened for use of violence and thirty were interviewed in-depth about masculinity and their use of violence. The boys identified characteristics of an "ideal man," which included physical strength, wealth, ability to be the breadwinner for his family, heterosexuality, active sex life, in control of his life, and in control of his woman. Almost all of the boys reported that they were like this ideal man, with the exception that they had no ability to be a breadwinner and had no wealth. The boys conveyed that it was important to be the breadwinner in the future for their wives and children and that failure to be a provider would be detrimental to their manhood. In addition, "They described themselves as powerful fighters, womanizers, gang members, and protectors of women. Yet, they made it clear that they were not 'faggots,' 'bitches,' 'wimps,' 'woman-beaters,' or 'rapists'" (81). Overall, the author concluded that for these boys violence was used as a means of compensation when there was a threat to masculinity, and it was clear that the expression and maintenance of masculinity was tied to violence and domination. This does not necessarily imply that being boys *makes* boys more violent, but that such displays of violence may be a venue by which masculinity is expressed—that is, consistent with the interactionist perspective described by Anderson (2005), violence may be a vehicle for doing gender.

The interactionist perspective also highlights how even when men and women engage in the same behaviors, it is the perceived difference, or how we make meaning of those behaviors, that is important (Lorber, 1994). For instance, despite evidence that women are increasingly employed in highly valued leadership positions, the social meanings and interpretations attached to men's versus women's leadership are very different (Eagly and Johnson, 1990). Thus, it is difficult to assert that any behavior is truly gender neutral, as it is always performed by gendered actors in a social context shaped by gender norms and expectations. From this position, one could argue that men's and women's use of violence against intimate partners is inherently different because it has different meanings within a gendered social context (e.g., Osthoff, 2002).

The structuralist approach, as defined by Anderson (2005), conceptualizes gender as a "social structure . . . that . . . organizes social institutions, identities and interactions" (858). For example, gender operates in the social environment to organize roles and opportunities (e.g., employment opportunities, parenting roles, etc.) and determine how rights, responsibilities, and opportunities are assigned. Gender has been a central organizing category in the division of labor both inside and outside of the home (Davis and Greenstein, 2009). Historically, men and women have been assigned to different types of work with different levels of prestige and resources—a disparity that persists into the twenty-first century. Social structures thus serve to maintain gender differences and, further, to enforce the social inequality paired with gender differences. While it initially appears that social inequality is the result of established gender differences (e.g., unequal pay for labor is the result of gender differences in employment preference or skill), the differences between gender groups are actually the result of social inequality (e.g., unequal pay for labor is the result of gender-based employment discrimination). This social inequity arises and is sustained as gender structures social norms, expectations, and opportunities. Specifically, a structuralist approach to gender focuses on domination as the explanation for apparent gender differences (Kimmel, 2000; Messerschmidt, 1993) rather than assuming that innate gender differences are the source of social inequality (e.g., the idea that women choose professions based on innate leanings or characteristics that happen to offer lower pay).

From a structuralist standpoint, one would not aim to explain men's use of violence as caused by gender identity but would instead attend to the social structures that create different opportunities and rewards for the perpetration of violent behavior (e.g., Anderson, 2005; Kimmel, 2000; Messerschmidt, 1993). Whether taking an interactionist or structuralist approach, focusing on gender using an ecological lens can provide an important corrective to an exclusively individual-level understanding of gender often reflected in research on men's violence against women. These two approaches, framing gender as something enacted or achieved in social interactions or as something that fundamentally shapes the social spaces, opportunities, and experiences of men and women, both require an analysis of men's violence against women that includes the social context of that violence (rather than assuming that gender matters only for identifying the sex of the perpetrator and victim).

The arguments for interactionist and structuralist levels of analysis apply not only to gender but to other important aspects of social organization as well. Thus, while an argument can be made that gender figures prominently in the expression and maintenance of men's violence against women, it is also critical to examine gender in light of other ecological factors, including, for example, race and class.

Gender and Intersectionality

One of the important critiques to the feminist theorizing of the 1970s that brought a new emphasis to gender in both public and academic domains was the argument that gender does not operate in a vacuum but must be understood as located within other social and cultural contexts, such as race and ethnicity, class, sexual orientation, physical ability, and so on (e.g., Combahee River Collective, 1997; Moraga and Anzaldúa, 1983). In other words, people are not shaped solely by their gender identity. An exclusive emphasis on gender alone, it was argued, had the effect of flattening and equalizing all women's experiences, as if by virtue of their gender, women experienced the same forms of oppression and the same social reality. For example, the feminist catchphrase that "sisterhood is universal" could be seen on the one hand as emphasizing women's shared experiences (vulnerability to male violence, roles as sisters, mothers, and daughters, etc.) but on the other hand as suggesting that women's experiences are not differentiated based on other cultural and social contexts (Lorde, 1984/2012). Social constructionist arguments about gender as a performance or interaction have also been criticized for failing to take into account the ways in which gender, race, class, and other social locations structure people's concrete, lived realities and do not emerge only from performances of gender, and so on (Flax, 1992). Instead, it has been argued that a structuralist approach illuminates the ways that gender and other categories of social organization shape the opportunities and constraints that people face (e.g., the pay gap between men and women, the quality of schools in different neighborhoods, the social networks in which people are embedded).

While gender is theorized to be profoundly important in shaping experience, it is also clear that gender may matter differently for men and women in various social and cultural locations. For example, activists and researchers have argued that efforts to promote arrest when police respond to domestic violence differentially impact women and men of color (Coker, 2001; Ruttenberg, 1994). In communities with heavy police presence or histories of police brutality or hostility, and in the context of the disproportionate incarceration of African American men in the United States, pro-arrest and criminalizing policies may differentially impact men and women of color. Women may be placed in a bind, with their own gender-based victimization competing with their solidarity with and loyalty to their communities and to men of color.

Attention to the importance of social forces in addition to gender, such as race, culture, and class, has taken many forms in academic research (Sokoloff and Dupont, 2005). For example, Richie (1995) conducted in-depth, qualitative research with incarcerated, African American women. She argues that for the marginalized women she studies (and for the men in their lives as well), gender, race and ethnicity, and class interact to constrain women's choices and make them uniquely vulnerable to male intimate partner violence through a process she calls "gender entrapment." She writes, "Poor African American battered women in contemporary society are increasingly restricted by their gender roles, stigmatized by their racial/ethnic and class position, and constrained by the competing forces of tremendous unmet need and very limited resources" (2). Gender entrapment describes "the socially constructed process whereby African American women who are vulnerable to men's violence in their intimate relationship are penalized for behaviors they engage in even when the behaviors are logical extensions of their racialized gender identities, their culturally expected gender roles, and the violence in their intimate relationships" (4). Thus, for these women, Richie argues that their attempts to conform to mainstream gender role expectations and to follow cultural norms in their communities contribute to their violent entrapment. For example, loyalty to male partners and attempts to maintain stable intimate relationships may lead to women's participation in petty crimes at the insistence of their male partners.

At another end of the continuum, large-scale survey research has also investigated the relationships among gender and other socially structuring variables. For example, one study examines the influence of socioeconomic status and gender ideology on intimate partner violence (Atkinson, Greenstein, and

Lang, 2005). Sociologists have proposed "relative resource theory" to explain men's violence against wives, arguing that married men with fewer resources (e.g., employment, income level, occupational prestige, or educational attainment) than their wives use violence to compensate and to regain power in the relationship (Macmillan and Gartner, 1999; Messerschmidt, 1993). In this case, violence is understood as a form of "compensatory masculinity," an alternative process of establishing one's masculine identity when more traditional markers of masculinity are unavailable (i.e., being the primary "breadwinner" in the family). Atkinson, Greenstein, and Lang (2005) argue that the influence of relative resource deprivation is strongest for men who endorse traditional gender ideology. In other words, they think that men who believe that husbands should be the primary breadwinners (traditional gender ideology) are most likely to be negatively influenced by having relatively fewer resources than their wives and thus are the ones most likely to use violence as an alternative resource. In their study, using data from the National Survey of Families and Households, they find that relative resource inequality increases the probability of abuse *only* for husbands with traditional gender ideology, but not for husbands with egalitarian or more neutral gender beliefs.

In quite different ways, these studies provide evidence for the argument that gender interacts with other social and cultural factors to produce different effects and realities. Rather than thinking of gender as a constant—influencing everyone in the same way—studies focusing on the intersectionality of gender with other social locations show how gender and its influence can vary. Certainly, race and class—highlighted here—are not the only social statuses that intersect with gender (and one another). There are many complex questions to pursue with regard to physical ability, sexual orientation, and ethnicity and culture. The important point is that considering gender in light of other complex social realities is imperative. One way to do this is to look at the proximal environments in which given individuals operate.

One important context for how gender is understood and expressed is the immediate community within which individuals act. The peer group is one proximal environment that may be particularly salient in the community with regard to men's violence against women. Especially for adolescents, the influence of the peer context on attitudes about gender and partner violence and in shaping normative experiences is particularly important. Focusing on the peer context provides a rich illustration of how gender organizes young men's and women's experiences in a way that might encourage men's violence against women.

An Ecological View of Gender and Men's Use of Violence in the Peer Context

Multiple studies using both quantitative and qualitative methodologies have demonstrated that peer groups influence the development and maintenance of violence in general (e.g., Fergusson and Horwood, 1996; Haynie, 2001; Miller, 2009; White, 2009). Thus, peer networks, and particular aspects of how they are structured, have a potentially powerful impact on the behavior of group members. Importantly, one of the mechanisms by which peer influence may operate is through the ways in which social constructions and norms are codified and legitimized by peers, such that peers learn how to "do" gender and maintain gender inequalities. Indeed, gendered norms instantiated within peer networks may be especially important in the promotion of men's use of violence against women in particular. Most prominently, a peer-validated ideology of familial patriarchy, defined as a belief system that supports the victimization of women who violate male authority and power (i.e., violate a traditional gender ideology), has been theorized to promote men's use of violence against women (Miller and Brunson, 2000; Schwartz and DeKeseredy, 2000; Smith, 1988). A discourse of patriarchy supports "women's obedience, respect, loyalty, dependence, sexual access, and sexual fidelity" (Schwartz and DeKeseredy, 2000, 560) and in turn sanctions the use of male violence toward the attainment of these qualities. The peer context and peer validation of patriarchal norms can serve as a powerful vehicle through which boys are socialized to use violence against their female partners. In this way, gender as an ecological or social category operates within a peer context to influence individual behavior.

Indeed, empirical work has underscored the importance of the peer context in promoting men's violence against women. Quantitative work establishes a link between peer promotion of violence and individual men's use of violence. For example, a study of 713 married U.S. Army men from twenty-seven companies found that soldier-reported levels of violence against their wives was linked with the extent to which a climate of hypermasculinity was present within the peer context (i.e., soldiers' companies) and demonstrates how a peer group climate supporting inequality serves to promote gender oppression. That is, male soldiers were more likely to report acts of violence against their wives if their military peer group was characterized by a climate of "objectification and denigration of women through the consumption of pornography and the pervasive use of sexist language" (Rosen et al., 2003, 1048).

Similarly, data from the Canadian National Survey, including a representative sample of community college and university students, demonstrated an association between peer validation and violence against women (Schwartz and DeKeseredy, 2000). They found that male college students are more likely to report sexually or physically abusing dating partners if they also perceive their male peers as validating norms around violence against women. Specifically, this validation came in the form of male peers providing informational support about women's inferiority (e.g., male peers providing guidance to respond with force if a girlfriend challenges male authority or advising men that women owe it to them to have sex) and upholding patriarchal beliefs (e.g., male peers might approve of slapping a dating partner if she won't do what he says, if she insults him in public or private, if she refuses sex, if she is dating another man, if she hits him first in an argument). Indeed, these findings exemplify how rigid norms prescribing and validating men's use of violence serve to equate *doing* masculinity (i.e., being a man) with being violent against a partner.

Research has also been conducted with more specific social groups, such as college fraternities and sports teams, which are thought to exemplify a hypermasculine culture (e.g., Boeringer, 1996). For instance, fraternity networks report some support for gender inequity norms, including those around the victimization of women, and this peer validation is related to individual acts of violence (Schwartz and Nogrady, 1996). Members of fraternities are also more likely to use verbal coercion and substances to attain sex, and male athletes display greater rape proclivity (i.e., the propensity to rape if one will not be sanctioned; Boeringer, 1996). These contexts in particular may provide a number of benefits to their members, such as support and social status, making it difficult (and socially costly) to go against peer norms. Indeed, as written by Bernsetin, "fraternity codes of silence, demands for group loyalty and opportunities for group retaliation" give fraternities a unique status that makes exiting the peer network very difficult and creates a perception, likely couched in reality, that the activities of fraternity men are "above the law" (Berenstein, 1996). These components add complexity to the effects of fraternity-validated gender norms, especially given the strong norms around loyalty and silence that make legal action and social sanction against acts of violence against women much more difficult to accomplish. The fraternity setting can also be an example of how resource deprivation operates, because the college setting can provide a more equal playing field for young men and women (i.e., they all hold the social status of "student"). Thus, fraternal codes placing masculinity in high regard and promoting patriarchal beliefs can effectively work against this equal playing field and serve to justify male dominance.

Lending a theoretical framework to these findings, Godenzi, Schwartz, and DeKeseredy (2001) advanced a social bond and male peer support model around violence against women. This model holds that bonds or attachments to conventional institutions may work to promote violence against women, to the extent that such conventional settings uphold traditional ideologies about gender inequity. Importantly, these theorists argue that it is specifically attachment to, or bonding with, a network of peers within these conventional institutions that provides the vehicle by which gender inequity ideals are transmitted. Notably, this framework is not consistent with traditional sociological bonding theories advancing that a greater connection to social institutions is inversely related to violent acts (e.g., Hirschi, 1969); thus, the prosocial value of bonding may depend on with whom this bonding occurs and what norms and values are transmitted within a given context. Further, the model posits that not all individuals will be influenced in the same way by the norms advanced by their peers, because the degree of peer influence will be related to the degree to which the individual is bonded with, committed to, and actively involved with the peer network.

In-depth qualitative work also demonstrates and elaborates on the particular peer-validated norms that may be most salient to the promotion of violence against women. In this way qualitative approaches are particularly valuable because they provide more detailed explanation for *how* gender norms and expectations shape behavior. One exemplar is Miller's (2009) ethnography of black male and female inner city youth. In her book Miller distills two dominant norms codified by male peer networks that promote violence against their female partners. First, the "playa (player) ethos" involves a discourse around the sexual objectification and conquest of women, where male social status is directly related to the number and nature of sexual partnerships. The second norm, that of the "cool pose," reflects the mask of emotional detachment, aloofness, and toughness that males display toward their female partners. These norms around the sexual conquest of and emotional detachment from female partners are directly promoted by male peer networks and foster an ideology of hypermasculinity that Miller conceptualizes as "features of localized hegemonic masculinity" (188).

In turn, these norms create a gendered climate of jealousy and distrust within dating partnerships that, Miller (2009) argues, works to the disadvantage of girls, notably, by placing them at greater risk for physical and sexual victimization. The playa ethos maintains a sexual double standard "that rewarded male sexual exploits but sanctioned unconstrained female sexuality." In this context, girls would attempt to engage their partners but be confronted with detachment (the cool pose), which often led to conflict and girls' physical or sexual victimization (188). Perhaps most important, Miller's work demonstrates how peer-validated norms around gender inequity teach youth that intimate partner violence is a result of individual girls' flaws and deficits and indeed rewards males for perpetuating gendered norms in their actions. Miller's ethnography also provides an excellent example of how gender intersects with other prominent identities, such as being black and adolescent. In Miller's analysis, both black and youth identities are tied to other forms of powerlessness, given the limited access to resources in the inner-city neighborhoods she studied and the fact that youth have fewer legal and social rights. The young black women were thus characterized by multiple marginalities that located them among the lowest levels of social power.

Detailed interviews conducted by Benedict (1997) with athletes, survivors of assault, attorneys, and coaches underscores how external support of peer networks is an important component of the success of the peer-validation process. This work focuses on male athletic teams, in which norms around violence are not only supported by peers but also further sanctioned by coaches and officials who instruct athletes to "behave without fear of the consequences" (65). Labeling male athletes as "public heroes, private felons," Benedict highlights the ways in which peer networks are themselves embedded in broader social structures that influence, and are influenced by, the gender-based norms that exist within the peer group and exemplifies how gender structures the ecology in multiple meaningful ways. Similarly, other research has also demonstrated a link between the broader community context and peer networks, emphasizing the importance of the larger social context in which peer networks are embedded. For instance, one study finds that community violence has been linked to the perpetration of violence within men's social networks, and individual males who report exposure to both community and social network violence are at highest risk for intimate partner violence perpetration (Raghavan et al., 2009). Thus, as individuals are exposed to gendered norms that reinforce hypermasculinity or where violence against women is viewed as normal and justified in response to certain perceived violations by women, they are more likely to engage in such violence.

Conclusion

There is ample evidence that "gender matters" regarding men's perpetration of violence against women. Importantly, these conclusions emerge not simply from treating gender as an individual characteristic (e.g., comparing men's and women's use of violence to determine the relevance of gender) but by examining how gender organizes the ecology, or context, of heterosexual relationships. Violence against women then reflects an extension of men's social power and women's subjugation. The risk for the perpetration of violence may be particularly high for men who lack other social resources and sources of social power (e.g., with regard to social class or race). Men's violence against women may also be codified and enforced by the specific contexts in which men operate, including the norms and expectations transmitted by peer groups in which men are a part. This risk may be particularly high when these peer and community contexts are characterized by hypermasculinity and rigid gender norms.

Indeed, while there is evidence for contextual influences on men's use of violence, not all men perpetrate violence against women. This brings us back to our original assertion that while it is essential to focus on the gendered ecology in which men operate it is also imperative to include multiple levels of analysis to fully understand how and why men's use of violence against women persists while resisting conceptualizing gender simply as an individual attribute. This brings us to new questions and horizons not only about the source of individual differences among men living within the same social contexts but also about the countercultural spaces in which men (and women) operate that encourage nonviolence and social equity. Focusing on such spaces may provide a critical window into how we can encourage and manipulate the contexts in which boys and men operate to promote different social messages.

References

Anderson, K. L., (2005). Theorizing gender in intimate partner violence research. *Sex Roles, 52*, 853–865.

Archer, J. (2000). Sex differences in aggression between heterosexual partners: A meta-analytic review. *Psychological Bulletin, 126*, 651–680.

Atkinson, M. P., Greenstein, T. N., and Lang, M. M. (2005). For women, breadwinning can be dangerous: Gendered resource theory and wife abuse. *Journal of Marriage and Family, 67*, 1137–1148.

Benedict, J. (1997). *Public heroes, private felons: Athletes and crimes against women.* Boston: Northeastern University Press.

Bernstein, N. (1996). Behind some fraternity walls, brothers in crime. *New York Times,* May 6, A1, B6.

Boeringer, S. B. (1996). Fraternity membership, rape myths, and sexual aggression on a college campus. *Violence against Women 2*, 148–162.

Coker, D. (2001). Crime control and feminist law reform in domestic violence law: A critical review. *Buffalo Criminal Law Review, 4,* 801–860.

Combahee River Collective. (1997). A black feminist statement. In L. Nicholson (Ed.), *The second wave: A reader in feminist theory* (63–70). New York: Routledge.

Dobash, R. P., and Dobash, R. E. (2004). Women's violence to men in intimate relationships: Working on a puzzle. *British Journal of Criminology, 44,* 324–349.

Dutton, D. G., and Nicholls, T. L. (2005). The gender paradigm in domestic violence research and theory: Part 1; The conflict of theory and data. *Aggression and Violent Behavior, 10,* 680–714.

Eagly, A. H., and Johnson, B. T. (1990). Gender and leadership style: A meta-analysis. *Psychological Bulletin, 108,* 233–256.

Ehrensaft, M. K., Moffitt, T. E., and Caspi, A. (2004). Clinically abusive relationships in an unselected birth cohort: Men's and women's participation and developmental antecedents. *Journal of Abnormal Psychology, 113,* 258–270.

Fergusson, D. M., and Horwood, L. J. (1996). The role of adolescent peer affiliations in the continuity between childhood behavioral adjustment and juvenile offending. *Journal of Abnormal Psychology, 24,* 205–221.

Flax, J. (1992). The end of innocence. In J. Butler and J. W. Scott (Eds.), *Feminists theorize the political* (pp. 445–463). Routledge, New York.

Godenzi, A., Schwartz, M.D., & DeKeseredy, W.S. (2001). Toward a gendered social bond/male peer support theory of woman abuse. *Critical Criminology, 10,* 1–16.

Hammons, S. A. (2004). "Family violence": The language of legitimacy. *Affilia, 19,* 273–288.

Haynie, D. L. (2001). Delinquent peers revisited: Does network structure matter? *American Journal of Sociology, 106,* 1013–1057.

Heise, L. L. (1998). *Violence against women: An integrated, ecological framework.* Thousand Oaks, CA: Sage Periodicals.

Hirschi, T. (1969). *Causes of delinquency.* Berkeley: University of California Press.

Kimmel, M. S. (2000). *The gendered society.* New York: Oxford University Press.

Kimmel, M. S. (2002). Gender symmetry in domestic violence: A substantive and methodological research review. *Violence against Women, 8,* 1332–1363.

Lehrner, A., and Allen, N. E. (2008). Social change movements and the struggle over meaning-making: A case study of narratives of domestic violence. *American Journal of Community Psychology, 42,* 220–234.

Lehrner, A., and Allen, N. E. (2009). Still a movement after all these years? Current tensions in the domestic violence movement. *Violence against Women, 15,* 656–677.

Lorber, J. (1994). *Paradoxes of gender.* New Haven, CT: Yale University Press.

Lorde, A. (1984/2012). Age, race, class, and sex: Women redefining difference. In *Sister Outsider: Essays and Speeches* (114–123). Freedom, CA: Crossing.

Mears, D. P., Ploeger, M., and Warr, M. (1998). Explaining the gender gap in delinquency: Peer influence and moral evaluations of behavior. *Journal of Research in Crime and Delinquency 35,* 251–266.

Medina-Ariza, J. & Barberet, M. (2003). Intimate partner violence in Spain: Findings from a national survey. *Violence Against Women*, 9, 302–322.

Messerschmidt, J. W. (1993). *Masculinities and crime: Critique and reconceptualization of theory.* Lanham, MD: Rowman and Littlefield.

Miller, J. (2008). The playa and the cool pose: Gender and relationship violence. In J. Miller (Ed.), *Getting played: African American girls, urban inequality and gendered violence* (151–190). New York: New York University Press.

Miller J., and Brunson, R. K. (2000). Gender dynamics in youth gangs. *Justice Quarterly 17,* 419–448.

Moraga, C., and Anzaldúa, G. (1983). *This bridge called my back: Writings by radical women of color.* Watertown, MA: Persephone.

Osthoff, S. (2002). But, Gertrude, I beg to differ, a hit is not a hit is not a hit: When battered women are arrested for assaulting their partners. *Violence against Women, 8,* 1521–1544.

Raghavan, C., Rajah, V., Gentile, K., Collado, L. and Kavanagh, A. M. (2009). Community violence, social support networks, ethnic group differences, and male perpetration of intimate partner violence. *Journal of Interpersonal Violence, 10,* 1615–1632.

Richie, B. (1995). *Compelled to crime: The gender entrapment of battered, Black women.* New York: Routledge.

Rosen, L. N., Kaminski, R. J., Parmley, A. M., Knudson, K. H., and Fancher, P. (2003). The effects of peer group climate on intimate partner violence among married male u.s. army soldiers. *Violence against Women, 9,* 1045–1071.

Ruttenberg, M. H. (1994). A feminist critique of mandatory arrest: An analysis of race and gender in domestic violence policy. *American University Journal of Gender, Social Policy and the Law, 2,* 171–199.

Schwartz, M. D., and Nogrady, C. (1996). Fraternity membership, rape myths and sexual aggression on a college campus. *Violence against Women 2,* 148–162.

Smith, M. D. (1988). Male peer support for woman abuse: An exploratory study. *Journal of Interpersonal Violence, 6,* 512–519.

Sokoloff, N. J., and Dupont, I. (2005). Domestic violence at the intersections of race, class, and gender. *Violence against Women, 11,* 38–64.

Thorne, B. (1993). *Gender play: Boys and girls in school.* New Brunswick: Rutgers University Press.

Totten, M. (2003). Girlfriend abuse as a form of masculinity construction among violent, marginal male youth. *Men and Masculinities, 6,* 70–92.

Wasco, S., and Bond, M. A. (2010). The treatment of gender in community psychology research. In J. Chrisler and D. McCreary (Eds.), *Handbook of gender research in psychology: Vol. 2. Gender research in social and applied psychology* (613–642). New York: Springer.

West, C., and Zimmerman, D. H. (1987). Doing gender. *Gender and Society, 1,* 125–151.

White, J. W. (2009). A gendered approach to adolescent dating violence: Conceptual and methodological issues. *Psychology of Women Quarterly, 33,* 1–15.

Commentary

Shuki J. Cohen and Chitra Raghavan

Claims about Gender Parity and Domestic Violence
Six Blind Men and an Elephant

In part 2, the three chapters demonstrate the quest for increasing the sensitivity of current measures of domestic abuse and intimate partner violence (IPV) to include the subtle matrix of coercive forces in which they are embedded. Studies of intimate partner violence have consistently suggested that violent acts are just the tip of the iceberg in a coercive relationship. Thus, a focus on the assessment of violent acts may not adequately reflect the context of intimate partner violence and may lead to wrong conclusions regarding their prevalence or symmetry. Furthermore, failing to assess the subtle context of intimate partner violence may hinder understanding of the processes that give rise to them and undermine efforts to mitigate or prevent them.

The three chapters represent a gamut of approaches to this problem. Tehee, Beck, and Anderson use sophisticated quantitative methods to show that the measurement of more subtle forms of violence reveal a different pattern than that of severe forms of violence. Stark provides a metasynthesis of the issue. Using qualitative methods, he deconstructs existing studies, makes plain the underlying assumptions of various methodological and data analytic strategies, and finally synthesizes and recontextualizes research findings to argue for a new theoretical model (see similar efforts in Finfgeld, 2003; and McCormick, Rodney, and Varcoe, 2003). Finally, Allen, Davis, Javdani, and Lehrner present a critical review of the literature and take this arc of argument even further and reflect on the asymmetry of the very construction of gender roles in modern Western societies.

Tehee, Beck, and Anderson begin their subject conventionally—they provide a concise summary of the empirical studies that have fueled and or supported either side of the gender parity conundrum in intimate partner violence research. Gender parity refers to the finding, consistently reported in the research literature, that men and women use the same rate of violence against their partner. They comment briefly on the adequacy of these methodological approaches and then, taking a true and tried strategy, identify the "fatal flaw" that many adherents of gender parity highlight.

While Stark and Tehee and others clearly share similar views regarding the inadequacy of the current state of research to tap intimate partner violence, their approaches differ. Stark writes with the historicity of a humanist—he traces the origins of political movements that have emblazoned violence against women on their banner, and he presents data tracing how knowledge (both supporting and disputing gender parity) is transmitted through generations rather than created radically (Sherrat, 2006) and, following the humanist tradition of reasoning, footnotes on the subtext of labels. Small curiosities, generally seen as digressions at best and poor form at worst by conservative social scientists, are significant in this type of approach. These digressions inform the reader how nuances have shaped knowledge and how this knowledge has been transmitted, thereby mending the seeming rupture that some of the research literature inadvertently created between history and knowledge making. This allows the reader to interpret more fully the investment, values, and ultimately meaning of arguing for or against gender parity.

In contrast, Tehee and others' argument against gender parity is based on empirical data and the methodological flaws that might have given rise to results of studies that suggested parity. For example, the authors point out that many articles that support gender parity either conflated severe violence with any physical violence, overused high school and college dating samples, did not use matched data from married or cohabiting couples, or excluded samples that provided data on women's victimization (e.g., Archer, 2000). Accordingly, applying the deficit model (Creswell, 2009, 106), the authors propose to address this flaw by using data from couples in custody mediation who were married or cohabiting at the time of the conflict. The strengths of this study are multiple— the sample is quite large (N = 827); data are used from both men and women who report on perpetration and victimization, therefore allowing comparisons; the sample is drawn from the community and therefore is more representative than a clinical or court-mandated sample; and the sample is at high risk for violence because the couples are separating. Further, the authors support the results of simple descriptive comparisons with more complex multivariate analyses that afford better methodological control on variables whose correlation may lead to confounding results. As the reader can see, Tehee and others wander down a methodologically sophisticated road to highlight their point dramatically, while simultaneously conforming to conventional behaviorally based social science research paradigms.

Specifically, Tehee and others first present data on only lower-level acts of physical abuse. When they do so, men and women do not statistically differ from each other. Tehee and others then conclude, albeit with multiple cautionary statements, that "this finding supports a limited definition that women are just as likely as men to perpetrate this form of abuse." However, unlike previous research efforts, the authors do not stop here. Tehee and others continue their analyses, this time adding multiple other indicators and covariants of abuse, including psychological abuse, sexual coercion, coercive control, and extreme violence, which they label as escalating violence. When a fuller analysis is conducted by comparing mean scores on the different subscales, the authors find that women are victimized at statistically significantly higher rates than are their male partners taking into account these indicators. The results are in stark contrast to the first part of the study, which suggest that men and women are equally violent.*

Next, Tehee and others consider one solution that has been offered to address gender parity—the notion that different kinds of abuse exist between couples and that these differences are defined by different motivations for violence as well the power differential within the couple. This formulation arguably accounts for both gender parity and asymmetrical violence. Within this formulation (which Stark implicitly suggests is apologist), most violence is perpetrated by men but a certain number of couples perpetrate and are in turn victimized at similar rates and without severe consequences. Tehee and others test five of these theoretically derived types of violent constellations (or typologies) using latent class analysis. The authors conclude that none of the patterns that emerge are consistent with the common paradigm whereby both male and female partners make equal use of low-level violence—a claim that stands at the heart of the gender parity debate. Instead, the authors find that there is a statistically significant tendency for the contentious couple to have a clear perpetrator and

---

*This phenomenon, whereby gender parity is found in overall tallies of behavior, but gender differences are found on more subtle analysis, is not limited to intimate partner violence. For example, using verbal behavior, Cohen (2009) shows that apparent gender parity in self-centeredness (based on prevalence of its linguistic markers) disappears once the temporal pattern of these markers are taken into account. Thus, unlike male speakers, female speakers avoid using markers of self-centeredness (e.g., "I," "me") in succession, but rather "dilute" or "pad" them with words with no particular attribution. In contrast, male speakers utter self-centeredness words in rapid succession, albeit with the same overall frequency as female speakers.

victim and that the dynamics of abuse differ qualitatively in each couple constellation or type (identified here as a statistical latent class). Finally, while four of the five groups indicate men as a clear perpetrator, the authors find that in 17 percent of couples, women are more coercive and violent than their male partners. The authors reiterate their caution—that relying on physical abuse alone can be misleading and might result in irresponsible public policies and that, at least in this particular sample, there appears to be no gender parity. Rather, the bulk of violence is perpetrated by men against their female partners.

Stark, in turn, argues against gender parity using nonbehavioral paradigms, using multiple intertwined and interdisciplinary arguments. In the first leg of his argument, which he weaves throughout the chapter, he traces the motivation to defend the gender parity claims in the history of the ideological power struggle around women's rights. For Stark, the journey begins long before we address partner abuse and coercive control—we must first understand the stakeholders that fuel the gender parity assumption and their values, the society that is creating the stakes and providing the meaning of why these debates happened in the first place.

Stark, using many of the same studies as do Tehee and others and highlighting many of the same flaws (i.e., how excluding severe victimization biases reporting) comes to a radically different conclusion. Whereas Tehee and others argue for better methodology in the form of better behavioral measures of violence, Stark argues for a paradigm change in the field that dispenses with the reliance on behavioral measures altogether, thus ridding the research community from the last vestiges of radical behaviorism. Claiming that "everything starts from the definition," he attempts to redefine what is considered abuse. His primary criticism of current approaches is that both parties (those who support gender parity and those who do not) limit their data to individual victim and offender relationships and ignore how systemic inequalities and preexisting power structures of masculinities and femininities shape relationships. Stark argues that current society markedly privileges men and masculinities in a way that ultimately gives rise to fundamentally biased interpretations when men hit women compared to when women hit men. Thus, relying solely on the severity of violence (however it may be defined) and demonstrating that this level of violence is used more often by men than women is inadequate for demonstrating the lack of gender parity. Indeed, all that behavioral tallies indicate is sex parity— men and women may use violence at the same rates but this does not relate in any way to gender parity because the same behavioral tactics have radically different meanings, contexts, and outcomes when enacted in different power contexts.

While Stark implicitly agrees with Tehee and others that abuse is multifaceted, he categorically argues against their behavioral approach and advocates instead for a paradigm shift that rewrites the ontology of abuse. First, Stark proposes that we do away with the neat criminal-justice model that ties the field to the most recent violent incident. Instead, he suggests a comprehensive examination of the history of abuse within the relationship. Next, he proposes that we examine the extent of "entrapment" that women suffer within the relationship, using a model of coercive control in which the men isolate, intimidate, and trap the women. Within this model, examining isolated incidents of severe or less severe violence is irrelevant. Instead, we should examine the role of physical violence as a tool for maintaining the entrapment. Finally, Stark argues that the notion of entrapment cannot exist in the same way for men with women who are coercers because of the prevalent sexual inequalities in the social world we live in and that attempting to search for symmetries is absurd and a historical perversion of women's struggle for equality.

Allen and others' chapter aims at boosting the greater ecological validity to the methodological attempts to characterize and gauge intimate partner violence through a critical examination of the social context in which gender is constructed and performed. Following social constructivist tenets, Allen and others argue that the very experience and praxis of intimate partner violence are shaped by gender norms that have been constructed by society and internalized by the individuals within the couple system. Thus, in lieu of attributing male violence against women to biological determinants of masculinity, Allen and others' ecological lens follows Anderson's conceptual review (2005) in regarding this violence as either interactive (whereby violence is associated with perceived threats to the masculine social image) or structural (whereby violence is an integral part of men's performance of their societal roles, afforded to them through social structures of opportunities, privileges, and reinforcements). Later, Jones makes similar arguments in her chapter, where she measures structural violence but argues that it affects not only men who hit women but also sexual minorities, implying that all individuals internalize that violence is an integral part of constructing masculinity across gender and sexual orientation. Also within the ecological theories of gender, the intersectionalist approach to gender parity further attempts to draw attention to the multiplicity of categories that each individual might belong to and the constant simultaneous interaction among them. These categories arguably shape the individual experience of violence along a complex intersection of motivations, affiliations, roles, and interests. For example, the dilemma that battered minority women, living within a community that is subjected to chronic police harassment and brutality, experience when contemplating asking authorities for help cannot be reduced to their gender, race, ethnicity, or class alone. Rather, the individual experience, interpretation, and reaction to gender violence are ultimately a function of a complex intersection of all these (and potentially other) categories operating simultaneously. These arguments are later echoed by Gillum and DiFulvio's participants through focus groups and finally by Gentile in her chapter.

In sum, the three chapters represent a comprehensive and integrative array of attempts to improve existing methodologies for gauging the prevalence of intimate partner violence in general and gender parity in particular. This array of approaches is consistent with sociological and philosophical models of scientific progress. According to these models (e.g., Kuhn, 1962), scientific progress is a combination of a greater qualification of the theory at hand, brought about by designing better measures and demonstrating exceptions to that theory, combined with a mounting critique of the particular context in which the findings that support this theory were obtained. The end result in our case is the reinterpretation of the earliest feminist work on violence and abuse and, in some sense, a fundamental transformation of the way questions are being asked or the way the terms that supported the theory are being currently defined. The newer revisitation of this feminist paradigm might then prove too incommensurable with the previous one and could lead the scientific community to abandon the old theory and view another set of questions as a valid focus of research. Therefore, the three chapters might reflect a trend toward a paradigm shift in the research of intimate partner violence that seeks to move away from the easily observable (yet decontextualized and potentially misleading) data to the more pervasive and ubiquitous—albeit largely transparent—matrix in which intimate partner violence takes place.

References

Anderson, K. L., (2005). Theorizing gender in intimate partner violence research. *Sex Roles, 52,* 853–865.

Cohen, S. J. (2009a). Gender differences in speech temporal patterns detected using lagged co-occurrence text: Analysis of personal narratives. *Journal of Psycholinguistics Research, 38*(2), 111–127.

Creswell, J. (2009). *Research design: Qualitative, quantitative, and mixed methods approaches.* (3rd ed.). Thousand Oaks, CA: Sage.

Finfgeld, D. L. (2003). Meta-synthesis: The state of the art—so far. *Qualitative Health Research, 13,* 893–904. doi:10.1177/1049732303253462

Kuhn, T. (1962). *The structure of scientific revolutions.* Chicago: University of Chicago Press.

McCormick, J., Rodney, P., and Varcoe, C. (2003). Reinterpretations across studies: An approach to meta-analysis. *Qualitative Health Research, 13,* 933–944.

Sherratt, Y. (2006). *Continental philosophy of social science: Hermeneutics, genealogy and critical theory from ancient Greece to the twenty-first century.* Cambridge: Cambridge University Press.

Critical-Thinking Questions

1. Why is Allen, Davis, Javdani, and Lehrner's chapter (chapter 5) closer to a critical literature review, while Stark's chapter is closer to a metastudy? Illustrate with one concrete example taken from each of the chapters.

2. How are Stark (chapter 4) and Tehee, Beck, and Anderson (chapter 3) similar or different in their definitions of partner violence? Provide one example.

3. Does the Tehee and others' study support or weaken gender symmetry claims? Why?

4. How are Cook and others' work (part 1) and Tehee and others' research similar in terms of research philosophy?

5. Tehee and others' sample comprises men and women who have been mandated into mediation and are generally drawn from lower-working-class populations. How might class considerations of the sample in Tehee and others' study influence the results?

6. As with virtually any research on partner violence, the results of these studies are likely to influence policy, legislation, and courts' attitude concerning domestic violence. Thus, a misinterpretation of these results can cause an unintended harm to society. For example, how might the preliminary results from Tehee and others' work be misconstrued if not supported by the couples' data?

7. Can you think of a subsection in society that might misconstrue the results of these studies?

8. Why is it important to understand coercive control when there is mediation?

9. Now that you have a better understanding of the difference between sex and gender, return for a minute to Serafim and Saffi's study (part 1, chapter 2). Serafim and Saffi find that "female responders did not think that restricting men from working was a form of violence, while male responders considered being restricted as a form of violence." Similarly, they note that "female respondents believed that searching the female

partner's handbag without her knowledge was a form of violence, but male responders did not agree with this statement." Is this a gender or a sex difference? Why?

Advanced Questions

1. How can a metasynthesis lead to better evidence-based practice compared to "one-shot" qualitative studies? (Hint: think about how we generalize studies.)
2. Each of these three chapters contemplates sex and gender at different modes of measurement (e.g., self-report vs. structural). Select and compare two levels and discuss the implications for the results you are likely to find.
3. In terms of statistical techniques, consider the factor analysis in chapter 1 with the latent class analysis in chapter 3. What do each of these techniques bring to the table in terms of knowledge about partner violence? (Hint: start with what each of these techniques aim to do.)

III DATING VIOLENCE AMONG SEXUAL MINORITIES

Learning Objectives

1. Understand how intimate partner violence is conceptualized in same-sex relationships.
2. Extend our understanding of the differential impact of sex and gender on intimate partner dynamics in same-sex relationships.
3. Understand the challenges of conducting research in same-sex intimate partner violence populations.
4. Understand how at times the research questions and the selected methodology are difficult to separate. In this case, understand how the research conclusions are in part constrained by sampling complexities.

Cassandra A. Jones, University of Bristol, U.K.

6 Neighborhood Violence, Peer Networks, and Dating Violence in Urban Sexual Minority College Students

Intimate partner violence (IPV) research has focused largely on understanding the prevalence, risk factors, and consequences of violence occurring between partners in a home. But there has been increasing recognition in the literature that IPV and its effects are not isolated to the relationship in the home. The effects may radiate out to other social contexts, such as the place of employment (Lloyd, 1997; Swanberg, Logan, and Macke, 2005; Tolman and Wang, 2005) or friends and family (Riger, Raja, and Camacho, 2002). Additionally, there has been an increasing recognition that the reverse may occur as well; events and individuals outside of the relationship may influence violence within a relationship. Studies have used successfully social disorganization theory and male peer support theory to explain how outside factors may influence IPV.

First put forward by Shaw and McKay (1942) and later refined by Sampson and Groves (1989), social disorganization theory posited that neighborhood characteristics, such as socioeconomic status, employment, and resident stability, reduced the ability of neighborhood social organizations to impose social control, and this reduced ability led to higher rates of neighborhood crime. A small body of literature has utilized social disorganization theory to show that neighborhood characteristics and neighborhood rates of crime were positively associated with rates of IPV within homes (Benson et al., 2003; Benson et al., 2004; Cunradi et al., 2000; Fox and Benson, 2006; Miles-Doan, 1998; Miles-Doan and Kelly, 1997; Van Wyk et al., 2003).

Further refinements to social disorganization theory (Sampson, Raudenbush, and Earls, 1997) proposed collective efficacy as a process that could be activated to enforce informal social control. Local residents in a neighborhood who are more willing to intervene to maintain the values of the neighborhood and who trust one another experience a high degree of social cohesion from the continual reinforcement of common values in the neighborhood. Subsequent studies did find a link between collective efficacy in neighborhoods and rates of IPV in homes, such that stronger collective efficacy led to reduced rates of IPV (e.g., Browning, 2002). However, as noted by Raghavan and others (2006), the relationship between collective efficacy and IPV may not be as straightforward as originally thought. Collective efficacy did not specify which values neighborhood residents work toward. In a highly disadvantaged neighborhood, residents may allocate neighborhood resources to eradicate public crimes such as drug crimes, creating an informal social control to limit these crimes. With little resources allocated toward eradicating IPV, it may flourish. Therefore, the relationship between collective efficacy and IPV may not be a direct one.

Raghavan and others (2006) suggested witnessing violence in the neighborhood may mediate the relationship between collective efficacy and IPV. Neighborhoods with lower collective efficacy are characterized by more widespread public violent incidents. The widespread violence outside of the home may normalize the use of violence within the home. While the results of the study did not fully support the suggested mechanism, the results did show a direct, positive relationship between witnessing neighborhood violence and IPV.

Further investigating the relationship between witnessing neighborhood violence and IPV, Raghavan and others (2009) employed social disorganization theory and male peer support theory. Male peer support theory proposed two processes to explain how male networks of social support providers may influence dating violence (DeKeseredy, 1988; DeKeseredy, 1990a; DeKeseredy and Schwartz, 1993; Schwartz and DeKeseredy, 2000). The first suggests that men who affiliate with violent male networks are more likely to perpetrate violence against women. Men may learn from their male support providers that violence can be used against women, particularly when women threaten their authority or power (DeKeseredy, 1990b; DeKeseredy and Schwartz, 1993; DeKeseredy et al., 2006). The second process proposed by DeKeseredy and colleagues focuses on the information that male networks supply about acceptable behaviors in a relationship. The information examined was "guidance and advice that influence men to sexually, physically, and psychologically assault their partners" (DeKeseredy and Kelly, 1995, 44). They found that associating with male networks who verbally endorsed and perpetrated dating violence predicted men's violent behavior against female partners (DeKeseredy, 1990b; DeKeseredy and Kelly, 1995; Schwartz et al., 2001).

In their application of social disorganization theory and male peer support theory to heterosexual dating violence, Raghavan and others (2009) found witnessing neighborhood violence was associated with male networks of violence and both were associated with perpetrating dating violence. Further, the relationship between witnessing neighborhood violence and dating violence was partially mediated by male network violence. Additional analysis of male peer support theory examined if men reported using less violence or more violence if female networks reported victimization and if female network victimization functioned similarly to male network violence perpetration. The authors reported that while male network violence was associated overall with higher participant violence, the relationship of violence use to female victimization was more complex. Specifically, African American men were more likely to report increased violence use when women in the networks reported victimization, whereas Asian men used less violence when women in the networks reported victimization. These authors suggest that how straight men affiliate with men and women, and the types of messages that same-sex and cross-sex social support providers transmit, are likely to vary across ethnic groups.

Male peer support theory has been applied successfully to same-sex dating violence (Jones and Raghavan, 2012). Similar to Raghavan and others (2009), Jones and Raghavan found male network perpetration and female network victimization were associated with dating violence. Jones and Raghavan noted that while male peer support theory holds true for sexual minorities, the violent messages and identification with male peers likely differs as a function of sexual orientation. These results suggest that male peer support theory may generalize to nonheterosexual contexts, albeit with differences arising from the gendered value of the support to the participant.

Expanding on Jones and Raghavan, I consider how the neighborhood environment outside of the home interacting with social support may affect dating violence in gay men, lesbians, and bisexual women. Specifically, I wished to examine if the relationship between witnessing neighborhood violence and dating violence is mediated by dating violence among networks of social support providers. Accordingly, I proposed two models as follows. In model 1 the independent variable is witnessing violence, the mediating variables are network perpetration and victimization, and the dependent variable is perpetrating dating violence.

Hypothesis 1a: Witnessing violence is associated with perpetrating dating violence.

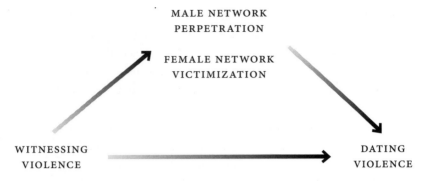

Figure 6.1 Proposed relationships among witnessing violence, network violence, and dating violence

Hypothesis 1b: Network perpetration and network victimization are both associated with perpetrating dating violence.

Hypothesis 1c: Once network perpetration and network victimization are entered into the model, witnessing violence will no longer contribute to dating violence. Such a relationship would indicate that the relationship of witnessing violence to perpetrating dating violence is mediated by network violence. No specific hypothesis was proposed to differentiate the role of network victimization and network perpetration in relationship to dating violence.

Next, I proposed a second model with dating victimization as the dependent variable. All other relationships were identical as in model 1.

Methods
Procedure

Data was collected from undergraduates enrolled in either an introductory psychology class or a mandatory life skills class at a large urban university in the Northeast. To participate, students had to be enrolled at least part-time and be eighteen years or older. All students received class credit for their time; students who chose to not participate read a paper on healthy relationships.

Participants

Participants were 88 college students drawn from a larger sample of 1,906 students. Participants were included if they self-defined as gay, lesbian, or bisexual or if they indicated currently being in a same-sex relationship. The final sample included 21 bisexual women with male partners (23.9 percent), 36 gay men (40.9 percent), and 31 lesbian women (35.2 percent). The average age was 19.4 (*Mdn* = 18.0, SD = 4.0). The sample was diverse and international: 26.4 percent were born outside the United States and the ethnic breakdown was as follows: 50 Latina/o (57.6 percent), 10 white (11.8 percent), 9 black (10.6 percent), 8 mixed (9.4 percent), 5 other (5.9 percent) and 4 Asian (4.7 percent). Finally, the majority of the sample fell in low to middle socioeconomic classes with yearly income less than $30,000 (43.8 percent), between $30,000 and $60,000 (36.2 percent), and over $60,000 (20.0 percent).

Measures

Neighborhood Violence

Witnessing violence in the neighborhood was assessed using the adult version (personal communication, Buka, 2002) of the My Exposure to Violence Scale (Selner-O'Hagan et al., 1998). Scores ranged from 0 to 10, with 0 indicating no violence and 10 indicating at least ten acts of violence in the past twelve months. The average number of violent acts witnessed was 2.79 (SD = 2.00).

Networks of Violence

A measure of networks of violence developed by Raghavan and others (2009) was used to identify participants' social support providers and whether the social support providers themselves reported dating violence. Participants were given the following instructions: First, think of the women in your support group when answering the following questions. Have any of your female support members experienced the following from their partner, husband, or boyfriend in the past twelve months that you know of? Participants rated on a 3-point scale (0 = never to 2 = three or more times) the extent to which female support members experienced four types of violence: physical, verbal, sexual, and emotional or controlled behavior. Participants then identified their relationships to female social support members as friend, sister, mother, other family such as aunt, or other.

Following completing questions about female social support members, participants were prompted with the following instructions: Please think about the men in your support group when answering the following questions. Have any of your male support members done the following to their partner, wife, or girlfriend in the past twelve months that you know of? Participants reported male support members' perpetration of violence using the same format. Participants identified male social support members as friend, brother, father, other family such as uncle, or other. Thus, I assessed only female support members as recipients of violence and male support members as perpetrators of violence.

The study was conducted in phases. The earlier phase of the scale had dichotomous answers, while the later phase was measured on a three-point scale. The same process used by Raghavan and others (2009) to combine the phases was used for this study. The resulting variables were used in analyses: male networks of dating violence perpetration ($M = 0.51$, $SD = 0.92$) and female networks of dating violence victimization ($M = 1.04$, $SD = 1.25$).

Dating Violence

Participants completed the Revised Conflict Tactics Scale (CTS2) to assess dating violence in the past twelve months, by noting the frequency of each act on a 6-point scale (0 = never happened to 6 = happened more than twenty times). Each response was coded at the midpoint of the frequency category (Straus et al., 1996). Perpetration and victimization were calculated by summing twelve items for each variable. The internal consistency for perpetration and victimization subscales was high ($\alpha = .85$ and $\alpha = .87$, respectively. The resulting perpetration ($M = 1.03$, $SD = 2.14$) and victimization variables ($M = 0.99$, $SD = 2.00$) were used in all analyses.

Results

Overall, 83.9 percent of participants witnessed at least one incident of violence in their neighborhood, 55.6 percent reported relying on a close female support member who was victimized, 33.7 percent reported relying on a male support member who had perpetrated dating violence, about half reported perpetrating and receiving dating violence. See table 6.1 for means broken down by sexual orientation. The only significant mean differences were in female network victimization. Follow up Mann-Whitney tests were conducted to evaluate pair

Table 6.1 Average number of incidents across sexual orientation

	Sexual orientation		
	Lesbian women (SD)	Bisexual women (SD)	Gay men (SD)
Violence witnessed in neighborhood	2.97 (2.63)	2.58 (2.32)	2.90 (2.77)
Female network victimization	1.39 (1.36)	1.38 (1.31)	0.48 (0.89)
Male network perpetration	0.49 (0.96)	0.73 (1.13)	0.40 (0.73)
Dating violence perpetration	1.52 (2.92)	1.04 (1.91)	0.59 (1.25)
Dating violence victimization	0.23 (0.31)	0.23 (0.32)	0.12 (0.20)

Table 6.2 Analysis of the average number of incidents

	Levene's test for equality of variance		Analysis of variance				Kruskal Wallis	
	F	Sig.	df	Mean square	F	Partial eta squared	df	Chi-square
Female network victimization	6.93	.002					2	11.54*
Male network perpetration	2.05	.13	2	0.64	0.76			
Dating violence perpetration	4.30	.02					2	3.14
Dating violence victimization	5.20	.007					2	2.25
Neighborhood violence witnessed	0.62	.54	2	1.37	0.21			

* $p < .05$

wise differences among lesbian women, bisexual women, and gay men. Type I error was controlled for by using the Bonferroni approach. Bisexual women reported more female support members who were victimized than gay men reported (Mann-Whitney 171.00, $p = 004$). Lesbian women reported more female support members who were victimized than gay men reported (Mann-Whitney 270.50, $p = 003$).

Table 6.3 Correlations for dating violence, dating violence in networks, and neighborhood violence

	Female network victimization	Male network perpetration	Dating violence perpetration	Dating violence victimization	Violence witnessed in neighborhood
Female network victimization	—	.57***	.37***	.42***	.20*
Male network perpetration		—	.43***	.33**	.34**
Dating violence perpetration			—	.70***	.25*
Dating violence victimization				—	.12
Violence witnessed in neighborhood					—

Notes: * $p < .05$; ** $p < .01$; *** $p < .001$

To test my primary study goals, I first ran correlations separately for each group. However, the small sample size did not present with enough statistical power to uncover potential differences, and most associations were not statistically significant. Thus, I combined the three groups, gay men, lesbian women, and bisexual women, for the remaining analyses.

To test model 1, I first examined how witnessing neighborhood violence is associated with dating violence perpetration and if this relationship is moderated by network victimization or network perpetration. For the mediating relationship to hold true, witnessing violence and network violence should be associated. As can be seen in table 6.3 , participants who reported higher levels of witnessing violence also reported higher levels of network victimization and network perpetration.

Second, I regressed dating violence perpetration against witnessing violence. This relationship was significant. Third, I added male network perpetration in the second step and female network victimization in the third step to test the model in figure 6.1. Female network victimization did not contribute to dating violence. Male network perpetration did contribute significantly to dating violence. Further, the relationship of witnessing violence and dating vio-

Table 6.4 Multiple regression predicting dating violence with networks of violence as mediator

	B	SE	β	t
Male network perpetration	.64	.31	.27	2.05*
Female network victimization	.34	.22	.19	1.57
Violence witnessed in neighborhood	.13	.10	.14	1.29
Model				
df	1, 75			
R²	.23			
Overall F	7.27***			

Notes: $^* p < .05; ^{**} p < .01; ^{***} p < .001$

Table 6.5 Multiple regression predicting dating violence victimization

	B	SE	β	t
Female network victimization	.59	.21	.35	2.82**
Male network perpetration	.29	.28	.13	1.01
	Model			
df	1, 76			
R²	.19			
Overall F	9.03***			

Notes: $^* p < .05; ^{**} p < .01; ^{***} p < .001$

lence changed from significant to nonsignificant, suggesting a fully mediated relationship. Thus model 1 predictions were founded.

I next tested Model 2. First, I examined how witnessing neighborhood violence affects dating violence victimization. Since the two variables were not significantly correlated, a mediation model was ruled out. I next examined if there was a direct relationship of network violence to dating violence victimization. I regressed dating violence victimization against male network perpetration and female network victimization. Female network victimization did contribute to dating violence victimization, but male network perpetration did not.

Discussion

The findings suggested how people and events outside of a relationship may influence dating violence within LGB relationships. These sorts of events may be particularly important for urban sexual minorities who live in complex chaotic neighborhoods and who are likely to have their sexualities contested as much as acknowledged and accepted. As predicted, exposure to more violence in the neighborhood lead to perpetrating more dating violence in a combined group of gay, lesbian, and bisexual participants. I found that exposure to more violence in the neighborhood led to male social support providers perpetrating more dating violence, which in turn led to LGB students perpetrating more violence against their partners. There appears to be a "matching" phenomenon where perpetration in the network of support providers is associated with perpetration against intimate partners. These results are similar to what others have found in community and college student populations; however, Raghavan and others (2009) found that network victimization mattered in complex ways to dating perpetration, which I did not find. One explanation for this could be related to sexual orientation. However, differences could also be attributed to sample size and treating different groups as homogenous. When Jones and Raghavan (2012) examined the strength of the association between network victimization and dating perpetration for lesbian women and gay men separately, they found a medium effect size for lesbian women and a small effect size for gay men. Additionally, Jones and Raghavan examined the association between network victimization and perpetrating sexual dating violence, finding a medium effect size for gay men and a small effect size for lesbian women. These preliminary results suggest that network victimization may have a different influence across sexual orientation. Future studies should recruit a sufficient number of individuals so that the influence of witnessing neighborhood violence and network violence on dating violence may be examined separately for lesbian women, gay men, and bisexual women.

Contrary to prediction, exposure to more violence in the neighborhood did not lead to more victimization. There was a direct relationship between network violence victimization and dating violence victimization. Network violence victimization may normalize dating violence for both LGB college students and straight women who experienced dating violence. As noted by Raghavan and others (2009), studies have found that straight women who experienced dating violence minimized the violence, blamed themselves, or encouraged one another to stay with their partners. This normalizing phenomenon found for straight women may be occurring for LGB college students as well. Future studies should investigate the information social support networks provided to LGB college students to see if a similar normalizing phenomenon is driving the direct relationship between network violence victimization and dating violence victimization.

Conclusion

The study contributed to the literature on dating violence within LGB relationships in several important ways. First, it measured dating violence occurring in LGB couples attending a nonresidential college. Second, it included the influence of neighborhood violence and female and male networks of social support providers on dating violence and therefore extended and linked previous research to provide a more comprehensive picture of the LGB community and dating violence. Third, the sample of LGB students was largely ethnic minorities and low-income individuals, who were underrepresented in literature.

Despite its strengths, several limitations should be noted. One, the sample size was small, so the results should be considered preliminary. Two, the study did not examine the sexual orientation of social support providers or the frequency of contact with social support providers. Third, the study did not measure if social support providers were both perpetrators and victims of violence. Current research indicates that young people frequently are both perpetrators and victims of dating violence, though the context of each tends to differ (Allen, Swan, and Raghavan, 2009; Kimmel, 2002). Social support providers who experience the context of perpetration and the context of victimization may influence the target differently than a social support provider who only perpetrates or who only experiences victimization. Adding these aspects to analyses of social support providers will further elucidate the relationship between witnessing neighborhood violence, networks of violence, and dating violence.

References

Allen, C. T., Swan, S. C., and Raghavan, C. (2009). Gender symmetry, sexism and intimate partner violence. *Journal of Interpersonal Violence, 24*(11), 1816–1834.
Benson, M. L., Fox, G. L., DeMaris, A. and Van Wyk, J. (2003). Neighborhood disadvantage, individual economic distress and violence against women in intimate relationships. *Journal of Quantitative Criminology, 19*(3), 207–235.
Benson, M. L., Wooldredge, J., Thistlethwaite, A. B., and Fox, G. L. (2004). The

correlation between race and domestic violence is confounded with community context. *Social Problems, 51*(3), 326–342.

Browning, C. R. (2002). The span of collective efficacy: Extending social disorganization theory to partner violence. *Journal of Marriage and Family, 64*(4), 833–850.

Cunradi, C. B., Caetano, R., Clark, C., and Schafer, J. (2000). Neighborhood poverty as a predictor of intimate partner violence among White, Black and Hispanic couples in the United States: A multilevel analysis. *Annals of Epidemiology, 10*(5), 297–308.

DeKeseredy, W. (1988). Woman abuse in dating relationships: The relevance of social support theory. *Journal of Family Violence, 3,* 1–13.

DeKeseredy, W. S. (1990a). Male peers support and woman abuse: The current state of knowledge. *Sociological Focus, 23*(2), 129–139.

DeKeseredy, W. S. (1990b). Woman abuse in dating relationships: The contribution of male peer support. *Sociological Inquiry, 60*(3), 236–243.

DeKeseredy, W., and Kelly, K. (1995). Sexual abuse in Canadian university and college dating relationships: The contribution of male peer support. *Journal of Family Violence, 10*(1), 41–53.

DeKeseredy, W., and Schwartz, M. D. (1993). Male peer support and woman abuse: An expansion of DeKeserdy's model. *Sociological Spectrum, 13,* 393–403.

DeKeseredy, W. S., Schwartz, M. D., Fagen, D., and Hall, M. (2006). Separation/divorce sexual assault: The contribution of male support. *Feminist Criminology, 1*(3), 228–250.

Fox, G. L., and Benson, M. L. (2006). Household and neighborhood contexts of intimate partner violence. *Public Health Reports, 121,* 419–427.

Jones, C. A., and Raghavan, C. (2012). Sexual orientation, social support networks, and dating violence in an ethnically diverse group of college students. *Journal of Gay and Lesbian Social Services, 24*(1), 1–22.

Kimmel, M. S. (2002). "Gender symmetry" in domestic violence. A substantive and methodological research review. *Violence against Women, 8*(11), 1332–1363.

Lloyd, S. (1997). The effects of domestic violence on women's employment. *Law and Policy, 19*(2), 139–167.

Miles-Doan, R. (1998). Violence between spouses and intimates: Does neighborhood context matter? *Social Forces, 77*(2), 623–645.

Miles-Doan, R., and Kelly, S. (1997). Geographic concentration of violence between intimate partners. *Public Health Reports, 112*(2), 135–141.

Raghavan, C., Mennerich, A., Sexton, E., and James, S. E. (2006). Community violence and its direct, indirect, and mediating effects on intimate partner violence. *Violence against Women, 12*(12), 1132–1149.

Raghavan, C., Rajah, V., Gentile, K., Collado, L., and Kavanagh, A. M. (2009). Community violence, social support, ethnic group differences, and male perpetration of intimate partner violence. *Journal of Interpersonal Violence, 24*(10), 1615–1632.

Riger, S., Raja, S., and Camacho, J. (2002). The radiating impact of intimate partner violence. *Journal of Interpersonal Violence, 17*(2), 184–205.

Sampson, R. J., and Groves, W. B. (1989). Community structure and crime: Testing social- disorganization theory. *American Journal of Sociology, 94*(4), 774–802.

Sampson, R. J., Raudenbush, S. W., and Earls, F. (1997). Neighborhoods and violent crime: A multilevel study of collective efficacy. *Science, 277,* 918–924.

Schwartz, M. D., and DeKeseredy, W. S. (2000). Aggregation bias and woman abuse: Variations by male peer support, region, language and school type. *Journal of Interpersonal Violence, 15,* 555–565.

Schwartz, M. D., DeKeseredy, W. S., Tait, D., and Alvi, S. (2001). Male peer support and a feminist routine activities theories: Understanding sexual assault on the college campus. *Justice Quarterly, 18*(3), 623–649.

Selner-O'Hagan, M. B., Kindlon, D. J., Buka, S. L., Raudenbush, S. W., and Earls, F. J. (1998). Assessing exposure to violence in urban youth. *Journal of Child Psychology and Psychiatry, 39,* 215–224.

Shaw, C. R., and McKay, H. D. (1942). *Juvenile delinquency and urban areas.* Chicago: University of Chicago Press.

Straus, M. A., Hamby, S. L., Boney-McCoy, S., and Sugarman, D. B. (1996). The revised conflict tactics scale (cts2). Development and preliminary psychometric data. *Journal of Family Issues, 17*(3), 283–316.

Swanberg, J. E., Logan, T. K., and Macke, C. (2005). Intimate partner violence, employment and the workplace. Consequences and future directions. *Trauma, Violence and Abuse, 6*(4), 286–312.

Tollman, R. M., and Wang, H. (2005). Domestic violence and women's employment: Fixed effects models of three waves of women's employment study data. *American Journal of Community Psychology, 36*(1/2), 147–158.

Van Wyk, J. A., Benson, M. L., Fox, G. L., and DeMaris, A. (2003). Detangling individual-, partner-, and community-level correlates of partner violence. *Crime and Delinquency, 49*(3), 412–438.

Tameka L. Gillum and Gloria T. DiFulvio,
University of Massachusetts Amherst

7 | Exploring Dating Violence among Sexual Minority Youth

Dating violence is defined by the Centers for Disease Control and Prevention (CDC) as physical, sexual, or psychological violence that occurs within the context of a dating relationship (CDC, 2006). Research reveals a disturbingly high prevalence of dating violence among U.S. youth (Eaton, Davis, and Barrios, 2007; Howard, Wang, and Yan, 2007; Sears, Byers, and Price, 2006; West and Rose, 2000). Data from the Youth Risk Behavior Survey (YRBS) estimate victimization rates at 10 percent (Eaton et al., 2006; Eaton et al., 2007; Howard et al., 2007), while community-based assessments have found prevalence rates for perpetration and victimization as high as 19–67 percent (Sears et al., 2006; West and Rose, 2000).

Research to understand dating violence among sexual minority youth (lesbian, gay, bisexual, transgender, queer, or questioning) has been minimal but reveals disturbing results. Analysis of Massachusetts Youth Risk Behavior Survey data revealed that sexual minority youth were significantly more likely than their heterosexual counterparts to experience dating violence (35 vs. 8 percent) (Massachusetts Department of Education, 2006). Using a national sample of adolescents reporting exclusively same-sex sexual or romantic relationships, Halpern and colleagues (2004) reported that nearly 25 percent identified as experiencing some form of abuse. A community-based assessment of sexual minority youth, aged thirteen to twenty-two, indicated that between 38–57 percent of gay and bisexual males and females surveyed had experienced dating violence (Freedner et al., 2002). Though these studies suggest high prevalence rates, little is known about the nature and manifestation of such violence among this population.

Research suggests that individuals who experience intimate violence are at increased risk for adverse mental and physical health outcomes (Amar and Gennaro, 2005; Campbell, 2002; Heintz and Melendez, 2006; Kramer, Lorenzon, and Mueller, 2004; Plichta, 2004). Teen dating violence has been linked to increases in risk behaviors such as early sexual activity, unprotected sex, alcohol and drug use, and a greater number of lifetime sex partners (Eaton et al., 2007; Howard et al., 2007; Ismail, Berman, and Ward-Griffin, 2007). Additionally, individuals victimized as adolescents are at increased risk for victimization during their college years (Smith, White, and Holland, 2003). These problems are compounded for sexual minority youth, who are already at risk for negative mental and physical health outcomes as a result of the social stigma associated with societal homophobia (Meyer, 2003; Sandfort, Melendez, and Diaz, 2007), even more so for sexual minority persons of color, who face the assaults and insults of racism as well.

Adolescence is the period in which individuals form their unique identities, including developing one's sexual identity and experiencing dating relationships. For sexual minority youth, developing a positive sexual identity in the context of a homophobic and heterosexist environment is even more tenuous during this already difficult period of development. Not conforming to socially approved dating practices may lead to teasing, ostracism, and violence. Additionally, such experiences may lead to internalized homophobia in sexual minority youth (Marrow, 2004). Internalized homophobia has been linked to less favorable perceptions of relationship quality and to both victimization and perpetration of intimate partner violence (Balsam and Szymanski, 2005; Otis et al., 2006; Tigert, 2001).

Gendered dating norms have been linked to the perpetration of male violence against females (Ismail et al., 2007; Schechter, 1982). Despite the desire to believe that such dated notions no longer impact relationships between males and females, recent research indicates that youth are still influenced by such social norms (Ismail et al, 2007; Johnson et al., 2005). Identity development of sexual minority youth also occurs within this context and may shape their perspective of relationship norms.

Another concern is that youth may not turn to adults or formal help sources when experiencing dating violence and do not receive adequate assistance when they do. Victims of dating violence have indicated encountering skeptical or dismissive attitudes upon revealing their abusive experience (Ismail et al., 2007; Weisz, Tolman, and Callahan, 2007). Fear of disapproval or rejection by family, peers, and school administrators on the basis of their sexual orientation (Marrow, 2004) is an additional barrier for sexual minority youth, who may be more likely to remain silent than their heterosexual peers because in the process of reporting, they would have to "come out" to anyone from whom they sought assistance.

The detrimental effects of dating violence coupled with the unique vulnerability of sexual minority youth calls for increased attention to this issue in both research and practice. To effectively target prevention and intervention efforts, research is needed that explores the issue from the perspective of sexual minority youth. One particular area of interest is to understand the unique factors that contribute to dating violence among this population. This study was designed to explore the perceptions and meanings of dating violence among sexual minority youth. For the purposes of this research, sexual minority youth were defined as individuals between the ages of eighteen and twenty-four who identify as lesbian, gay, bisexual, transgender, queer, or questioning or who indicate dating or being sexually intimate with a member of the same sex.

Methods

The data presented here are from a larger study (n = 109) designed to explore perceptions of dating violence and associated health outcomes among sexual minority youth.

Sample and Recruitment

Participants were recruited through flyers posted in strategic places on a large rural New England university campus and through active recruiting at campus-based queer groups and activities and community events. Participants completed surveys at the project office and were then asked if they wished to be contacted for participation in a focus group. Two focus groups were conducted, one with female participants and one with male participants. Limited enrollment of transgender individuals in the overall study prohibited our ability to include this unique perspective in focus group results. Special procedures were followed in a successful effort to assure that focus group participants were not involved with one another to reduce the possibility that two individuals involved in an abusive relationship would participate in a group together.

Focus group participant (n = 18) demographics were similar to that of the overall study sample and are as follows: eleven females, seven males; sixteen white (89 percent), two black/African American (11 percent); ages nineteen to twenty-three, mean = twenty; and six gay (33 percent), four bisexual (22 percent), three lesbian (17 percent), two pansexual (11 percent), two nonorientation conforming (11 percent), one queer (6 percent).

Analysis

Reports from focus groups were electronically recorded and transcribed verbatim. Focus group data were examined using thematic analysis with an emergent coding approach (Miles and Huberman, 1994). The analysis identified salient themes representing participant perspectives on the prevalence of and reasons for dating violence among this population. For the purposes of this research, dating violence was not defined for participants, as they were asked how they would define dating violence. Consistent with the literature, participant responses identified physical, sexual, and psychological dating violence. With this understanding of the definition, we proceeded to ask participants questions regarding prevalence and contributing factors.

With the first round of coding, focus group transcripts were read and coded independently by both authors and a third reader trained in qualitative methodology. Each coded for emerging themes regarding dating violence prevalence and perceived reasons for its occurrence. A list of codes was generated as a result of each individual's coding process. These three separate coding schemes and supporting quotes were compared for assessment of similarities and discrepancies. Discrepancies were resolved and, when necessary, codes were redefined and renamed and a uniform coding scheme was created. Once a final coding scheme was reached through this process, the authors recoded all transcripts in accordance with the final coding scheme. Codes were then independently grouped into themes by the authors. Themes were subsequently compared and finalized. Identified themes are presented in the following section.

Results
Prevalence

When asked about the prevalence of dating violence among sexual minority youth, most participants endorsed a belief that such violence was either more prevalent or the same as their heterosexual counterparts. One male participant expressed this as follows:

> I just think it is more common that gay men could be, or not just necessarily gay men but like homosexual couples could be, in more violent situations than heterosexual. There's so much at stake with coming out and keeping a lot of stuff in.

Similarly, a female participant stated,

> I think there's more potential for it to happen because you're at the same physical level and so that if a girl hits a guy that will be the end of it and like it will be resolved, but if a girl hits a girl, you may be going at it for a while. Like, you're going to hit her right back. . . . If a guy hits you, you might be afraid to hit him back and you might get out of the situation. . . . There's a lot of potential . . . for physical abuse in the same-sex relationship.

Those participants believing that the prevalence of dating violence within same-sex relationships was the same as among their heterosexual peers agreed with one male participant who stated, "I'd have to say from personal experience it's fifty-fifty."

Reasons for Dating Violence

Participants were asked their perceptions of the reasons dating violence happens in sexual minority youth relationships. Responses identified four themes: homophobia (both societal and internalized homophobia), negotiating socially prescribed gender roles, assumed female connection, and other relationship issues.

Homophobia

For sexual minority youth, there is a constant negotiation of "self as other" in the context of a larger culture of homophobia and heterosexism. According to the youth, the intense stigma associated with "being other" than heterosexual is one of the most important contexts for understanding the existence of violence in same-sex dating relationships. This culture of homophobia may keep them from coming out to others or lead to feelings of isolation or shame about their sexual identity. These factors associated with homophobia place stress both at the individual and relational level. Participants identified both societal and internalized homophobia as reasons for violence in same-sex relationships.

SOCIETAL HOMOPHOBIA   Societal homophobia contributes to fear and stigma among sexual minority youth. This may result in youth choosing to stay in a violent relationship due to fear of reporting the abuse or fear that reporting the abuse will lead to their identity becoming public to family and friends. Societal homophobia also results in a lack of awareness about violence in same-sex relationships and the minimization of such violence.

Participants described needing to understand themselves against a larger cultural discourse that has universally presented heterosexual identities as "normal" and as the only acceptable sexual orientation, while those that identify as lesbian, gay, or bisexual are rendered invisible and viewed as deviant or unnatural. As one woman stated, "it's not made visible. . . . It [dating violence] happens so often because it's not really culturally okay yet to be gay."

This invisibility may lead to a perception of limited dating options. One male participant identified the following reason for remaining in an abusive relationship.

> In a gay relationship, you almost in a way have a lot more invested because the numbers in the pool are just so much smaller. So you almost feel like, oh, this is kind of like, for me, it's an emotionally kind of abusive relationship, but maybe you can come out of it. Like I'm just thinking if I was a heterosexual, I would never have considered that. I never would have been like, well, I mean, there's really a small pool to date out here, that would never be a thought in my mind.

Reporting dating violence to the police may not be an option for sexual minority youth. They discussed how a larger culture of homophobia leads to fear of reporting violence to authorities. There is a perception that if youth report same-sex violence, they may not be taken seriously or could be revictimized by the police. As one male participant stated,

> I've heard of people saying I'm afraid to go to the police or the authorities or whoever's in charge because they won't be sympathetic because it's a gay relationship or they won't understand, or they'll ridicule me.

Because youth may not be "out" to family and friends, they say that they may endure abuse because reporting it may result in having to tell their parents about their relationship. Telling parents may result in being cut off financially, being kicked out of the home, or a disconnection from family members. As a male participant explained,

> [in] a closeted relationship, the prospect of fear really makes it even worse. . . . It's a fear that parents will find out, that they'll be moved out of the house, that they'll be cut off from financial funding; all of these issues go together.

Another young woman talks about needing to hide her identify from her parents:

> Like I can't afford to be on my own right now. . . . I can't take that risk. There's no possible way I would be able to survive on that risk. Love is great, but like sometimes at the end of the day I hopefully can pay my bills.

Homophobia results in a silencing of sexual minority identities in social discourse about violence. This silencing serves to maintain heterosexual dominance and thereby further alienate sexual minority youth. The lack of same-sex models makes it difficult for youth to know what abuse looks like or leads to a minimization of abuse that may occur in a dating relationship. This is demonstrated in the following exchange:

FEMALE PARTICIPANT: Like a man beats his wife like that is a big thing, more than hearing about it from a man beating a man in a same-sex relationship.

FEMALE PARTICIPANT: And it's seen as more of a problem, I think, the man hits his wife then if two fags are beating each other or two dykes are going at it, whatever, who cares. Crazy gays. If a man beats his wife, it's like, "whoa, abuse."

FEMALE PARTICIPANT: Maybe it's like because you assume that they would be the same size, that, oh no, like, two lesbians are fighting, let's go watch.

FEMALE PARTICIPANT: Yes, it's not as if they're going to hurt each other, you know, because they're both girls.

FEMALE PARTICIPANT: Society is like you might as well kill each other anyway, you know, better off gone anyway so, who cares.

This pervasive silencing and discrediting of same-sex relationships in the national discourse results in sexual minority youth feeling as if their relationships are viewed as inferior to heterosexual relationships and therefore physical violence in these relationships is perceived as less important. As one male participant stated,

> Until the government allows gay people to serve openly in the military, until gay people are allowed to marry in the United States, you're never going to be considered equal and that goes all the way down to physical violence. Your physically violent relationship is not the equal of a heterosexual physically violent relationship.

The dynamics of homophobia and heterosexuality as the privileged orientation may provide permission or tacit support for the victimization in dating situations. According to these youth, the omission of dialogue about the existence of same-sex relationships and the tacit approval of homophobia by a larger society through silence and overt policies contribute to the existence of violence in same-sex relationships.

INTERNALIZED HOMOPHOBIA Several participants discussed how societal homophobia becomes internalized, resulting in a discomfort with self and their same-sex relationships. Participants stated that this discomfort or shame with one's sexual identity might be associated with violence in a relationship. One male participant stated,

> As gay people we have different ways of coming out or coming to our identities and . . . thinking about the ways we think about relationships and the ways in which we have had to kind of identify something outside of a norm. I think it allows for more of these things [violence].

Another male participant stated, "I think that a lot of violence stems from insecurity. Like if you don't feel good about yourself or the relationship, then you might lash out."

Being unable to express one's identity—whether in a heterosexual or same-sex relationship—may also lead to expressions of violence.

> I think [dating violence] has lots to do with the internalization of how you feel about being in that relationship and especially like how comfortable you are with your own gender, your own body. And I think people can have a lot of resentment towards themselves, towards their bodies, and towards their identities, and especially like for me, being in a lot of straight relationships . . . in [those] relationships, any violence that I exhibited towards the guy has always been my resentment towards him for not being able to express like a huge part of myself, which is like having feelings for girls. There's always having feelings for girls and the part of me that can't express [that] and that's definitely led to violence in [those relationships]. Like not knowing what you think or not always being okay with the relationship that you're having.

"Internalized homophobia" may lead to feeling the need to hide or deny one's sexual orientation in an attempt to fit into a heterosexual norm. Within this context, individuals continually negotiate the degree to which they are "out" in the world. Being in a same-sex relationship means considering a partner's "out" status and the affect this status may have. Differences here may create tensions within couples. One female participant described it like this:

> It comes down to controlling coming out. . . . My girlfriend had that situation where I was like I just want to come out, and she just looked at me like, whoa, where are you going with this? She's like you can come out as gay, but you better not [tell] people you're in a relationship or anything like that. Like you can't do that. And I was just like, I don't understand. She was like, "you have to understand the risk."

Similarly, another female participant stated,

> People are really different in homosexual relationships, like in queer relationship[s] because expressing yourself is big. That's a big, big part of you, whereas in like a

heterosexual relationship, like you're not really trying to express your sexuality, I guess, and at times like your sexuality is already known, whereas like in a homosexual relationship, you want to be known as such, want to identify as such, this other person's like, no, you can't identify this. You can't look like that. That's against the law in my book. So like that's a form of abuse.

Being in a same-sex relationship may reinforce a status as "other" such that these youth often feel marginalized, disconnected, and even targeted. Resisting this otherness can be so strong as to lead to abusive or violent behavior. One woman described her anger that emerged as her girlfriend expressed an interest in dressing in more stereotypical male ways. She feared that being seen with a more masculine partner would expose her as "other."

> She was like, "I want to wear ties." I was looking at her like, "I'm not going outside with you wearing ties." . . . For the longest time I couldn't understand. I was so angry with her, and it was just because I'm bisexual and already I don't want to be seen as other. I'm already other, like in the community, period. . . . But, I have the pleasure of being able to not . . . have my gayness be so [obvious]. You just don't see it. It doesn't come across at all I guess and I was comfortable with that, but if . . . she has a tie on and we're walking together. . . . It just turned into a very disgusting argument, very disgusting time.

Similarly, another female participant described how her past abusive partner tried to control her gender expression so the two could appear as friends rather than as girlfriends.

> I was in a relationship over the past summer, like, she was pretty abusive and controlling. . . . I had long hair and she told me if I cut it she would dump me. . . . I think she didn't want to be identified with a more masculine female because she was in the military, so no one could know she was gay.

Negotiating Socially Prescribed Gender Roles

Both male and female participants described a process of negotiating socially prescribed gender roles as a reason for relationship conflict, sometimes contributing to violence in same-sex partnerships. This included gender role or expression conflicts, changes in or fluidity of gender roles, need for one partner to assert a dominant role, and the association between being dominant and abusive. Participants described an imposition of heterosexual relationship molds on same-sex relationships and attempts by one or both parties in a relationship to conform to this mold. A female participant stated,

My girlfriend originally identified as gender queer. So like for the first year or so we were together, we're both sort of like femmy or whatever and, all of a sudden, she's like presenting really masculine, and she passes as a guy all the time, and I like just got okay, like completely with I'm with a woman, ya da ya da, the whole gay thing and like now when people see me they're like, oh, straight heterosexual and like I'm trying to deal with being perceived that way again, because I don't want to pretend or be in a closet or be viewed that way. So it's sort of hard to deal with that.

Conflicts also arose when defined "roles" were in place and one partner attempted to change or modify their previously defined role. A male participant stated this as follows:

A relationship can start off as honeymoonesque in the beginning and then change to a nightmare because the roles that one person wants to hold can change halfway through a relationship, and it could add severe amounts of stress to a relationship and lead to abuse.

Related to this, some participants attributed violence to being the means by which one partner asserts his or her dominant role in the relationship to fit gender stereotypes. One female participant articulated this as follows:

I think a lot of people think that you can't be dominant without being either verbally abusive or like readily make it known that you're the dominant one in the relationship between two girls.

Assumed Female Connection

A factor the emerged unique to female participants was the theme of an assumed female connection. Females asserted the idea that between two females there is an assumption of a shared connection that comes with the expectation that they should automatically understand each other, limiting the need for communication or to explain themselves. Female participants expressed that when this does not occur within the relationship, tensions develop sometimes, leading to abuse. This is exhibited by the following exchange:

FEMALE PARTICIPANT: I was going to say as far as the communication piece, how it can manifest itself, I'm talking about girls. She should be able to understand me. We both have the same periods. We both get moody the same way. Why don't you understand? What the fuck is wrong with you? Why don't you get it, you know what I mean, and I'm going to be angry at her and not sensitive. If I was dating a man, it's like he's just not going to get it. I'm just going to let this go and go want to talk to my home girls.

FEMALE PARTICIPANT: I do but I don't. Like if you've been gay your whole life, I definitely don't know how to do my hair. I don't know how to do my makeup. I don't have these emotional-like actions. . . . I think here is the first time I got extremely emotional or something. So I think in that sense a lot of the times I don't understand what the hell she's saying. Like what?

FEMALE PARTICIPANT: A lot of times she's probably like what the fuck are you saying, you know what I mean?

FEMALE PARTICIPANT: Exactly.

FEMALE PARTICIPANT: And I'm, hmm . . . like I don't know. Who knows?

FEMALE PARTICIPANT: This kind of a little bit relates to what [another participant] was saying that connection, so there's kind of like that female connection, what you were talking about, and connection you assume leads to a shared understanding, and [it] doesn't necessarily.

Other participants expressed similar sentiments: "I mean same sex couples . . . you have to deal with . . . like expecting the other person to understand you because they're the same gender."

Other Relationship Issues

In addition to discussing factors perceived to be unique to dating violence among same-sex couples, participants also identified factors similar to dynamics experienced in heterosexual couples. These include incompatibility, one person not being ready for a relationship, stress, class differences, lack of clarity regarding relationship status, and jealousy. This is represented by the following: "Some people just aren't good together. So sometimes the reason for the violence is because they push each other's buttons" (male participant).

Participants, also stated that these factors may manifest differently or more intensely in same-sex relationships than they do in heterosexual dating relationships. For example, when speaking of jealousy a female participant indicated that if one female is dating a bisexual female, the idea that she would be jealous of potential males and females adds to this dynamic. She expressed this as follows: "Plus you have double the jealousy if you're dating a bisexual girl. They're always looking at dudes and girls, like that jealousy level is just like up there."

Discussion

This study makes an important contribution to the literature, as it qualitatively explored dynamics of dating violence among sexual minority youth, including factors that youth identify as contributing to its occurrence. Consistent with the literature (Freedner et al., 2002; Massachusetts Department of Education, 2006), participants in this study perceived dating violence prevalence among sexual minority youth to be at least equal to but mostly more prevalent than among their heterosexual peers. These findings are important for two reasons. First, they reinforce the presence and magnitude of dating violence among sexual minority youth, supporting the need for prevention and intervention efforts targeting this population. Second, they provide support for the contention that sexual minority youth are aware that this is an issue within their community and consequently may be receptive to interventions targeting this issue.

Participants identified the process of navigating socially prescribed gender roles as a source of tension that sometimes led to violence. It is not surprising that heterosexual gender roles and relationship molds impact same-sex relationships. As indicated earlier, we live in a culture where socially prescribed gender roles constructed around male dominance and female submissiveness prevail and continue to influence today's youth (Ismail et al., 2007; Johnson et al., 2005), with gendered dating norms having been linked to the perpetration of violence in intimate partnerships (Ismail et al., 2007; Schechter, 1982). Consequently, as discussed by the youth in this research, these norms shape their perspective of what their relationships should resemble. This is especially true given the dearth of public models of healthy lesbian and gay relationships and the exclusion of LGBT sexualities in school-based sex-education classes (Marrow, 2004).

These norms impact youth in same-sex relationships in significant ways. Some sexual minority youth consciously resist these norms, while others ascribe to them. Having individuals with these differing positions in a relationship creates a source of conflict as they negotiate this space. These norms also influence same-sex relationships through the male-dominant, female-submissiveness model, where "masculine"-identified females and males assert their dominant role through the use of aggression and control tactics.

Participants in this study also identified homophobia, both societal and internalized, as a contributing factor to dating violence in same-sex relationships. Consistent with the literature, youth perceived that coping with these experiences places additional stress on relationships, contributing to dating violence. The concept of "minority stress" helps us to understand this relationship. The impact of an oppressive culture has been termed "minority stress" (DiPlacido, 1998; Meyer, 2003) and has been linked to such negative outcomes as increased isolation, shame, depression, substance abuse, and suicide (Allen and Oleson, 1999; Herek et al., 1997; Lock and Kleis, 1998; Shidlo, 1994). As operationalized by Balsam and Szymanski (2005) in their study of domestic violence in women's same-sex relationships, minority stress includes both experiences of heterosexist discrimination (societal homophobia) and internalized homophobia. The authors found a relationship between homophobia and intimate partner violence. One finding in particular was an identified association between experiences of discrimination (one aspect of minority stress) and perpetration of psychological and physical and sexual aggression against a partner. Research has identified that sexual minorities experience multiple stressors, including stigma, prejudice, and discrimination (Balsam and Szymanski, 2005; Marrow, 2004; Meyer, 2003). Balsam and Szymanski (2005) inform us that the stress of living a heterosexist society contributes to the use of violence in relationships. Youth in this study also identified societal homophobia as a factor in whether they report dating violence to others (including family, police, or peers).

For sexual minority youth, developing a positive sexual identity, often in the context of a homophobic and heterosexist environment, adds an additional challenge to the already fragile period of adolescent development. Not conforming to socially sanctioned dating practices may lead to teasing, ostracism, and violence for LGBT youth (Marrow, 2004). This experience may lead to the development of internalized homophobia, another component of minority stress, in sexual minority youth (Ryan and Futterman, 1997). Internalized homophobia has been conceptualized as the negative feelings or self-hate that results from growing up in a homophobic environment that devalues those who identify as a sexual minority (Bohan, 1996; Shidlo, 1994). Internalized homophobia has been linked to both victimization and perpetration of same-sex intimate violence and less favorable perceptions of relationship quality (Balsam and Szymanski, 2005; Otis et al., 2006; Tigert, 2001). Youth identified the impact that internalized homophobia has on relationships, including concerns about the other partner being too "out" or trying to control the look of the other partner so as not to be identified as a sexual minority.

A surprising theme that arose from this work was the identification of an assumed female connection contributing to relationship tension when violated. Participants talked about an underlying assumption in relationships between females that they understand and relate to one another simply on the basis of their same gender positions. If this assumption exists it is likely to lead to a lack of adequate communication in the relationship. This is particularly concerning as healthy communication is important for relationship quality and longevity in both same-sex and heterosexual intimate partnerships (Mackey, Diemer, and O'Brien, 2004).

Worthy of reinforcement here is one youth's comment that societal devaluing of sexual minorities and same-sex relationships fosters a lack of attention to dating violence in this population. His words highlight the message that discriminatory policies that cast sexual minorities as second-class citizens and their relationships as unworthy of legal recognition and its associated rights and privileges has many detrimental affects, including placing these individuals at heightened risk for negative consequences of dating violence through inadequate acknowledgement and response. Research supports the detrimental impact of these discriminatory policies on the mental health of sexual minorities (Hatzenbuehler et al., 2010), which likely also impact relationship quality.

Understanding sexual minority youth's perceptions of dating violence in the context of their same-sex dating relationships is important to enhancing our understanding of this phenomenon and the unique factors that should be addressed through prevention and intervention efforts. This research suggests that sexual minority youth experience dynamics unique to them and their relationships that cannot be effectively addressed through existing dating violence prevention programs that use and presume a heterosexual dating context for all youth. This study, therefore, makes a significant and useful contribution to the dating violence literature and the informing of dating violence services and programs for sexual minority youth.

References

Allen, D. J., and Oleson, T. (1999). Shame and internalized homophobia in gay men. *Journal of Homosexuality, 37*(3), 33–43.

Amar, A. F., and Gennaro, S. (2005). Dating violence in college women: Associated physical injury, healthcare usage, and mental health symptoms. *Nursing Research, 54*(4), 235–242.

Balsam, K. F., and Szymanski, D. M. (2005). Relationship quality and domestic violence in women's same-sex relationships: The role of minority stress. *Psychology of Women Quarterly, 29*, 258–269.

Bohan, J. S. (1996). *Psychology and sexual orientation: Coming to terms.* New York: Routledge.

Campbell, J. C. (2002). Health consequences of intimate partner violence. *Lancet, 359,* 1331–1336.

Centers for Disease Control (CDC) (2006). Understanding teen dating abuse fact sheet. Atlanta: CDC.

DiPlacido, J. (1998). Minority stress among lesbians, gay men, and bisexuals. In G. M. Herek (Ed.), *Stigma and sexual orientation* (138–159). Thousand Oaks, CA: Sage.

Eaton, D. K., Davis, K. S., and Barrios, L. (2007). Associations of dating violence victimization with lifetime participation, co-occurrence, and early initiation of risk behaviors among U.S. high school adolescents. *Journal of Interpersonal Violence,* 22(5), 585–602.

Eaton, D. K., Kann, L., Kinchen, S., Ross, J., Hawkins, J., Harris, W. A., Lowry, R., et al. (2006). Youth risk behavior surveillance—United States, 2005. CDC *Morbidity and Mortality Weekly Report, 55*(SS-5), 1–108.

Freedner, N., Freed, L. H., Yang, W., and Austin, S. B. (2002). Dating violence among gay, lesbian, and bisexual adolescents: Results from a community survey. *Journal of Adolescent Health, 31*(6), 469–474.

Halpern, C. T., Young, M. L., Waller, M. W., Martin, S. L., and Kupper, L. L. (2004). Prevalence of partner violence in same-sex romantic and sexual relationships in a national sample of adolescents. *Journal of Adolescent Health, 35,* 124–131.

Hatzenbuehler, M. L., McLaughlin, K. A., Keys, K. M., and Hasin, D. S. (2010). The impact of institutional discrimination on psychiatric disorders in lesbian, gay, and bisexual populations: A prospective study. *American Journal of Public Health, 100*(3), 452–459.

Heintz, A. J., and Melendez, R. M. (2006). Intimate partner violence and HIV/STD risk among lesbian, gay, bisexual and transgender individuals. *Journal of Interpersonal Violence, 21*(2), 193–208.

Herek, G. M., Cogan, J. C., Gillis, J. R., and Glunt, E. K. (1997). Correlates of internalized homophobia in a community sample of lesbians and gay men. *Journal of the Gay and Lesbian Medical Association, 2,* 17–25.

Howard, D. E., Wang, M. Q., and Yan, F. (2007). Psychosocial factors associated with reports of dating violence among U.S. adolescent females. *Adolescence, 42*(166), 311–324.

Ismail, F., Berman, H., and Ward-Griffin, C. (2007). Dating violence and the health of young women: A feminist narrative study. *Health Care for Women International, 28,* 453–477.

Johnson, S. B., Frattaroli, S., Campbell, J., Wright, J., Pearson-Fields, A. S., and Chen, T. L. (2005). "I know what love means": Gender-based violence in the lives of urban adolescents. *Journal of Women's Health, 14*(2), 172–179.

Kramer, A., Lorenzon, D., and Mueller, G. (2004). Prevalence of intimate partner violence and health implications for women using emergency departments and primary care clinics. *Women's Health Issues, 14*(1), 19–29.

Lock, J., and Kleis, B. N. (1998, June). A primer on homophobia for the child and adolescent psychiatrist. *Journal of the American Academy of Child and Adolescent Psychiatry, 37*(6), 671–673.

Mackey, R. A., Diemer, M. A., and O'Brien, B. A. (2004). Relational factors in understanding satisfaction in the lasting relationships of same-sex and heterosexual couples. *Journal of Homosexuality, 47*(1), 111–136.

Marrow, D. F. (2004). Social work practice with gay, lesbian, bisexual and transgender adolescents. *Families in Society, 85*(1), 91–99.

Massachusetts Department of Education. (2006). 2005 Massachusetts youth risk behavior survey results. Boston: Massachusetts Department of Education.

Meyer, I. H. (2003). Prejudice, social stress, and mental health in lesbian, gay, and bisexual populations: Conceptual issues and research evidence. *Psychological Bulletin, 129*(5), 674–697.

Miles, M. B., and Huberman, A. M. (1994). *Qualitative data analysis.* (2nd ed.). Thousand Oaks, CA: Sage.

Otis, M. D., Rostosky, S. S., Riggle, E. D. B., and Hamrin, R. (2006). Stress and relationship quality in same-sex couples. *Journal of Social and Personal Relationships, 23*(1), 81–99.

Plichta, S. B. (2004). Intimate partner violence and physical health consequences: Policy and practice implications. *Journal of Interpersonal Violence, 19*(11), 1296–1323.

Ryan, C., and Futterman, D. (1997). Lesbian and gay youth: Care and counseling. *Adolescent Medicine, 8*(2), 207–374.

Sandfort, T. G. M., Melendez, R. M., and Diaz, R. M. (2007). Gender nonconformity, homophobia, and mental distress in Latino gay and bisexual men. *Journal of Sex Research, 44*(2), 181–189.

Schechter, S. (1982). *Women and Male Violence.* Cambridge, MA: South End Press.

Sears, H. A., Byers, E. S., and Price, L. (2006). The co-occurrence of adolescent boys' and girls' use of psychological, physical, and sexually abusive behaviours in their dating relationships. *Journal of Adolescence, 30*, 487–504.

Shidlo, A. (1994). Internalized homophobia: Conceptual and empirical issues in measurement. In B. Greene and G. M. Herek (Eds.), *Lesbian and gay psychology: Theory, research, and clinical applications* (176–205). Thousand Oaks, CA: Sage.

Smith, P. H., White, J. W., and Holland, L. J. (2003). A longitudinal perspective on dating violence among adolescents and college-age women. *American Journal of Public Health, 93*(7), 1104–1109.

Tigert, L. M. (2001). The power of shame: Lesbian battering as a manifestation of homophobia. *Women and Therapy, 23*(3), 73–85.

Weisz, A. N., Tolman, R. M., and Callahan, M. R. (2007). Informal helpers' responses when adolescents tell them about dating violence or romantic relationship problems. *Journal of Adolescents, 30*(5), 853–868.

West, C. M., and Rose, S. (2000). Dating aggression among low-income African American youth. *Violence against Women, 6*(5), 470–494.

Commentary

Chitra Raghavan and Shuki J. Cohen

Dating Violence among Sexual Minority Youth

In this section, we focus on the methodological challenges associated with the study of dating violence in sexual minorities. The scientific study of dating violence in these populations has historically been slower, largely because same-sex relationships have not enjoyed the same cultural and legal legitimacy as their heterosexual equivalents. This legal and social marginalization has simultaneously hampered acknowledgement of violence in same-sex relationships and, accordingly, slowed research, prevention, and intervention. Apart from these external constraints, the marginalization and stigma associated with belonging to a sexual minority increase the vulnerability to partner abuse from within the community in the form of denial and minimization of violence, reduced resources for support, and culturally specific tactics such as one partner outing the other, thus exposing them to a hostile community. Because of these sociopolitical concerns, the methodological challenges to dating violence research are considerably heightened where sexual minorities are concerned.

The first fundamental problem is in the definition of the population itself. Should we investigate partner violence as a phenomenon that occurs between anyone engaged in an intimate relationship whether queer or straight? Or should we use sexual preference as a criterion that defines this population category in empirical research? Is the definition of a group by sexual preference alone a reflection of societies' obsession with sexual behavior? And if we assume sexual preference to be a legitimate research criteria, can we equate male same-sex violence with female same-sex violence and transgendered violence? A second fundamental problem is what represents abuse. Most partner violence research has assumed that there is both functional and behavioral equivalence in violent tactics across gender and cultural contexts. However, a few researchers have argued that this universalism fails to capture the contextualized nature of abuse and therefore the meaning and consequences of the abuse, whether the context is male to female (Stark, 2006) or male to male (Raghavan et al., 2011).

Finally, the methodological focus on young adults introduces several additional complexities to the study of intimate partner and dating violence among sexual minorities. Studies suggest that sexual orientation among young adults today is experienced and expressed as more fluid and relies less on secret communities, which typified older models of sexual minority socialization habits. As such, the paucity of research in this field may reflect either a true lack of established and reproducible models or the fact that youth perceptions and behavior often exhibit a level of fluidity and novelty that established models cannot yet capture.

Both chapters in this section respond to some of these intellectual challenges, albeit using different methodological positions. Jones, a doctoral candidate in social policy in the United Kingdom, grapples with these questions by introducing sociological and neighborhood measures into the conventional quantitative methods of studying individual victims. In contrast, Gillum and DiFulvio use focus groups to understand what sexual minorities themselves think is partner violence and why it happens. Gillum and DiFulvio's approach suggest that different models may be warranted for sexual minorities and that insider perspective is important. However, both authors separate male and female same-sex groups, suggesting that gender and sexual orientation should not be conflated.

Jones's correlational study rests on the premise that intimate partner violence in sexual minorities is embedded within the exposure of LGBT individuals to general violence in their environment and important peer relations. This framework, as she notes, has been routinely used to explain both IPV and dating violence in heterosexual populations. Her model suggests that while sexual orientation is important in determining the substance of peer messages and the importance (and type) of peer attachment, causal mechanisms of dating violence are similar for straight and queer populations. She thus takes a more liberal postpositivist approach that acknowledges differences in the details but not necessarily in the fundamentals of intimate relationships.

Jones's sampling procedure is worthy of particular attention. She attempts to test a model that includes sexual minority students who did not differ from their heterosexual counterparts in other domains such as club membership or campus gay activism. Her inclusion criteria therefore ruled out any purposive sampling that might target gay-friendly classes, clubs, or campus activities. Instead, Jones surveyed almost two thousand students enrolled in either mandatory introductory life skills classes or introduction to psychology courses. Her final sample numbered eighty-eight college students, which is close to the original survey sample that Gillum and DiFulvio acquire through purposive sampling (n = 109).

Why go to so much trouble? Jones wishes to be able to generalize some of the relationships she finds in her sample to the average LGBTQ student, not just the student who is active and "out" regarding sexual orientation. Additionally, although not directly tested, Jones wishes to see if similar mechanisms to dating violence exist across sexual orientation. Alternatively, at the very minimum, Jones can rule out the possibility that her results are due to sampling individuals who widely identify themselves as sexual minorities and that her sample includes a wide range of LGBTQ students. Her sampling strategy illustrates both the difficulty in obtaining large enough samples of sexual minorities to permit sophisticated quantitative testing and the difficulty of obtaining a minority sample that can produce generalizable results.

Jones eligibility criteria are also worthy of particular attention. She includes participants who may not self-identify as gay or queer but were in same-sex relationships. Additionally, she includes participants defined as sexual minorities but who were not at the time in same-sex relationships. Thus, her definition of a sexual minority is a mix of both self-identification and current sexual practices. While this more complex definition of sexual minority is likely to be more ecologically valid than self-selected or self-identified LGBTQ youth, it also includes women currently with male partners. Some researchers may consider this to be "fuzzying" the boundaries, but others are likely to agree that criteria focusing only on sexual behavior or identity are rigid and do not reflect the reality of complex sexual identities.

Substantively, Jones's study is unique for two reasons. First, she frames the problem of dating violence as a social problem that is not unique to same-sex populations and therefore shares correlates and causal factors with heterosexual violence. Thus she approaches the problem as a universal experience, one influenced by neighborhoods and peer messages. Second, she frames the correlates of dating violence as structurally embedded in society rather than as individually caused or related uniquely to being gay or queer (although she doesn't rule out these factors). While structural explanations for same-sex violence are common, they usually focus on homophobic violence, not on generalized exposure to violence. One advantage for her focus is that her sample is a commuter sample and is largely poor and urban. Thus, her participants are likely to be exposed to considerable street violence and peer experiences of violence. And while homophobia matters, it may matter less or differently in a city where same-sex relationships have long been accepted.

Jones investigates whether witnessing violence in participants' neighborhoods is associated with either perpetrating or receiving dating violence. She further investigates if this relationship is attenuated by associating with female peers who themselves are victimized or with male peers who themselves are perpetrators. She finds that the relationship is not straightforward and that witnessing violence and its relationship to dating violence is mediated by affiliation with violent male peers but not victimized female peers. These results are different from previous findings (Raghavan et al., 2009), where straight men (controlling for their ethnic group membership) are more likely to perpetrate violence when they associate with both violent men and victimized women, suggesting that gender and sexual orientation do matter in how peer affiliation operates. Jones also finds that witnessing violence facilitates dating violence but not dating victimization. Overall, her results suggest that while the "neighborhood theory" is a useful framework for understanding dating violence, gender and sexual orientation play significant roles also.

One difficulty Jones encounters is that of sample size. While her sample is adequate for the analyses she proposed, she notes that she is unable to test her models while controlling for gender and sexual orientation. Thus, some of her results may be unclear because her group is treated as homogenous when they may not be. This difficulty underscores the need to obtain a sexual minority sample large enough to work with but still generalizable.

Gillum and DiFulvio turn to focus groups to better understand their sexual minority youth. Focus groups have become an important method of inquiry to understand the perspective of hard-to-reach and minority groups (Kitzinger and Barbour, 1999). Gillum and DiFulvio in their study do precisely this—they explore the perceptions and meanings of dating violence among sexual minority youth. As the authors note, this work is important because most of the extant research on dating violence is about heterosexual couples, producing theoretical models that were never intended to apply to other contexts.

As this chapter illustrates, purposive sampling can be the best approach when information is sought from small or difficult-to-access populations. It may also be the only valid option where identifying a large representative sample is not feasible. But purposive sampling should not be viewed as a fallback or panacea method. It may well be the best approach when a deep and contextualized understanding of the experiences or perceptions of particular groups is the desired. In this case, Gillum and DiFulvio recruited their participants strategically on a university campus to maximize their sample prevalence of sexual minorities. Just as Jones wishes to generalize her results, generalization is largely irrelevant to Gillum and DiFulvio.

As the reader might have inferred by now, focus group methodology is labor intensive (e.g., Morgan and Krueger, 1993). In this study, participants were recruited in two steps—a survey followed by eligibility and interest in a focus group. Groups were then electronically recorded, transcribed verbatim and then coded independently by three specifically trained coders, coding disputes were then resolved, and then recoded. Following the second full recoding, the authors searched the data individually for themes, which they then compared and finalized. While the sample size is small in comparison to what Jones assesses, the labor is not.

One of the hallmarks of focus groups is the intimacy that group interaction produces. By sampling people who share similarities (in this case sexual orientation), a peer group is created, which may confer a safer environment for members to express themselves honestly (Barbour, 2005). Further, focus group members interact with one another as well as the moderator and thus produce interactive data (Kitzinger, 1994). Unlike survey data, focus group data reflect a co-constructed reality and are argued therefore to better reflect participant realities than meaning that might be imposed by either an interviewer or a survey. In this study, participants discussed personal events that included shame, victimization, rejection, and suffering, allowing readers a glimpse of the realities that shaped their perspective. Further, we see a powerful example of dialoguing in the data, where female participants interact and develop their views on how same-sex relational violence is discredited. The participants affirm one another's views while developing their theories and opinions on how and why women who hit women are not taken seriously. By following this dialogue, we also understand the process of consensus (also present in Gentile's chapter in part 4).

It is interesting to speculate what a focus group strategy might have produced with Serafim and Safi's participants. While both authors used qualitative strategies and asked the same question—what does domestic violence mean for you or how do you define domestic violence—Serafim and Safi's findings reflected a lack of consensus on the definition, whereas Gillum and Difulvio note much consensus. Some of these definitional differences are clearly cultural, but we also may ponder the extent to which groupthink, a function of internal homogeneity but also a desire to please and conform that arises when group members feel connected, might have influenced Gillum and DiFulvio's participants (Sim, 1998). There is nothing inherently wrong or inferior about consensus; however, just as homogeneity creates safety, it can also promote conformity and thus ultimately mar our understanding of the phenomenon.

Several of the participants' responses provide interesting insight. First, Gillum and DiFulvio find a degree of consensus on why violence occurs but also obtain insight into why participants believe so. Other than factors shared with heterosexual populations, participants talked about their experiences and struggles with internalized and societal homophobia as one of the reasons for why dating violence occurs. Methodologically, this is particularly interesting because assessment of homophobia tends to run along disciplinary lines—psychologists are more likely to focus on internal psychic processes and sociologists are more likely to examine larger structural processes. However, these interviews suggest that for participants, the reality is carved differently, and they view the two levels—internalized and externalized—as interdependent. Thus, perhaps, future studies need to consider both levels of analysis in predicting dating violence. Finally, in contrast to Jones' study, none of the participants evoke peer or group experiences of street violence as contributing to dating violence, either because it is irrelevant for this sample or, perhaps, because the neighborhood influences are not directly experienced or processed as internal constructs.

Second, responses suggest that another reason for why violence occurs is that men and women in same-sex relationships are physically matched in strength. This view suggests that the participants adhere to a rather concrete and behavioral definition of domestic violence, which is in fact quite mainstream. Behavioral definitions of domestic violence are routinely critiqued (see Stark, 2006, ch. 5). As such, the views expressed in studies we have discussed are interesting. Could they reflect the internalization of more hegemonic views that tend to define and explain domestic violence by physical strength and discrete acts of abuse? Or, in fact, are such views accurate and reflect a different reality in queer communities than in heterosexual ones? It will be interesting in future studies to examine if and how same-sex participants also identify with and or view tactics such as domination, intimidation, and coercive control as central to abuse or if coercive control is particular to male-to-female abuse.

Third, some of the responses concerning reasons for tolerating abuse mirrors the reality and reasoning of other minority female victims in extant research. For example, participants note a reluctance to report violence to police for fear of homophobic retaliation. Such realities have also been reported in minority and immigrant women who are reluctant to seek formal help either because they do not trust the criminal-justice system or because seeking help from outside the community betrays their community (e.g., Moss et al., 1997). Taken together, these results suggest that minority status adds a complex layer of complications and stressors, and when there is violence, these vulnerabilities may increase exposure to and acceptance of violence.

To conclude, the two chapters utilize very different methodologies and frameworks to better understand violence in sexual minorities. Jones uses correlational data and a neighborhood framework to understand dating violence and finds similar patterns in heterosexual and queer participants. Gillum and DiFulvio use focus groups and find that responses largely reflect participants' awareness of the broader system of power and gender inequality that privileges heterosexuality. Further, participants' responses suggest that interpersonal power dynamics in sexual minorities play a unique role in violence causality. Both authors use radically different frameworks with what on the surface appears to be similar populations: sexual minority youth who attend college. However, the two different contexts—one urban and poor, and the other residential—may in fact suggest that both authors selected apt methodologies and frameworks to answer their research questions. The different samples and responses also raise the important issue of whether dating violence models differ not only across sexual orientations but also within the intersectionalities of class, gender, and socioeconomic status.

References

Barbour, R. (2005). Making sense of focus groups. *Medical Education, 39*(7), 742–750.

Kitzinger, J. (1994). The methodology of focus groups: The importance of interaction between research participants. Sociology of Health and Illness, 16(1), 103–121.

Kitzinger, J., and Barbour R. S. (1999). Introduction: The challenge and promise of focus groups. In R. S. Barbour and J. Kitzinger (Eds.), *Developing focus group research: Politics, theory, and practice* (1–20). London: Sage.

Kuzel, A. J. (1992). Sampling in qualitative inquiry. In B. F. Crabtree, W. L. Miller (Eds.), *Doing qualitative research* (31–44). Newbury Park, CA: Sage.

Morgan, D. L., and Kreuger, R. A. (1993) When to use focus groups and why. In D. L. Morgan (Ed.), *Successful Focus Groups.* London: Sage.

Moss, V., Pitula, C. R., Campbell, J. C., and Halstead, L. (1997). The experience of terminating an abusive relationship from an Anglo and African American perspective: A qualitative descriptive study. *Issues in Mental Health, 18,* 433–454.

Raghavan, C., Beck, C., Anderson, E. R., and Brewster, K. O. (2011, November). *How are violence tactics gendered? Examination of partner violence behaviors in male same sex relationships.* Paper presented at the annual meeting of the American Society of Criminology, Washington, DC.

Raghavan, C., Rajah, V., Gentile, K., Collado, L., and Kavanagh, A-M. (2009).

Community violence, social support networks, ethnic group differences, and male perpetration of intimate partner violence. *Journal of Interpersonal Violence, 24,* 1615–1632.

Sim, J. (1998). Collecting and analyzing qualitative data: Issues raised by the focus group. *J Adv Nursing, 28*(2), 345–352.

Stark, E. (2006). Commentary on Johnson's "Conflict and control: Gender symmetry and asymmetry in domestic violence." *Violence against Women, 12*(11), 1019–1025.

Critical-Thinking Questions

1. Are the racial and class makeup of the two studies (chapters 6 and 7) similar or different?
2. How might the racial and class makeup of both studies affect the findings?
3. How might masculine gender socialization be associated with violence perpetration in both studies?
4. While the quantitative assessment of domestic violence boasts higher replicability, reliability, and accuracy, the qualitative analysis of domestic violence boasts higher ecological validity and nuance.* What would be the risks that policy makers are running by privileging one method over the other?
5. When using focus group methodology, how can we tell that experience is genuine and personal versus a parroting of societal or media-bound notions (a phenomenon dubbed as the "availability heuristic")? How might such an availability heuristic affect the conclusions of the study?
6. How is Jones's study positivist?
7. Similarly, compare which participants were considered eligible in both studies. Provide a strength and limitation of each study's eligibility criteria with an eye to ecological validity.
8. Compare the sampling strategies used in Gillum and DiFulvio's study with Jones's. Provide a strength and a limitation of each of their sampling strategies.
9. In your view, is Jones's study generalizable to all populations or only to select ones?
10. In Jones's study, data on peers is obtained through self-reports provided by the participant. Would this be considered an individual level of measurement or some other level?

*Replicability is the extent to which experimenters will obtain the same results if they use the same experimental paradigms and conditions that produced these results in the first place.

11. According to Jones's results (see figure 6.1), is witnessing violence associated with intimate partner violence or is it causing it?
12. From Gillum and DiFulvio's results, what can you say about the relationship between gay identity and same-sex violence?

Advanced Questions

1. How would a public health administrator (whose mandate is to reduce violence in communities and peer groups) differ from a clinical psychologist (whose mandate is to treat individuals) when addressing same-sex intimate partner violence?
2. Returning to chapter 5, in what ways does Tehee and others' study contain elements of feminist scholarship and yet remain positivist?
3. Which element of Jones's study would be enriched by a focus group?

IV | SYSTEMIC REVICTIMIZATION

Learning Objectives

1. Returning to the learning objectives in part 1, expand the understanding of the role of the expert and survivor rather than the layperson in defining domestic violence and the role of the scholar in the research narrative as expert, advocate, and participant.
2. Expand the understanding of intimate partner violence and domestic violence by explicating the larger context in which it unfolds.
3. Expand the understanding of how sex and gender are conceptualized within the larger framework of power dynamics.

Katie Gentile, John Jay
College of Criminal Justice

8 | "You Don't Recognize Me Because I'm Still Standing"

The Impact of Action Research with Women Survivors of Domestic Violence

Gender-based violation of human rights is the greatest human rights scandal of our times (Amnesty International report from 2004, quoted in Evans and Lindsay, 2008, 355).

I dread the question, but it is predictably asked in each class I teach or speak in and even in social conversations when I mention working with women in violent relationships: "Why don't they just leave?" or the related "Why do they stay?" Each time it is asked with genuine bewilderment or occasionally contempt, as if the battered women in question had never considered such a straightforward solution. I am amazed that no one ever asks, "Why do men hit their partners?" This choice of focus says something significant about our expectations of masculinity and violence, and it maintains victim blaming as an enduring response to domestic violence. Foisting the responsibility for violence securely onto survivors impacts how we assist survivors and what we examine in research, where identifying individual risk factors in women (and now men) is typical. We tend to ignore the fact that community and criminal-justice systems consistently fail women (see Haaken, 1998, 2008; Riger, 1999; Burman, 2004; Slote et al., 2005) and that leaving does not end violence; it escalates it (Stark and Flitcraft, 1988). Reflecting these biases, domestic violence is continually pegged as a women's issue, not a human rights issue, which, in a patriarchal culture, guarantees limited scope and coverage. As Slote and others (2005) observed, using human rights discourse expands accountability to include governmental systems that condone and repeat violence against women. A human rights approach also serves to "re-politicize" (1391) the issue and highlight the overlapping categories of gender, race and ethnicity, class, and sexuality.

The mission of most domestic violence (DV) work is crisis driven, focused on getting women and children to safety. Beyond this essential task, survivors rarely participate in policy creation or trainings for criminal-justice personnel (Wilcox, 2007). They are still stigmatized for having been in a violent relationship and if they have children, they are often accused of having put them in danger. Wilcox notes that it is important to create contexts where survivors can provide mutual support so as not to be labeled or to experience themselves as exclusively helpless victims in need, romanticized heroines acting as independent agents who alone survived against the odds, or as independent agents who chose or provoked violence. In psychological research these individualized categories of victim or agent are typically dichotomous and used to reinscribe oppositional gender roles. Men's violence is seen as individual pathology (e.g., as borderline and antisocial disorders, see Fonagy, 2003; Bateman and Fonagy, 2008), not as a collective cultural activity (Haaken, 2008). As many feminist and postcolonial theorists have observed, this ideal of an autonomous subject, either helpless or violent, is a strategy that serves to uphold patriarchal colonization (Alcoff, 1991; Anzaldúa, 1987; Kaplan, Alarcón, and Moallem, 1999; Mohanty, 2004; Hook, 2008). Contextualizing violence within the culture helps to destabilize these categories and illuminates how resistance emerges in relation to power (Foucault, 1972; Hoy, 2004). However, focusing exclusively on the social can lose the nuanced forms of resistance that, in the face of oppression, can appear to be self-destruction or even complicity (Collins, 1990; Gentile, 2007).

One methodological way around this dilemma has been participatory action research, engaging participants in the research process. Although action research is a key method for feminist research on DV issues, there are often many problems with engagement and implementation (see Haviland, Frye, and Rajah, 2008 for a review; Riger, 1999; Slote et al., 2005). Organizationally, one consistent problem is that the research focus and levels of collaboration are usually set by the researcher (Josselson, 1996), which reinforces the power hierarchy action research often claims to challenge and deconstruct. In the literature on DV collaboration there is a repeated attempt to equalize hierarchies of researchers and advocates (staff of the participating DV organization). Some have attempted this through crossing boundaries, engaging survivors to participate, translating academic research requirements, and developing research ideas as a team (Haviland, Frye, and Rajah, 2008). DV researchers have to negotiate with both advocates and survivors, which requires addressing multiple levels of power struggles, including preexisting ones between advocates and survivors.

Surviving violence and abuse also impacts ones psychological and relational functioning (understanding that these are inextricable). Trauma can have a lasting impact on psychological capacities of symbolization, which are central to articulating one's experience and actively participating in research (Gentile, 2007). Riger (1999) noted the potential for secondary trauma for advocates engaged in action research, but the potential for survivor retraumatization has slid under the radar in favor of the assumption that participation is necessarily liberatory. There is little to no critical analysis of the impact of participation on survivors.

This chapter describes focus group research and explores the experiences of participating in an action research project. The participants were all women, and either members of Voices of Women Organizing Project (VOW) or staff of that organization, which is the lead initiative of the Battered Women's Resource Center (BWRC) in New York City. Members are all identified survivors; staff are paid employees who may or may not be survivors or members. In collaboration with Ramona Ortega, Kristen Renshaw, myself, and others, VOW developed an interview protocol to document human rights violations against battered women with cases in the New York City family court system. All participating women self-identified as having been abused by their male partners. This family court study is unique because the research focus itself was generated by the survivors. VOW advocates, staff, and members created and implemented the project, and the researchers were consultants.*

In the first section of this chapter I outline the research protocol and present a brief summary of the study findings. As Oliver (2004) observes, to explain the contradictory effects of oppression we need a theory of the unconscious "that operates between the psyche and the social, through which the very terms of psychoanalysis are transformed into social concepts" (xiv). I outline the theoretical foundation of this chapter, which integrates relational psychoanalytic and feminist theories as the approach to action research. Then I shift to discuss the research experiences of some VOW members; VOW executive director, Susan Lob; and myself, as we shared them during one two-hour focus group. As a participant I also spoke individually with members and Susan Lob (approximately one hour each), and one member chose to contact me by e-mail. As I explore here, psychoanalytic theory in particular has a great deal to offer action

---

*The author was not paid for her participation.

research, as it involves the analysis of interpersonal dynamics and is well situated to explore the experiences of participation in action research. Using this particular theory of inquiry I will highlight some of the complex processes that enable the *action* of participatory action research to be empowering.

Voices of Women Organizing Project

VOW was created by the Battered Women's Resource Center to bring survivors of domestic violence together to work to end violence against women and improve the services and legal systems that abused women and their children rely on for safety and justice. VOW helps survivors reclaim their power by helping them create a community through personal growth and opportunities for social action. VOW works to help survivors identify their own needs and the needs of other survivors. This form of grounded knowledge construction about themselves and others becomes a foundation for members to speak publicly about domestic violence. The organization trains survivors to speak to lawmakers, criminal-justice personnel, other survivors, and current victims. They do educational programming for the community and public outreach to schools, colleges, and other organizations. They learn to collectively draft public statements about policy and organize civil actions for change. As a group they document institutional failures, testify at hearings, and write position papers. They work to help women create a life outside of violence while reflecting on that violence and placing it within a cultural context of patriarchal, racist, classist, and homophobic violence. They integrate education with the creation of an activist community oriented toward the goal of systemic change in line with Freire's (1972) ideas of liberation pedagogy.

Justice Denied: Vow Family Court Research

After years of working on a number of different issues, VOW sought to focus their attention on one particular system. To identify that system they conducted focus groups with their members. From these focus groups VOW members decided to hone in on housing and child welfare and family court. For the latter, they wanted to document the stories they were hearing about how the family courts reinscribed violence against women. VOW staff wrote a Sociological Initiatives Foundation grant to fund the research as part of VOW's Battered Mothers' Justice Campaign. VOW members were paid to implement the research, and they provided a small stipend for the women they interviewed. Although outside researchers, including myself, consulted about the grant, it was primarily written by the staff who, with VOW members, administered it. This is a distinct shift from most action research projects, where the economic power is held by the academic researcher. Because it was designed to place the VOW members in the center with the academic researcher on the side as a consultant, my participation had to be limited to promote the action of the members. Taking this backseat made for a unique action research project, but it also meant that for me, there were times when my ability to participate in meetings had to take a backseat in favor of more direct tenure-generating activities. Members were involved in every step. I was considered the consultant; they controlled the research agenda, timeline, and setting. Not surprising, this clear shift in formal power did not impact informal power, as will be described momentarily.

The survey was designed collectively by VOW members and staff in a series of focus groups to develop short answer questions. They also translated it into Spanish. They then piloted the survey with other members of VOW, making changes and repiloting it. After a number of editing cycles, Ramona Ortega (at the time working with the Human Rights Project of the Urban Justice Center) and I organized trainings for the members who would be administering the surveys. I conducted one training with Kristen Renshaw and Ramona did the other two and helped further refine the survey. After the data was collected she helped train the VOW members to code the data, and she oversaw the analysis and helped write the report. By participating in every aspect of the research project, VOW members had the opportunity to acquire a variety of research skills and to thoroughly "own" the research project and resulting report. This also guaranteed their input at every level of the research, which is important toward collaboration and knowledge building (Haviland, Frye, and Rajah, 2008).

To recruit women with active cases in family court, VOW members designed fliers they thought would attract participants and distributed them to child welfare and domestic violence agencies and family court. The fliers had a contact number for VOW. When a woman called wanting to participate, a VOW staff member paired her with the member of VOW who would conduct the interview. The VOW member and the participant would agree to meet in a safe public space. The office administrator always knew when a member was conducting an interview and would await her call at the end of each one. The VOW member would debrief with the administrator in person or over the phone immediately after the interview. VOW also established monthly process groups to help the members digest their experiences.

In the end the members conducted more than one hundred interviews, completing one hundred surveys for analysis. The surveys took about one to two hours to complete. The survey itself required short answers, but the process was quite long and involved because vow members were committed to capturing the complicated circumstances that most survivors find themselves in. For instance, a woman may be in court five different times with five different judges for five different issues all related to DV with the same partner. The survey had to reflect this complexity.

The final report is aptly titled "Justice Denied: How Family Courts in NYC Endanger Battered Women and Children," cowritten by vow with the Human Rights Project of the Urban Justice Center (available on the web at www.vow bwrc.org). Like the family court study in Massachusetts (Slote et al., 2005), vow found a number of significant problems with the family court system that regularly endangered women and children. Their report exemplifies the complexities of researching and writing about gender-based human rights violations, which are rarely straightforward and cloaked in "naturalized" categories of identity (Bourdieu, 1978).

First, the courts do not follow the law or their own policies and procedures. vow found common ex-parte communication between the judge and other parties, less than 20 percent of the women they interviewed had been allowed their own witnesses, transcripts did not reflect what happened in the court, and most women could not afford to purchase copies. Law guardians did not always meet with their clients, almost half of the clients felt their lawyers did not understand domestic violence, and many mothers lost custody based on unsubstantiated allegations against them. Most of these mothers were prevented from seeing the evaluations that lead to their children being removed.

Second, similar to the Massachusetts family court study (Slote et al., 2005), vow found that decisions by the court often endangered children. A full 80 percent of the respondents said their abuser threatened to take away the children and 10 percent said they quit reporting abuse out of fear of losing custody. Mothers were often told by their lawyers, a law guardian, or judge not to oppose visitation, even when the women felt it was unsafe for them or the children and when it was unsupervised. The NYC child welfare agency often did not help. Close to 10 percent of the women reported that their children were abused in foster care, and over half claimed that Administration for Children's Services (ACS) did not help them reunite with their children. Child support was a hot issue, and 58 percent said asking for it resulted in a retaliatory custody battle from their abusive partner. Child support was ordered in only half of the cases when it was requested.

Third, the report found a court system that continues to minimize violence against women and refuses to hold abusers accountable. Even though all the women interviewed self-reported as victims of domestic violence, the court recognized only 52 percent of them, and 25 percent of the women were told not to mention DV in the court, half by their own attorney and half by court personnel such as mediators. In all cases the occurrence of DV was seen as jeopardizing the woman's but not the abuser's case. Women's reports of child physical and sexual abuse were typically used against them by triggering accusations of "parental alienation" against the mother.* Close to half of the women had their respective confidential addresses revealed in court, seriously endangering them and their children and forcing some of them to move. The court setting itself was also a problem. Many felt unsafe in the waiting areas, in the conference rooms with their batterers, and while waiting in long lines to get through metal detectors. In general, all of the women described being retraumatized by their experiences in family court.

Fourth, they found a sexist, classist system that rewarded wealthy men. In all, 90 percent of the women had a court appointed attorney, and 23 percent said their lawyers were not present for all of their proceedings. Fathers were not held accountable when they missed court dates and meetings. If women needed court interpreters their cases were often delayed. Interpreters are not always licensed and did not always translate accurately, and there are no mechanisms to impact this practice. Income seemed to be a factor in custody decisions. Of the women surveyed a trend emerged where those who lost custody were more likely to not speak English (when the father did); more likely to be an immigrant (the father a citizen); more likely to have no public job (the father working in the criminal-justice field, child welfare, or to have other similar connections to the system); more likely to be of color (the father white); or more likely to have been a full-time caregiver (father working outside the home). A full 37 percent of the women who lost custody of their children were the primary caregiver.

Based on these findings, the writers of the court report make a number of suggestions. They call for enforcement of all laws and procedures of the court, including opening the courts to independent evaluators, adding domestic violence experts and survivors on task forces that appoint judges, and having judges evaluated more frequently. They recommend that family court decisions

---

*"Parental alienation" (also known as Parental Alienation Syndrome, or PAS) was first coined by Gardner in the 1980s. It is used in DV cases to imply that a mother is turning a child against the father with false accusations of abuse.

and procedures protect children more effectively. This requires exploring the reasons why a child might not want to visit the violent parent and creating an independent review panel to deal with complaints about law guardians and to hold them accountable. They mandate trainings on DV for the guardians so they can understand the complex psychological manipulations common in these cases. They call for all allegations of DV to be taken seriously, including while ex-partners are in the courthouse. They suggest creating an advisory board of survivors to help family court address safety issues more effectively. They call for the creation of different ways for survivors to testify without facing and being intimidated by their abuser. They recommend that the physical space be made secure, with working alarms in bathrooms and guards and escorts for women, including those without current orders of protection. Lastly, they call for court proceedings to be fair and just, which requires addressing the gender, race, and class discrimination, trainings for all court personnel, and regulation to ensure that judges with patterns of discrimination are not reappointed. The report has resulted in VOW members presenting their findings at conferences and press events and garnering television and print media coverage. They have met with chief administrative judges and continue to work with family court officials.

Action Research

Action research has helped bridge the gulf between advocates, survivors, and researchers (Riger, 1999). It emerged out of Freire's (1972) ideas of liberation and Lewin's ideas of psychological group theory (Burman, 2004). Despite the centrality of Lewin to its development, psychology has lagged behind other fields in utilizing action methods for research. Action research has been described as a methodology with a goal of "recovering oppressed voices through the agency of non-Western people to reconstruct both history and knowledge production . . . while raising serious questions about the politics of speaking for and writing about others" (Frisby, Maguire, and Reid, 2009, 19). Giving voice to the voiceless and challenging the objectification of participants has also been a focus of much feminist research (Alcoff, 1994; Fine, 1994a, 1994b, 1996, 2006; Fine et al., 2004; Fonow and Cook, 1991; Mies, 1991; Stacey, 1988; Stanley 1996; Tolman and Brydon-Miller, 2001), which has noted how most studies fail to address the politics and power involved with representing participant experience (Alcoff, 1994; Bar-On, 1996; Burman, 2004; Fine, 1996; Lather and Smithies, 1997; Mishler, 1979; Naples and Clark, 1996; Visweswaran, 1994). Action research attempts to address these inequities through participation; however, as Stacey (1986) rightly pointed out, merely asking for a collaboration does not address issues of power, authority, or representation, and in fact it can provide new and perhaps more destructive forms of exploitation. It can be used to better mine participants or to "fix" research with the participant's stamp of approval functioning as a kind of intellectual shield for the researcher. As Spivak (1986) writes, "the other is simply a name that provides the alibi for erasing the investigator's intervention into the construction and representation of the narrative" (229). Josselson (1996) notes that even when we ask for the participation of those we research, this participation is still structured around the researcher's frames of interpretation.

In DV research there are historical tensions between researchers and advocates that impact collaboration, for instance, the tendency for researchers to focus primarily on how the study fits into the literature, while advocates focus on social change (Haviland, Frye, and Rajah, 2008; Riger, 1999). Researchers may swoop in, collect data, and leave without a trace. This impacts not just the relationship, or lack thereof, but it supports hierarchal power by highlighting researchers' lack of contact with the subject of their study, ability to come and go as they please, and a potential lack of commitment (Haviland, Frye, and Rajah, 2008). This can also reinscribe trauma. Even in action research the tools of analysis are only one part of the equation; one must create the space for sustained action, and this requires community building (Fisher, 2000). Thus, reflection alone, even when it is coupled with research-related action, may leave participants in a new oppressive situation.

Fine (1994b) has proposed that feminist researchers position themselves in the hyphens between self and other to generate knowledge, but we need to remember that we are integral to creating that hyphen. Furthermore, to engage in a dynamic relationship, we must nurture one to develop, which is complex and is a large epistemological leap that has profound ramifications in terms of research training and implementation. It requires not just social skills, as Riger (1999) described, but advanced skills in interpersonal dynamics. With this particular shift, qualitative research is propelled into the epistemological realm of relational psychoanalysis, a form of inquiry that focuses on the space between that is neither you nor I, but uniquely and continually changing, improvised, and cocreated.

Relational psychoanalytic theory emerged out of a coming together of British Object Relations (e.g., theorists such as Donald Winnicott, Ronald Fairbairn, Harry Guntrip, Melanie Klein, and others) and the interpersonal school represented by Harry Stack Sullivan (Aron, 1996). Relational theory holds the idea that there are two minds-bodies in the room, and each contributes to the creation of the therapeutic dynamic. The space of analysis is the interaction, with the understanding that each party participates in its creation. It is a form of inquiry focused on creating the space for subjectivities to emerge, understanding that they do so only in relationship. This emergence occurs only as an atmosphere of mutual engagement is created (Cohen, 2009b).

There is a vast difference between action research and psychoanalysis or psychotherapy; however, relational *theories* of psychoanalysis have a great deal to offer feminist action research. First, as Sampson (1996) notes, transformative relationships must be embodied. To embody a research relationship the researcher must enter into the analysis to collaborate with a distinct body, a distinct position of knowing. The "anchoring of subjectivity in *its* body is the condition of coherent identity, and, moreover, the condition under which the subject *has a perspective* on the world" (Grosz, 1995, 89, emphasis in original). Relational psychoanalytic theory provides a model of active engagement with participants, identifying selves not as unitary but as collections of complex and often contradictory self-experiences, each of which contribute to meaning making. This is important. As Humphrey (2009) observed, in much action research, participants have multiple identities of advocate, researcher, and even survivor or, in my case, advocate, activist, researcher, and clinician. These different self experiences influence knowledge production and the research relationship. Being able to engage multiple self experiences is also relevant from a postcolonial perspective (see Hook, 2008; Stopford, 2007). If we incorporate intersectionality (Collins, 1990) and liminality (Anzaldúa, 1987) into research we must also analyze the multiple shifting positions of self experience involved in these intersections for both the researcher and the participants.

Focusing the analysis on the relationship, the hyphen, also opens the door to acknowledging the unconscious, something researchers have been flirting with for years. For instance, Riessman (1995) has noted that language is not transparent, implying that participants may not always say what they mean. Lather (2001) focuses on the unconscious of the researcher, contending that even textual interpretation involves the unconscious. The psychosocial research methodology developed in part to incorporate the unconscious (Jefferson and Hollway, 2000). This approach also attempts to articulate "a place of suture" (Frosh and Baraitser, 2008) between the psychological and the social, as both contribute to the production of the subject, yet they are typically theorized separately. Psychosocial methods involve attending to contradictions, inconsistencies in stories, topics participants avoid, or changes in tone of voice, facial expressions, and other telling signs of emotional shifts. Through these disjunctions unconscious motivations and ambivalences can be inferred. Despite its widespread use, psychosocial researchers, like most psychology researchers, are not specifically trained in psychoanalysis nor are they always well versed in psychoanalytic theories of relationality and the unconscious (see, e.g., Layton, 2008). In most psychosocial research, the unconscious may be a focus of inquiry but only the unconscious of the participant. The researcher maintains an objective stance. This stance toward the unconscious can create an even more invasive form of inquiry, as the researcher can appear like an omniscient mind reader. Additionally, the unconscious is conceptualized as being an individual, not a relational construct. So psychosocial methodology is one way of including the unconscious while linking the psychological and social, but the researcher can remain objective and distant and the power dynamics inherent in data collection and analysis can be quite problematic.

Relational psychoanalysis conceptualizes the unconscious not as an isolated discrete entity located within the participant but emerging only in relation to others (Bass, 2001) as a product of relating. It is, as Frosh and Baraitser (2008) quote of Nasio (1992), "a constantly active process that exteriorizes itself incessantly" (357). The unconscious includes cultural proscriptions and identities, such that it becomes a form of knowledge, a "feel for the game" (Bourdieu and Wacquant, 1992) that is carved on our bodies and psyche as we are shaped and shape the world around us. It can be the repository of the unspeakable or of culturally unsanctioned identifications (Butler, 1993). However, it is important not to interiorize the unconscious (Gentile, 2007). It is a relational phenomenon that comes into being as we act on the world. Given these ideas about collaborative participation and the complexity of socially generated self-experience, the research process can be approached more as Lacan (1956) described and Frosh and Baraitser (2008) also note, like an endless quilt with different points of buttoned-down meaning where knowledge can emerge from within different relationships.

About Trauma and Processes of Symbolization

Including the unconscious as a factor in research problematizes the process of collaboration and the goal of "recovering oppressed voices" (Frisby, Maguire, and Reid, 2009, 19). Assuming the voiceless will just speak within the context of research ignores both the history of colonization and violence that renders them the voiceless targets for research to begin with and the history of academic authorities participating in the continual pathologization of survivors of violence. Additionally, the psychological impact of trauma and violence can handicap processes of symbolization, interrupting the goal of becoming voiced within the research (Gentile, 2007).

There has been much written about the impact of trauma on our abilities to create chronological narratives (Gentile, 2007; van der Kolk, 1994) and thus to use symbolic forms of expression (Fonagy and Target, 1996; Davies and Frawley, 1992; Gentile, 2007). This disruption has multiple levels, for experiences can be beyond signification based on psychic processes being overwhelmed or by experience being beyond the possibilities for cultural signification. Not being able to contain traumatic experience within symbolic forms can itself be retraumatizing, for these experiences do not cease to exist for us. Instead, they are often held within the body, where they may continually play themselves out in relationships to our selves, our bodies, and other people (Davies and Frawley, 1992; Gentile, 2007; Gentile et al., 2007).

There are a number of levels to how the cultural structures available for symbolization render certain experiences nonnarritavizable. First, language itself is unreliable in that speaking creates a unique experience but it does not mirror experience (see Frosh, 2007), for something always slips through the cracks of words (Gentile, 2007). Additionally, words temporally link experiences of the past with those of the present and future, such that in speaking experiences we are also, to some extent, (re)experiencing differing temporal affective states simultaneously, like a series of embodied echoes (see Loewald, 1980; Gentile, 2006, 2007). Telling one's story is empowering because it provides the opportunity to reconceptualize one's past. It is, after all, the basis of Freud's "talking cure," but it is not without its own costs, as one also relives the violence on some level of consciousness.

Narrative forms of symbolization are also shaped by culture. This means the ways in which we symbolize experience emerge from within cultural constructs of oppression and privilege such that certain experiences may be more readily symbolizable, while others are rendered abject (Kristeva, 1982). Some experiences have rigid cultural narratives for symbolization; for instance, the victimization of women is a category of experience often symbolized and made sense of through victim blaming. This reinscribes trauma through revictimization. As Bergson (1913/2001) observes, such linear causality collapses duration and capacities for reflection. Speaking one's experience, then, is quite complicated and loaded. Additionally, as Bhabha (1994) and Kaplan, Alarcón, and Moallem

(1999) note, speaking from the cultural margins can disrupt the center, but it also functions to reinscribe the marginalized identity and position of the speaker. Researchers need to be aware of and attend to the multiplicity of potential social and psychological challenges to speaking one's experiences within the research process, understanding that, as Massumi (2002) notes, these challenges are simultaneously conditions of emergence and becoming. They create the conditions for recognition even as they must be deconstructed.

Holding all theses issues in mind, I conducted a two-hour focus group and an hour-long interview with members of vow. The following section is an analysis of my and their reflections on our experiences of the trainings and the action research.

Reflecting on the Experiences of Action Research

At the request of vow's executive director, Susan Lob, I worked with Kristen Renshaw, the vow social work intern, to facilitate a day-long training with vow members around research issues. We sought to collaboratively engage vow members to help them best create the conditions for other survivors to tell their stories, knowing the method needed to be valid to produce legitimate, influential results. I had previous contact with some of the women and was aware of the many potential power pitfalls of collaborations but thought my identity as a director of the Women's Center, thus an advocate and counselor for women survivors, made me an ally. When, during the training, one of the members made repeated comments about "the system" not understanding their experiences I assumed she meant the judicial system they were going to examine. When she made the comments in reference to the research process, insisting that people who are part of the system cannot understand the questions that need to be asked and what they needed to do to engage the interviewees, I began to realize she was talking about me. I was not an ally. I represented "the system" that could not understand what needed to be done.

There were multiple gulfs between myself, a white academic researcher, and the survivors, primarily women of color (see Renzetti, 1997). Even though Kristen Renshaw and Susan Lob both identified as white women, Susan was the founder of vow and Kristen had worked for a year with them. They were both treated as allies by vow members. By the time I met with the members, they had worked for two years on their project. They already knew how they wanted to conduct the interviews. They already knew what they wanted to ask. I could only disrupt their plans. Additionally, the audacity of an academic coming in to the vow space to "train" them on how to interview survivors when they themselves were survivors was troubling to them and to me. I could imagine their questions about me: Was I another researcher who would not understand the nuances of domestic violence? Would I honor and respect their knowledge of DV or assume mine as a researcher and clinician was more valuable? Was I going to suddenly hijack this research that they had worked so hard on developing? Would the many levels of my social privilege blind me to their knowledge while providing me with the power to promote my own? Weren't these class, ethnic, and race issues the exact ones they were trying to fight against with the family court research? If so, what was I doing there?

Even though Kristen and I tried to set up the day as one of dialogue where these questions and others could be voiced, we also knew it was not a dialogue initiated by the members. Therefore my experiences that I thought made me a clear ally—as an advocate, a provider of crisis intervention and ongoing counseling for students in violent relationships and my victim-centered research (e.g., Gentile, 2006, 2007, 2010; Gentile et al., 2007)—were moot points. All that mattered to the vow members I was trying to engage was that I had to understand their particular experiences with DV or I had to have had my own. As the day progressed, I was continually baited with questions and potential allusions to my dating history and whether I had experiences with violence. Having had an experience of violence was key to safety for good reason, as noted; without this shared history the women had a good chance of being misunderstood and misrepresented. Additionally, as I noted, I was "other" to the women on many levels, so sharing a history of DV might have enabled a connection for them. They were in a position where they had to accept my expertise. vow staff had discussed needing researcher input. The members didn't have much of a choice and even if they agreed and wanted this input, ambivalence was inevitable. As noted previously, the model of research interaction I expected to uphold was not to be a blank screen and, as I found, withholding information when the members were clearly asking for it felt and was sadistic. I did answer their call for contact by stating that, yes, I had some experiences of relationship violence, but I provided no details. I described working with many women whose experiences mirrored theirs as reflected in their questions. I again acknowledged the survivors' expertise in the subject and the potential for the study to be groundbreaking and influential. It is important to note that I did not answer their questions or provide my opinions in hopes of being trusted or let into their confidence. That would have been manipulative. I answered them out of respect for our evolving dialogue and relationship. Sustained unfolding time, not immediate spatial depth, was most important in developing our relationship.

As a group, three of the women considered me "as much of an ally as they needed to." Two other women were more suspect. They provided stories of how their words had been twisted and distorted throughout their lives by "helpers," counselors, lawyers, and judges supposedly on their side. As they described, the identified allies are the worst and most dangerous because they gain a woman's trust and then use her words against her in shelters, with lawyers, and in court. There was no way for me to be an easy ally for them.

Riger (1999), Haviland, Frye, and Rajah (2008), and Slote and others (2005) describe the importance of each participant having an acknowledged expertise. I could and did recognize that of VOW's staff and members. The staff recognized mine by inviting me to assist them; however, for the members, recognition of my expertise was loaded and it did not nor could it result in a deeper collaboration during the training. My expertise was the problem; it represented the many ways in which they had been betrayed, revictimized, and put in danger by "well-meaning" psychologists, researchers, and other professionals supposedly out to help them. Additionally, my expertise would result in my desire to change the survey they had worked so hard on and to alter the ways in which they had planned to conduct the interviews. In my mind, the surveys needed to be shorter, more organized (according to more linear research instrument models), and the interviews were forms of data collection that needed to be done methodically. Similar to Frisby, Maguire, and Reid's (2009) experiences with action research, the members chaffed at the rigidity of academic protocols for research and documentation. Shortening the survey meant cutting questions, which meant a member's experience might not be represented in the survey. I was motivated by my strong desire to see them produce a valid report people would read that would change how survivors are treated in family court. However, as noted earlier in terms of research, the models of linearity are decidedly masculinist and Western, not reflective of the complexities of human rights violations and gender-based violence. Therefore, part of me also thought maybe this survey needed to be complicated and seemingly unwieldy. I found these conflicting needs difficult to balance. By presenting my dilemma to the members and "translating" (Haviland, Frye, and Rajah, 2008) the importance of research validity for their message, we were able to come to a center point of agreement about editing the survey a bit. Clearly, recognizing expertise is a complicated process.

Another issue that came up repeatedly throughout the training was when and how would they share their survivor identity with the interviewees? Would they do it by describing VOW at the beginning? Would they say they were volunteering with VOW, implying they may not be survivors? They began to question whether being a survivor would be enough common ground to gain trust. And would the quest for trust trump maintaining boundaries? We discussed these boundary issues throughout the day and decided it would be important to introduce themselves as members of VOW and therefore also survivors, understanding that doing so was motivated by research honesty and not to gain trust.

Agentic subjectivity can emerge from recognition (Benjamin, 1995), but this notion alone does not contain the space within which to explore the multidimensional forms that power takes in terms of culture, race, class, ethnicity, gender, and so on. To be in the position of researcher, thus, can be tantamount to "conferring" recognition on the other, which may (re)interpolate us within a relational scene (or discourse) of a rescuing colonizer of disadvantaged "others" (Oliver, 2001). It would be another form of ventriloquism, not a way of learning to listen (Spivak, 2010, 16).

Instead, relationally acknowledging that there was no "existing representational space in which" the VOW members could make themselves heard itself became a form of listening (Cornell, 2010, 101) in concert with what Oliver (2001) describes as a double process of witnessing—being an eyewitness to an incident and bearing witness to something "that can't be seen" (197). I actively engaged as a novice to their expertise, without denying my own in an attempt to create the conditions for a potential ethical moment of deconstruction that could remind "us of the ungraspable otherness that remains beyond our reach and yet in the deepest sense also constitutes who we are, the otherness in relation to which we are both indebted and unable to know the full extent of our accountability" (Cornell, 2010, 105).

So to work together I had to own the collective history of my role, including its power, status, and abuses, and they had to trust me enough. I did not have the exclusive power to choose how I would be seen and engaged with by them. Of course, this relational struggle, as we pointed out, might mirror some of their interviews, where the interviewees might have difficulty trusting them as the researchers. Articulating this connection in the moment "translated" (Haviland, Frye, and Rajah, 2008) this aspect of the research and pulled them spatially closer, as they now shared my experience in a way that was immediate for them.

After the report was published, I contacted VOW staff to see if they would be interested in talking to me about their experiences of the family court research. The staff checked with the members, some of whom were very interested in sharing their experiences. They wanted to meet with me as a group first. We organized a focus group to discuss the experiences of participating in the research. There are pros and cons to focus group methodology (Morgan and Krueger, 1993), but it was the format chosen by the members for this exploration of their experiences and it made methodological sense, given that the research training had also occurred in a group setting. Members of vow work together as a collective, and this seemed appropriate and comfortable for them. The questions I entered the discussion with were general and meant to stimulate our conversation. They were as follows:

- What was the process of interviewing like for you?
- What did you find challenging about it?
- What did you find rewarding?
- Were you surprised by any responses from the women?
- How was it doing the analysis and writing the report?
- What did you learn about the topic?
- What did you learn about yourself?

I did not get beyond the first question, for as the women began reflecting on their experiences they went through the list with their descriptions. These members had met regularly throughout the year to discuss their research and their reactions to it. vow provided a space for them to meet and process their experiences. Differences in opinion were most likely already ironed out. They presented as a united body. They function well as a group. This also means I did not get individual nuances or conflicting differences in meaning making.

Having said that, I assumed the women were telling me what they had already discussed as a group and individually while debriefing. During our individual interview, Susan Lob said that she believed the members were more open in particular about how much the process had hurt. I had not shared with them my particular interest in any painful responses to the research participation, nor had I asked about this in my questions. So my presence as an outsider to vow may have created a space for them to be more open about their experiences of retraumatization. They are a grassroots activist organization. I am a psychologist who they know conducts research but also provides clinical support to survivors. They may have also keyed into my multiple identities and felt they could or should open up about these experiences. While our training meeting was marked for me by a feeling of running the gauntlet, this meeting felt open and collegial. The previous power struggle receded and was replaced by a boisterous sharing of what it was like to be a researcher. This empowerment was complicated and not a guaranteed outcome of the action of the research process.

Retraumatization

KIM: I relived my own journey, holding my breath.

TANYA: One interview, she just kept crying. I had to take time with [the] interview. I went dancing after that night. I wanted to save her.

PATRICE: I would type one or two interviews, then need a break. You can't go fight the universe every moment.

Retraumatization in research like this is inevitable, whether the participants are trained academic researchers or trained activists.* Although we discussed retraumatization during the training and Susan Lob had set up process meetings for the women, no one was prepared for how deeply it would impact them. During the trainings the urgency to bring the problems of the family court to light and fix the system occluded exploring other potential experiences. During the training the only future trajectory imaginable was that of a rescuer. The members were going to identify participants in trouble, listen to their stories, witness their experiences, and make the injustices public, outing a deeply flawed system. In doing so, they would rescue the women by providing social ties to VOW, hoping it would help the women as much as it had helped the members. Davies and Frawley (1992) describe "rescuing" as one of the potential roles people take in the clinical setting in relation to survivors of violence, and it is especially common when both parties are survivors. It is important to understand that this relational position is healthy and agentic and not just a psychological defense. It is a resistant motivation and response to helplessness, and it served the members well.

All but one of the women was years away from her own court experiences.

---

*Here I must add that I use the term *retraumatization* with caution. The incidences of violence the members described hearing about during the interviews were at times so horrific and terrifying I could barely contain myself. Using the term *retraumatization* can function to locate the problem, again, in the survivor, as if she is somehow less competent in handling stressful stories. In fact, one would not need a history of domestic violence to be deeply disturbed by some of their stories. In fact, I would say one *should* be disturbed by them. Such a history would just make this response more complicated. Additionally, as noted earlier of the unconscious, such affective responses emerge from relational spaces, not from within individualized subjects.

For each, doing the interviews brought them right back to their own experiences of helplessness in the face of a system that does not work despite its claims of "justice." They were dealing with reliving their own violent relationship(s), their own struggles in the court, experiences of losing custody of their children, and their own hopelessness. As noted earlier, experiences of trauma and violence are often unsymbolizable psychically and culturally (Gentile, 2007), such that when one is confronted by similar circumstances, one often relives the past in the present in a deep and oftentimes unspeakable way. Additionally, the members had been organizing and protesting actively for years, so the coping mechanism of rescuing, while operating, did so alongside the knowledge that systemic change is frustratingly slow.

There were different levels of trauma to the members' experiences. First was the frustration with the system. Patrice noted, it was "challenging to know in this world people are still ignoring these issues." Thereasa added succinctly, "the court system is versatile. It will batter you on whatever level you are on. To me it was confirmation that the system beats you down more than the man [your partner] did." One of the ways the court batters women is, as Kim said, the "symptomology of DV [the symptoms of PTSD that many survivors suffer from] is used against us in the court and system." They all nodded. As Kim noted, and their report supported, "if you are vigilant you are seen as paranoid. That renders everything you say questionable. If you are numb you are not emotional enough. There is no way to win." Tanya was particularly upset by her contact with the court system. She said, "court was worse than I thought. It took everything to not break down and cry, because even though I knew the large picture hadn't changed. I thought little pieces had. I could feel myself thinking, there is no hope. It will never change. My challenge was to keep my hope. There were so many little things like bad representation or how women are subject to arrest if the kids don't want to go with the abuser for visitation. They are often scared too. Then if they don't go, the woman can be arrested." As they repeated time and time again, the women's lives were in the hands of court personnel who seemed to not understand or respect the dynamics of domestic violence, and they continued to victimize the survivors. Here the parallel process between the way the courts treat women and the way batterers treat women is clear to them.

But it was not merely the court system they witnessed as not having budged. As Thereasa noted, "Everyone asks you why didn't you leave, as if you deserve no help because you didn't do what they think you should have done or what they think they would have done. Why don't you leave? Well, in order to leave you need a home and if you are disabled there are only so many houses you can go to." Lorna added, "You go around in circles in the city. You leave everything and don't know where you will sleep. Shelters also abuse women. The rules are patronizing. You never know if they are on your side." Kim added, "They murder your soul. When you have extraordinary experiences you are dubbed the crazy one." Here the members were reliving the past in the present, as their language indicates. Slippages from "were" to "are," past to present, from "the women" to "you" or "I," and from general to personal made the back-and-forth of temporality the members were experiencing clear. As many have described, our experiences of time are not linear (Grosz, 1995, 2004; Massumi, 2002), but when traumatic experience impacts symbolizing capacities what is identified as the past can overwhelm the present (Gentile, 2007). Of course, these slippages also function to support their report's claim that not much in the treatment of survivors has changed. Whether the experiences they discuss are theirs or those of their interviewees, it doesn't really matter. Survivors are objectified and interchangeable to the courts.

Although the struggles they heard or experienced with the interviewees triggered their memories, which came flooding back, Tanya brought in a positive side. "I saw so many survival skills the women didn't even know you had." Here, when she shifts from referring to the women she interviewed to vow members and herself ("you"), she let on that seeing these resilient women was a mirror for her as she realized just how much she had been through and survived. As Kim described, "I felt like I was reliving everything with details. It took a while, three to four interviews to get used to it. I just kept thinking, by participating maybe I'll get something improved, and it will have been worth it." The other members echoed this sentiment. Some could conduct only one or two interviews because it was overwhelming. A common coping mechanism was to keep their focus on the future—social change. They contained their anxieties and pain by playing with their temporality to self-regulate (see Gentile, 2006, 2007), propelling themselves into the future goal to tolerate the present anxieties.

The experience of the members illustrate Evans and Lindsay's (2008) observation that "recovery" is a poor word to describe the healing process survivors endure. This language is heavy with cultural attitudes toward quick fixes and twelve-step programs to put the event "into perspective" to "move on." It implies that a person can and should return to a past state of self, but this can happen only if they erase their experiences of violence. Survivors are expected to play with time by erasing the experiences of violence to return to a past previctimized state of being. This approach locates the recovery exclusively in the woman, taking the abuser and the culture completely off the hook. It assumes the women experienced only one perpetrator who can easily be erased to resuscitate a past without violence. It relies on a fantasy world without everyday patriarchal, gender-based violence against women. Additionally, safety, a requirement to moving on, is never guaranteed. Indeed, danger mounts when a survivor leaves and the threat follows her throughout her life. Each VOW member had a story of being contacted by their abuser years after they left. And violence against women and gender-related violence permeates all of popular culture from novels to music, television to films. Even walking by a magazine stand one is assaulted by images of women appearing to submit to a dominating other. There is no truly safe past state of being to return to.

With all these feelings of helplessness and temporal shifts, challenging some of the boundaries of the research protocol was inevitable. Tanya admitted, "It was much tougher interviewing than we thought. We began giving extra money to the interviewees." Kim then described giving them gifts. I asked if Susan Lob knew, and Tanya replied that, yes, she told her she gave them some of her own money, and Susan had told her it was not a good idea. Susan Lob described wanting to protect the VOW members from trying to rescue the interviewees and getting burned out. She wanted to help contain their responses by setting some limits on their giving. They settled on a compromise between the research protocol of paying the interviewees and the members' desires to help. They decided to give each interviewee the small sum of money, as planned, and some food bars, tissues, and a diary book. Kim aptly stated her struggle, "as interviewers we had a lot of power, yet we felt completely powerless to change the system for these women." Then on key to contain these feelings for the group, Tanya added, "Hopeless, not powerless." The other members nodded.

Like many researchers and organizers before them, the VOW members struggled with wanting to rescue their interviewees, to save them from their suffering while saving themselves from their own feelings of helplessness in relation to the courts, their interviewees, and their respective pasts. But in this case their responses were even more complicated. Watching someone suffer is painful. But this pain and the helplessness and powerlessness it engenders is only accentuated when the observer has experienced a similar situation. For the VOW members, they were witnessing women struggling to survive a situation they themselves had already survived. They clearly struggled with being in power in relation to women they experienced as being much less powerful. They struggled to hold onto the knowledge, perhaps even some survivor guilt, that they were out and had survived and these women were just beginning the journey. Here they articulated the divisions between themselves and the interviewees, and these were not comfortable. It seemed having gotten out alive became a form of uncomfortable privilege. A communal relief had to be employed to save themselves from the interviewees' feelings of hopelessness (or their own feelings of hopelessness and helplessness in relation to their interviewees). This created a necessary boundary between them and their interviewees. But these boundaries were held ambivalently for, as noted, the common experience of domestic violence was both the impetus for the research and the reason for the members' participation. To create a boundary between them would identify the interviewees as "other," bringing in to question the idea that their shared experience meant they could understand each other. Surviving was also the requirement for trust. Thus, they had to create gradations of what it meant to be a survivor to save themselves, yet remain connected and trustworthy. Their gifts functioned as a compromise that bridged their differences.

The Trust in Being a Fellow Survivor . . . Sort Of

Conducting the interviews also had challenges, as the members had to establish trust with their interviewees. This required reassuring the interviewees that the interview and data were not going anywhere but to vow and their mission of the court report. This trust usually occurred only, as all the women echoed, once the interviewees learned that they too were survivors. As described earlier, while in most academic research and even much action research (Humphrey, 2009) any personal ties to the subject matter of the research are rendered invalidating and therefore remain invisible, here they were front and center. The fliers vow members created stated the mission of vow clearly, it noted that all members are survivors, that members would do the interviewing, and the goal of the research. Each interviewer approached the women by stating they were a member of vow and providing enough information about vow's mission to contextualize the role of their interview within the family court research project. As such, they directly and immediately outed themselves as survivors. This action, they felt, was crucial to creating trust and rapport with the interviewees. According to them, it created a level of trust and intimacy important for both participants. As Lorna noted, although she herself works in a shelter and loves her work, the women she works with there do not know she too is a survivor. She enjoyed having this automatic bond with the interviewees and felt it helped the interview. Here the shared bond helped both parties feel less isolated and alone.

Bion (1959) outlined three relational structures around which groups tend to organize, one of which functions around the dynamics of fight or flight. These are the same dynamics common to survivors of trauma and violence. This type of group organizes itself around a commonly identified enemy from outside or an emotional experience the group as a whole is unified in avoiding. For the vow members the need to bond through a similar experience functioned to siphon off the fears of betrayal or distrust that were also undoubtedly present. But to open up about such painful, frightening, and ongoing experiences of violence, the women being interviewed needed to bond in relation to a common enemy. The courts and their horrid treatment of survivors provided a perfect and deserving target.

But It Was All Worth It

The women had spent months processing their feelings as a group. And they are clearly invested in vow, which is *their* organization. They are active and committed members of vow because they are active and committed women working hard for social change. So this research, with all its struggles, had a definite purpose that was always at the forefront of their thinking.

Kim said, "Yeah, it was hard but it felt good that there was an organization of survivors who really wanted change. It helped me and them feel not alone. For the women [interviewees] the reward was knowing they were participating in change. In an organization that is working for change and bringing . . ." "Truth to light," Tanya added. Lorna noted with pride, the research and the report has "put vow on the map, so they know we are watching." Kim added, "Now, when I run into judges who worked with me and called me crazy and didn't believe me, now I see them on committees and they say 'you look familiar.' I say, 'you don't recognize me because I'm still standing.'" Lorna said, "Thanks to vow I can be the woman I was supposed to be." Kim shared, "I felt like a champion with this work."

Patrice described the skills she gained through the research and how the activity of entering, coding, and analyzing data was healing. "I liked typing up surveys, and what I was doing was important and could create change. I got trained in spss, coding, and analysis. I knew I was part of vow and that made it hopeful for me."

This theme came up over and over again that what gave the women the hope to continue, to not be pulled down into their own memories of abuse, to not be overwhelmed by the helplessness of watching women continuing to go through the same struggles and abuse at the hands of the court system, was being identified members of a larger organization. As Kim said, "I never felt helpless or powerless. I always think about vow. It helped me through the interviews."

This organization is no typical "higher power" within which to feel safe. vow is not only an organization but also a generative, transformative collective. It is a source of pride and activism. It enables the women to remember their victimization and share an identity that is stigmatized in the wider culture. In doing so they reevaluate it and take control over the meaning of the identity. Being a survivor means being a member of vow and being connected to these other survivors. It means no longer being alone in the world or being a victimized woman in the margins of society. They have bridged the opposing categories set for them within the culture. vow is their generative hybrid space (Bhaba, 1994).

This group identity is also quite powerful. vow makes change happen. They have a track record. They train their members to talk to the very people who held them down within the court system. They talk to lawmakers. They influence policy. They talk to police officers and counselors. They make social change. So this new identity is collective and agentic. This is extremely important. As Wilcox (2007) noted, there are grassroots organizations that are informal networks and then there are the formal ones that make and implement the rules. It is rare that survivors are able to organize such that the informal networks influence the formal institutional structures. As she notes, it is imperative that these networks interact. vow has created a structure for this dialogue and influence. As Thereasa said clearly, "Don't talk about us without us." She added that as a member of vow, she does sit on some city committees for DV policy, and she sees vow making a change. As Tanya noted, "you want to give them the blueprint for survival, but that's why it's good to be part of it [the research]. We have proof. We are doing something and continue to fight. We *are* the proof." This statement said it all: they are the proof that change can and will happen.

The interview process also helped the women see their own individual strengths. Thereasa said, "Knowing I was on the other side of the table made me feel really empowered. Seeing them and their tunnel vision and remembering I was there and now I'm here. . . . It is still a healing process no matter where you are. It can take you back; you want to numb the pain out. I listen to music and take a bath. I remind myself I'm out of it. I have a roof over my head and a home that is mine." The women used the interviews also to anchor themselves in the present they have carved out for themselves now. This was necessary to counter their unconscious and conscious memories that returned full force during the interviews. Research was empowerment and social change. As Wilcox (2000) noted, it is imperative in action research to understand the individual and group power separately and interactively. The voices of the women indicate that they are holding well the tensions between these different forms of agency, but that the empowerment emerged from a complex process of reliving pasts in the present within an activist group that was available to contain and process these experiences individually and collectively. Thus the *action* in participatory action research is multifaceted.

Conclusion

vow brings the informal and formal networks that work with DV in New York City and New York State together, while sustaining themselves as individuals with creative differences. This is a model for social change and reminiscent of that outlined by Paulo Freire (1972). I wanted to explore how vow members experienced their action research project. As they described, action research is powerful and empowering, but they struggled with constant retraumatization, which, were they not processing individually and in groups at vow, might have been damaging. Also, only those members able to conduct the most interviews volunteered to participate in my focus group. A number of members conducted only one. They did not volunteer to be part of my focus group or to be contacted by me. It may be the others were too negatively impacted by the research experience to talk to me, they were not impacted at all or enough to talk, or they were outsiders to the group and were unable to bring in alternative views. So clearly this project has limits.

Action research is complex, containing within it the potentials for empowerment, transformation, new forms of knowledge, and retraumatization and its attendant harms and generative resistances. Relational theories of psychoanalysis can provide one way of beginning to unpack the layered process that is the action of participatory research.

References

Alcoff, L. (1994). The problem of speaking for others. In S. O. Weisser and J. Fleischner (Eds.). *Feminist nightmares women at odds: Feminism and the problem of sisterhood* (285–309). New York: New York University Press.

Anzaldúa, G. (1987). *Borderlands/La frontera: The new mestiza.* San Francisco: Aunt Lute Books.

Aron, L. (1996) *A meeting of minds: Mutuality in psychoanalysis.* Hillsdale, NJ: Analytic.

Bar-On, D. (1996). Ethical issues in biographical interviews and analysis. In R. Josselson (Ed.), *Ethics and process in the narrative study of lives* (Vol. 4, pp. 9–21). Thousand Oaks, CA: Sage.

Bass, A. (2001). It takes one to know one; or, whose unconscious is it anyway? *Psychoanalytic Dialogues, 11*(5), 683–702.

Bateman, A., and Fonagy, P. (2008). Comorbid antisocial and borderline personality disorders: Mentalization-based treatment. *Journal of Clinical Psychology, 64*(2), 181–194.

Bergson, H. (1913/2001). *Time and free will: An essay on the immediate data of consciousness.* Mineola, NY: Dover.

Bhabha, H. (1994) *The location of culture.* London: Routledge.

Bion, W. R. (1959). *Experiences in groups.* New York: Basic Books.

Bourdieu, P. (1978). *Outline of a theory of practice.* Cambridge: Cambridge University Press.

Bourdieu, P., and Wacquant, L. J. D. (1992). *An invitation to reflexive sociology.* Chicago: University of Chicago Press.

Burman, E. (2004). Organising for change? Group-analytic perspectives on a feminist action research project. *Group Analysis, 37*(1), 91–108.

Cohen, S. J. (2009). Healers on the fault lines: Trauma as a risky opportunity for growth, mental flexibility and the inclination to heal others. *International Journal of Applied Psychoanalytic Studies, 6*(3), 211–224.

Collins, P. H. (1990), *Black feminist thought: Knowledge, consciousness, and the politics of empowerment.* London: Routledge.

Cornell, D. (2010). The ethical affirmation of human rights: Gayatri Spivak's intervention. In R. C. Morris (Ed.), *Reflections on the history of an idea: Can the subaltern speak?* (100–116). New York: Columbia University Press.

Davies, J. M., and Frawley, M. G. (1992). Dissociative processes and transference countertransference paradigms in the psychoanalytically oriented treatment of adult survivors of childhood sexual abuse. *Psychoanalytic Dialogues, 2*, 5–36.

Evans, I., and Lindsay, J. (2008). Incorporation rather than recovery: Living with the legacy of domestic violence. *Women's Studies International Forum, 31*, 355–362.

Fine, M. (1994a). Dis-stance and other stances: Negotiations of power inside feminist research. In A. Gitlin (Ed.), *Power and method: Political activism and educational research* (13–35). New York: Routledge.

Fine, M. (1994b). Working the hyphens: Reinventing self and other in qualitative research. In N. Denzin and Y. Lincoln (Eds.), *Handbook of qualitative research* (70–82). Newbury Park, CA: Sage.

Fine, M. (1996). Writing the "wrongs" of fieldwork: Confronting our own research/writing dilemmas in urban ethnographies. *Qualitative Inquiry, 2*, 251–274.

Fine, M. (2006). Bearing witness: Methods for researching oppression and resistance; A textbook for critical research. *Social Justice Research, 19*(1), 83–108.

Fine, M., Weis, L., Pruitt, L., and Burns, A. (2004). *Off white: Readings of power, privilege and resistance.* New York: Routledge.

Fonagy, P. (2003). Towards a developmental understanding of *violence. British Journal of Psychiatry, 183*(3), 190–192.

Fonagy, P., and Target, M. (1996). Playing with reality: I. Theory of mind and the normal development of psychic reality. *International Journal of Psycho-Analysis, 77,* 217–233.

Fonow, M. M., and Cook, J. A. (Eds.). (1991). *Beyond methodology: Feminist scholarship as lived research.* Bloomington: Indiana University Press.

Foucault, M. (1972). *The archaeology of knowledge and the discourse on language.* New York: Pantheon Books.

Freire, P. (1972), *Pedagogy of the oppressed.* (M. B. Ramos, Trans.). New York: Herder and Herder.

Frisby, W., Maguire, P., and Reid, C. (2009). The "f" word has everything to do with it: How feminist theories inform action research. *Action Research, 7*(1), 13–29.

Frosh, S. (2007). Disintegrating qualitative research. *Theory and Psychology, 17*(5), 635–653.

Frosh, S., and Baraitser, L. (2008). Psychoanalysis and psychosocial studies. *Psychoanalysis, Culture and Society, 13,* 346–365.

Gentile, K. (2006). Timing development from cleavage to differentiation. *Contemporary Psychoanalysis, 42*(2), 297–325.

Gentile, K. (2007). *Creating bodies: Eating disorders as self-destructive survival.* New York: Analytic/Routledge.

Gentile, K. (2010). Purging as embodiment. In J. Petrucelli (Ed.), *Knowing, not knowing, and sort of knowing: Psychoanalysis and the experience of uncertainty* (265–280). London: Karnac.

Gentile, K., Raghavan, C., Rajah, V., and Gates, K. (2007). It doesn't happen here? Eating disorders in an ethnically diverse sample of low-income, female and male, urban college students. *Eating Disorders: Journal of Treatment and Prevention, 15*(5), 405–425.

Grosz, E. (1995), *Space, time, and perversion: Essays on the politics of bodies.* New York: Routledge.

Haaken, J. (1998), The recovery of memory, fantasy, and desire in women's trauma stories: Feminist approaches to sexual abuse and psychotherapy. In S. Smith and J. Watson (Eds.), *Women, autobiography, theory: A reader* (352–366). Madison: University of Wisconsin Press.

Haaken, J. (2008). Too close for comfort: Psychoanalytic cultural theory and domestic violence politics. *Psychoanalysis, Culture and Society, 13,* 75–93.

Haviland, M., Frye, V., and Rajah, V. (2008). Harnessing the power of advocacy-research collaborations. *Feminist Criminology, 3*(4), 247–275.

Hollway, W., and Jefferson, T. (2000). *Doing qualitative research differently.* London: Sage.

Hook, D. (2008). Postcolonial psychoanalysis. *Theory and Psychology 18*(2), 269–283.

Hoy, D. C. (2004), *Critical resistance: From poststructuralism to post-critique.* Cambridge, MA: MIT Press.

Humphrey, C. (2007). Insider-outsider: Activating the hyphen. *Action Research 5*(1): 11–26.

Josselson, R. (Ed.). (1996). *Ethics and process in the narrative study of lives* (Vol. 4). Thousand Oaks, CA: Sage.

Kaplan, C., Alarcón, N., and Moallem, M. (Eds.). (1999). Introduction: Between woman and nation. In C. Kaplan, N. Alarcón, and M. Moallem (Eds.) *Between woman and nation: Nationalisms, transnational feminisms, and the state* (1–18). Durham: Duke University Press.

Kristeva, J. (1982). *Powers of horror: An essay on abjection.* New York: Columbia University Press.

Lacan, J. (1956). *The psychoses: The seminar of Jacques Lacan* (Bk. 3). London: Routledge.

Lather, P. (1991). *Getting smart: Feminist research and pedagogy with/in the postmodern.* New York: Routledge.

Lather, P., and Smithies, C. (1997). *Troubling the angels: Women living with HIV/AIDS.* New York: Westview.

Layton, L. (ed). (2008). British psycho(-)social studies. Special issue, *Psychoanalysis, Culture and Society, 13*(4), 339–340.

Loewald, H. W. (1980). *Papers on psychoanalysis.* New Haven, CT: Yale University Press.

Massumi, B. (2002). *Parables for the virtual.* Durham: Duke University Press.

Mishler, E. (1979). Meaning in context: Is there any other kind? *Harvard Educational Review, 49*(1), 1–19.

Mohanty, C. T. (2004). *Feminism without borders: Decolonizing theory, practicing solidarity.* Durham: Duke University Press.

Morgan, D. L., and Krueger, A. (1993). When to use focus groups and why. In D. L. Morgan (Ed.), *Successful focus groups: Advancing the state of the art* (Vol. 156, pp. 3–20). Newbury Park, CA: Sage.

Naples, N., with Clark, E. (1996). Feminist participatory research and empowerment: Going public as survivors of childhood abuse. In H. Gottfried (Ed.), *Feminism and social change: Bridging theory and practice* (160–183) Bloomington: Indiana University Press.

Nasio, J. (1992). *Five lessons on the psychoanalytic theory of Jacques Lacan.* Albany: State University of New York Press.

Oliver, K. (2004). *The colonization of psychic space: A psychoanalytic social theory of oppression.* Minneapolis: University of Minnesota Press.

Price, J., and Shildrick, M. (Eds.). (1999). *Feminist theory and the body: A reader*. New York: Routledge.

Riessman, C. K. (1993). *Narrative analysis*. Newbury Park, CA: Sage.

Riger, S. (1999). Working together: Challenges in collaborative research on violence against women. *Violence against Women, 5,* 1099–1117.

Sampson, E. E. (1996). Establishing embodiment in psychology. *Theory and Psychology, 6*(4), 601–624.

Slote, K. Y., Cuthbert, C., Mesh, C. J., Driggers, M. G, Bancroft, L., Silverman, J. G. (2005). Battered mothers speak out: Participatory human rights documentation as a model for research and activism in the United States. *Violence against Women, 11,* 1367–1395.

Spivak, G. C. (2010). Can the subaltern speak? In R. C. Morris (Ed.), *Critique of postcolonial reason: Reflections on the history of an idea; Can the subaltern speak?* (21–80). (Rev. ed.). New York: Columbia University Press.

Stacey, J. (1988). Can there be a feminist ethnography? *Women's Studies International Forum, 11,* 21–27.

Stanley, L. (1996). The mother of invention: Necessity, writing and representation. *Feminism and Psychology, 6,* 45–51.

Stopford, A. (2004). Researching postcolonial subjectivities: The application of relational (postclassical) psychoanalysis to research methodology. *International Journal of Critical Psychology, 10,* 13–35.

Tronto, J. C. (1994). *Moral boundaries: A political argument for an ethic of care*. New York: Routledge.

Van der Kolk, B. A. (1994). The body keeps the score: Memory and the evolving psychobiology of posttraumatic stress. *Harvard Review of Psychiatry, 1,* 253–265

Wilcox, P. (2000). Researching in the community: Power relations in a study on domestic violence in England. *Research in Community Sociology, 10,* 141–164.

Wilcox, P. (2007). Survivors of domestic violence, community and care. In S. Balloch and M. Hill (Eds.), *Care, community and citizenship: Research and practice in a changing policy context* (121–140). Bristol: Policy.

Evan Stark, Rutgers University

9 | A Failure to Protect
Resolving the Battered Mother's Dilemma

On September 11, 1992, based on injuries observed on the hands of seven-year-old Daniel L., the principal of the Sandy Hook school reported a case of suspected child abuse to the Newtown police department and the Connecticut Department of Children and Families (DCF). Further investigation revealed numerous bruises on the boy's back, buttocks, legs, and arms. Daniel told police he had been struck recently with a belt and slapped by his mother, Lavonne L., and her live-in boyfriend, Miguel S., after he was found playing with a BB pistol.

When Daniel failed to return home as usual, Lavonne called the school and was told he had missed the bus. Shortly afterward, the police arrived at the house, accompanied by a caseworker from the DCF. Lavonne's four other children were taken into custody, including a newborn, and she and Miguel S. were placed in the back of a police car and taken to the station for questioning. A week earlier, the same DCF investigator had visited the home and found the baby in the basement washroom. Her report evoked Dickens:

> The baby, Candy, age 1 year, was lying on the mattress with a bottle in her mouth. She had a variety of blankets around her. She was noticeably dirty, has a smell about her. Diaper (cloth) soaked completely. A small bowl with bits of food on it lay on the mattress next to her. She cried a bit. Advised mother that child can't be left alone down here. . . . Mother said, "Ok, I respect your opinion, if that's what you

This chapter is based on the case of the *State of Connecticut v. Lavonne L.*, tried in Danbury Superior Court. As an expert witness hired by the State of Connecticut Office of the Public Defender, Dr. Stark's involvement included interviewing Ms. L, reviewing all relevant documents and investigative reports on the case, preparing a report on his findings, and testifying at Ms. L's trial. Quotes are taken from Dr. Stark's interviews as well as from a handwritten history prepared by Ms. L. of her relationship with Miguel S. A summary of Dr. Stark's notes was reviewed by Ms. L., modified to reflect her recollections, and approved for publication.

think, I'll take her out." When the mother didn't move . . . I moved aside the bed frame and mattress and lifted the baby out.

The cellar was accessible only from an outside bulkhead. The caseworker accompanied Lavonne around the house. Dickens redux:

> In the one bedroom, door closed, 3 year old Maria was playing in closet. She appeared fairly clean and dressed. The room was dark, with dirty smell, dirty sheets and bunk beds. Smelled of feces, although none were visible. Mother acknowledged she could not provide for Candy's needs. No services were recommended.

A hospital examination of the children revealed numerous suspicious bruises on the three- and four-year-old girls, most notably on the legs and back of Maria. Lavonne told detectives she had hit Daniel with a belt in the BB gun incident and insisted she was the only one to "discipline" her children, explaining that this was "how I was treated when I was a girl." Miguel also admitted hitting the children and using a belt on Maria. The couple was charged with four counts of risk of injury to a minor.

Lavonne was out on bail and staying at a battered woman's shelter when the public defender contacted me to do a domestic violence assessment. Her five children were in foster care, including the newborn, whose father was Miguel. He had been sentenced to "time served" (seventy-five days) and deported to Mexico. Lavonne faced eight years in jail. The state's attorney was offering three.

Each of Lavonne's children had a different father, and four of the fathers were from Mexico. A neighbor reported that the couple had left an earlier apartment in shambles and were stealing water. The stories in the local press had headlines like "Modern Day Medea?" It reminded me of the widespread hostility that had greeted Hedda Nussbaum in 1987 after her abusive partner Joel Steinberg killed Lisa, their adopted daughter (Brownmiller, 1989; Johnson, 1990). In that case, the mother had been hospitalized with nine broken ribs, a broken jaw, a broken nose, and numerous bruises (McFadden, 1987). Except for a single note in a police file, however, there was no evidence Lavonne had been abused by Miguel. Nor had Hedda ever abused Lisa. A plea bargain seemed Lavonne's best option.

What follows applies the coercive control model of abuse to a case study of Lavonne L.'s alleged criminal acts. In explaining the dynamics when children are hurt in abusive relationships, coercive control highlights three elements of the abusive situation: when abusers use children as an extension of their control of their mother ("child abuse as tangential spouse abuse"); the forced choices victims make between their own safety and the safety of their children ("the battered mother's dilemma"); and the extent to which victims make what they perceive as the best choice in highly constrained circumstances ("control in the context of no control").

Despite a growing recognition of the risks battered women face when they try to protect their children, many child welfare agencies still charge nonoffending battered mothers with "neglect" and place their children in foster care (Stark, 2002). In criminal courts, battered mothers are frequently held to the standard of *strict liability* simply because they are aware of the child's abuse or their partner's violent nature or even if, in a court's opinion, they *should* have been aware of either. These actions reflect the fact that state statutes criminalize omissions: only twelve states require an overt act to constitute child abuse ("commission statutes") and only three states (Minnesota, Iowa, and Oklahoma) have statutorily adopted an affirmative defense to the charge of failure to protect a child based on the parent's reasonable fear of severe injury to himself or the child.

In its basic contours, the dynamics of Lavonne's abuse mirror the experience of thousands of women involved in criminal or child welfare proceedings or in custodial disputes. In explicating women's experience in these contexts, the coercive control model supplements the examination of threats and physical violence ("coercion") with an analysis of "control," a generic term for the range of restrictions abusers impose to subordinate a partner, limit and regulate their decisional autonomy, exploit their capacities and resources, and isolate and humiliate them. In this analysis, what "makes" a battered woman is not being hit but being deprived of the means to effectively resist or escape when she is threatened or assaulted. In place of violence-induced injury or psychological trauma, the coercive control model highlights the harms that result when persons are denied basic rights and liberties in personal life. These harms reflect the ongoing nature of abuse and its cumulative effects. If men have a greater capacity or propensity than women to coercively control partners, this is because the continued privileges our society bestows on persons who identify as male reinforce structural inequalities in power in relationships.

Failure to Protect? *State of Connecticut v. Lavonne L.*

The news stories had not prepared me for the tall, striking, impeccably dressed, and articulate twenty-seven-year-old woman who met me at the Women's Center in the working-class valley town of Shelton, Connecticut. Lavonne's experience with "psycho guys" had not been positive. During her court ordered evaluation at the Yale Child Study Center, the psychiatrist had refused to interview Lavonne without Miguel in the room.

> Lavonne: He said Miguel would be handcuffed to the chair. I said, "I don't care if he's handcuffed to the wall." I told him in no uncertain terms that I didn't even want to be in the same building with this man. It was already court-ordered that it be separate. I made him call my attorney. . . . I spoke to him on the phone . . . and he told him, "they are to meet separately." So, the psychiatrist changed his tone.

Lavonne was afraid Miguel would return from Mexico (which he did) and was furious that DCF had taken her children. As the Yale interview suggested, however, she was capable of being assertive and self-protective. She showed no signs of depression, PTSD, battered woman syndrome, or another psychiatric disorder. Still, if she was so high functioning, why had she confessed to abuse, beaten Danny with a belt, and left Candy in a damp basement that was not accessible from the house?

Family Background

The youngest of three children, Lavonne L. no longer saw her father, an alcoholic who had rejected her. He told her, "I had my son and daughter. I didn't need you." Her relationship with her mother also remained tense. At fourteen, after her parents moved "yet again," Lavonne moved in with her boyfriend's family so she could finish high school. The boyfriend sexually assaulted her repeatedly. But she never told his parents (to whom she remains close), because she feared they would make her move out before graduation.

At eighteen Lavonne met Joe, Danny's father. She had her own condo, had a car, was working at a bank in the affluent town of Westport, and cared for her sister's daughter. The couple discussed marriage and Joe put a deposit on a ring. Though they used birth control, Lavonne became pregnant. Joe bolted when she decided to have the baby.

> Lavonne: Religion was part of it. That and I thought if I don't have Joe, at least I have a part of Joe. And when I told Joe, he said, well, that's your problem. [I told him,] I just wanted you to know you're going to be a father whether you're happy with it or not.

Lavonne was laid off and moved home with Danny. In the evenings, she often brought Danny to the diner where her mother and sister worked. A number of undocumented Mexican men lived at an adjacent boarding house. These men gravitated to the already bilingual mother. Stephanie was born two years after Danny, in 1987, the child of an immigrant Lavonne met at the diner. Stephanie was also premature and suffered from colic and a milk allergy that made her difficult to toilet train and moody. Stephanie's father helped care for her until he returned to Mexico when she was three.

When Lavonne became pregnant again, this time with a younger man, his older brother ordered him to return to Mexico. He returned shortly after his daughter's birth and gave her some financial support. The girl was named Katerina. Lavonne was still living with her mother when she met David, Candy's father. Lavonne and David dated for some time, lived together, discussed marriage, and planned to have a baby. Based on her prior experience, Lavonne insisted that David tell her if he had to return home. However, shortly after they became pregnant, David left suddenly. Lavonne later learned he had gone home to break a prior engagement, which he kept from her. But she felt abandoned and angry. In light of what happened next, it is ironic that Lavonne traced her attraction to the immigrant men to their gentleness and their "family orientation."

STARK: So when you say "family," what do you have in mind?
LAVONNE: I guess the family I was trying to create. . . . And that's the first
    thing that started me talking to most of these people is they started talking
    to my children and doing things for the children.

Lavonne was also rebelling against her father, who was openly contemptuous of Hispanics and blacks. By contrast, he had embraced Joe, the fiancé who had fathered Danny, as a "perfect Italian boy"—even the beer that was always in his hand felt familiar. In part, Lavonne's hunger for family reflected a home environment in which neither parent was affectionate. Her father was a quiet drunk who rejected her, and with her mother "it was either absolute silence or I'm going to sit here and yell at you." Lavonne had learned to manage a child's need for predictability in their environment by relying on external cues to establish trust (the "wedding ring" she and Joe picked out; the "words of love" spoken by the immigrant men in her life).

The scars Lavonne bore from sexual abuse as a teen and parental rejection were aggravated by having to approach potential partners with a premade family. She defended against these "hidden injuries" by developing the capacity for self-sufficiency (if not always for self-care) evident in her determination to finish school as well as to detach herself from physical and psychological pain. In obvious contrast to her parents, she picked boyfriends whom she could dominate, at least emotionally and intellectually. The impermanence of her partners was at least as much a byproduct of their problems with emotional commitment (Joe) and of the transitory loyalties of immigrant workers as it was of any ambivalence on her part. As Lavonne put it, "unfortunately, the only man who stuck around was the one I wanted to get rid of."

Lavonne had never been struck by a man before meeting Miguel. She used the same physical discipline methods with her own children she had witnessed growing up in an extended Italian family network, including spanking and an occasional slap. She wished she had learned alternatives and admitted "overreacting" by yelling a good deal while trying to toilet train Stephanie, unaware of her allergy. But there was no evidence of child abuse or neglect prior to her meeting Miguel. Apart from a report by Daniel that he was once slapped by David—an incident Lavonne cannot confirm—none of the other men she dated hit or otherwise mistreated the children. To the contrary, the men in her life treated the children more kindly than they did her.

The Relationship with Miguel

Before David left for Mexico, he asked Lavonne to teach his cousin Miguel some English, and they met almost daily. When David left, Miguel spent time with the children, attended birthing classes, and gave Lavonne general support in a difficult time.

> Lavonne: Actually, I think I had an instant attraction to him. Because he did something for me right off. I met him when he first came into the country. It was my birthday, and I was upset at David because David wasn't going to spend my birthday with me. And here we were at the checkout. Miguel, who I knew didn't have anything to speak of, when he found out it was my birthday, he bought me a rose. Because that's out of custom, because one man doesn't buy another's man's woman a gift.

Miguel offered to move into Lavonne's mother's house and "protect" her after David returned and warned he would come for their baby after the birth. He treated her with "respect" and initially slept on the living room couch. He was her "knight in shining armor." Her "knight" soon moved into her bedroom. Miguel made numerous suggestions about how Lavonne should live. She interpreted these as concern for her family's well-being. The account of Miguel's coercive control is subdivided into three phases. I describe only the most serious of the several hundred assaults Miguel committed during their two years together.

Phase 1: The Onset of Abuse, April–September 1991

During the first phase of their relationship, Miguel pressured Lavonne to remain at home and adopt the traditional role of the *señora*. He hit her on several occasions, often without warning, usually when he was drinking. Then he apologized and promised to change. Miguel's "respect" was expressed by proposals for how she could improve her life.

LAVONNE: David was hassling me, and he made suggestions about how to handle it. "You shouldn't really hang around the diner. It doesn't look good for you and your kids; you should keep them at home. . . . Better to have cooked meals at home, than out at the diner. You'll feel better about yourself if you take care of the house . . . and your kids."

STARK: So he had a real idea of what a traditional woman was like?

LAVONNE: Yeah.

STARK: And a lot of those things did make sense?

LAVONNE: Yeah. And I did feel better. Because the kids and I would be home.

Shortly after they began living together, Miguel suggested that Lavonne change Katerina's name to Maria after his grandmother. Lavonne complied because "it made us more like a family." She now recognizes how both staying home and changing her daughter's name facilitated Miguel's control by isolating her from friends and family who opposed the name change.

The first assault occurred several months later. After Lavonne protested, Miguel agreed to do his drinking at the boarding house. One evening, when Lavonne went to pick him up, David came down and tried to talk to her. She asked Miguel's permission, and he replied, "You do what you think is right." Lavonne was six months pregnant at the time with David's baby. An argument ensued, during which Miguel told David, "She's mine—she does what I tell her," and ordered Lavonne into the car. Then, Miguel told David, "I can do anything to her, and she's still mine." He told her to relax and stop crying, then suddenly slapped her across the mouth. Lavonne was shocked. Then, he told her to kiss him, which she did. On the way home, he broke both the dashboard and the windshield with his fist. Miguel passed out when they arrived. The next day he apologized and blamed the alcohol. She told him if he hit her again, they were through.

Two weeks later, David called. Although Lavonne did not talk to him, Miguel began to cry, then became furious, slapped Lavonne, and then hit her with the back of his hand until she bled. Lavonne called a cab and threw Miguel out of the house. A few weeks later, Miguel started calling every day, crying, telling her he "made a mistake" and promising not to drink. His explanation seemed credible since both her brother and uncle were violent when drunk. She allowed him to return.

Within days of his return, Miguel was pushing, shoving, and slapping Lavonne almost every day. The most common pretext was Miguel's claim that he had been "hassled" at work by David or other Mexicans because of their relationship. He was constantly correcting her behavior and the behavior of the children, explaining after beatings that "if your father had disciplined you and raised you to be a decent woman, you wouldn't be where you are in life today. Somebody has to do it."

Ironically, apart from the abuse, Lavonne felt her life was generally "calm" and family-like. Danny and Stephanie were in Head Start, and Lavonne had only Maria with her during the day. She was not going out "at all" any longer and spent her days cleaning the house and cooking for Miguel. She was treating him "like a king" and "giving him what he wanted before he wanted it," following an exact schedule that he required.

Lavonne and the children were now on AFDC (Aid to Families with Dependent Children). She would cash her check and turn the money over to Miguel, and he would give her money for food or clothes as he thought appropriate. She had to account for every penny and was not permitted to go to the store alone. If he couldn't go with her, her mother would do the shopping for her. She was learning to be a *señora*. During this phase of their relationship, Miguel hit Lavonne when her mother was out of the house or when she and the children were in bed. He never disciplined or hit the children. Still, Daniel and Stephanie were aware of the fights.

Phase 2: The Escalation of Violence and
Control, September 1991–January 1992.
In September 1991 Miguel raped Lavonne, eight months pregnant, shortly after she began spotting. At this point "fights" (pushing, shoving, etc.) became less common than "beatings," in which Miguel punched, kicked, and whipped Lavonne to "discipline" her. Everyone around Lavonne was aware of the abuse, including her children. Miguel increasingly directed how Lavonne disciplined the children. She became depressed, particularly after Candy's birth, was completely isolated, and attempted suicide.

Miguel wanted sex at least once a day, often two or three times. One night after intercourse, when Lavonne was seven and a half months pregnant with

Candy, she began to bleed. The doctor proscribed sex until after the birth. But several weeks later, Miguel returned from work and demanded sex, and when Lavonne told him, "I can't," he raped her, telling her he didn't care what happened to "David's baby." When Lavonne experienced contractions and bleeding, Miguel accompanied her to the hospital, staying with her "even to the bathroom," and attended the birth. This showed, she felt, that "he loved me more than anybody ever had." But when the doctor handed him a girl "who looks just like his father," he hissed, "I'd like to throw her right in the garbage because that's what she is, just like you." Within hours of her returning from the hospital after Candy's birth, Miguel insisted on sex. From this point on, he demanded sex regularly, forcing Lavonne if she refused, then beating her.

There were still "good times." When Miguel and Lavonne went away for a weekend, they planned to move to Mexico, buy a house, and create a "real family," a dream Lavonne held dear. Violence escalated one evening, presumably because Miguel had been taunted at work. She was in the process of changing. She knew she would be hit because "his eyes were black." "When he's like that," she says, "once he gets started, he doesn't stop." Although she begged him to "just talk," he pushed her around the bedroom, punched her, and "backhanded" her. Then he did something he would do frequently in the future: he removed his belt and began snapping it. He started by hitting her lightly with the belt, then harder. When she tried to get away, he kicked at her, hitting her in the face, blackening her eye. She fell to the floor, and he began to kick her. He stopped when her nose starting bleeding. This was just one month after Candy's birth. The beating caused a problem with Lavonne's ear, and she saw a doctor. The doctor recognized she had been beaten, but did nothing.

After this, Lavonne stopped crying or begging Miguel to stop when he hit her, both of which "infuriated" him. Although he was often drinking, he abused Lavonne when he was sober as well. One night, Miguel and his "best friend" returned home drunk and Lavonne served them dinner. When his friend asked why Lavonne had a black eye and was covered with bruises, pointing out that Miguel had everything a Mexican man could want ("she waits on you like a king"), Miguel brutally beat the man, "turning the house into 'a holocaust' with blood and broken furniture everywhere." Lavonne intervened to save the man's life and was herself struck. When Miguel realized what he'd done, they washed the man up and drove him home. They took him to a doctor several days later.

In November 2001, when Candy was two months old, Lavonne found out she was again pregnant, this time as the result of a rape. That night, Miguel punched her repeatedly in the stomach, causing her to miscarry. He said the miscarriage was her fault because she aggravated him. Then he demanded sex. Lavonne was completely isolated from her friends, whom Miguel believed were not good for her or else were jealous of what they had. He had gotten her a car for her birthday, which she taught him how to drive, and he occasionally drove himself to work. In general, however, she drove him to work, picked him up, and drove the children to school but was not allowed to drive the car alone or for any other purpose. He carefully monitored what she and the children ate, where they went, and how they dressed, insisting Lavonne wear only dresses, "never pants."

Miguel had started to spank and slap the children. At first they argued about whether this was right. Miguel insisted that since he was their father, he should discipline them. Lavonne stopped protesting. Concerned that Stephanie was not wearing appropriate clothes, the director of Head Start talked to Lavonne about abuse and warned that it could "overflow" and affect the children. Apparently the discussion was couched in such vague terms, Lavonne was not sure what she was talking about. In any case, her own need for help was not addressed.

Lavonne became increasingly depressed after Candy's birth, sensing she was "trapped" with Miguel and that "there was no way out." One night, when he insisted she drink with him, he put a tattoo of his name on her arm, to show the world she was his "now and always." Feeling degraded, that night she cut her wrist, stopping only when Candy began to cry. Seeing what she'd done, Miguel grabbed for the knife, they struggled, and her hand was cut. He called her crazy and bandaged her up. Looking back, Lavonne realizes that when she attempted to hurt herself, she was barely aware Candy was in the room.

On Christmas Day, 2001, Lavonne had Miguel arrested. She had driven him to work, but he needed to take a cab home because the brakes on the car were not working. When he returned, she was leaving to go to her grandmother's house for Christmas dinner with her mother and brother. Her mother and Miguel fought, and Miguel threatened Lavonne, who knew she would be beaten whether she stayed or left with her family. Then her mother put her in the car, as a way to protect her, she realizes now. Miguel tried to follow in her new car but was drunk and wrecked it. He left the car, then called her to come home, saying he had a knife, threatening suicide and talking about them both dying. Terrified, she called the police and returned home, where the police were waiting. They arrested Miguel for "evading responsibility" for the accident. They asked Lavonne to accompany Miguel to jail and to court the next day to help translate for him. When he was released, Miguel sent the children to their rooms, turned up the radio and told her, "You said you were afraid—I'm going to teach you to be afraid now." He beat her severely, then acted "as if nothing had happened." Shortly after Christmas, they moved out of her mother's into a house of their own.

Phase 3: Further Escalation of Violence and Control, January–September 1992

The move completed Lavonne's isolation from support. Miguel's control was total in their new house, and he now beat her with objects, threatened her with weapons, and burned her with cigarettes. A brief interlude followed the baby's birth. But shortly afterward, he extended his abuse to the children both directly and by demanding Lavonne escalate her discipline. Afraid Lavonne might kill him or leave, he ensured she was never with all the children alone. Less and less able to function as an autonomous adult, Lavonne neglected basic household chores, lost state assistance, and lived for a time without the most basic comforts. Her whole life was now focused on protecting herself and the children. She reached out to DCF and began planning an escape.

The beating by Miguel when they returned from court convinced Lavonne that Miguel could easily kill her. Reflecting the total level of control she experienced, she wrote, "After that, I listened to his every command. . . . I shower the children at certain times. I shower when he allows. I go to the bathroom when he allows. I have my hair styled how he wants. I sleep when he wants. Get up when he wants."

Miguel's use of objects extended to his throwing knives at Lavonne. One evening, when he held a knife to her throat, she kneed him in the groin, the first time she had retaliated. Miguel doubled up and cut her throat with the knife, which he then dropped. When she picked it up, he told her, "If you're going to use it, make sure I'm down for good."

Miguel put his cigarettes out on Lavonne's hand or arm. He would touch her skin with cigarettes to taunt her because she could smoke only at his discretion. He also hit her with bottles. The first few times he burned her with cigarettes she fought back. But then she realized that "if he doesn't get a reaction, he doesn't win." Scars from these assaults were still visible when we met.

After the knife incident, Miguel became fearful that she might kill him in his sleep or poison him. He insisted that she taste all food first, something his father had taught him. By this time, Miguel had destroyed or disposed of all possessions that in any way reminded him of Lavonne's past.

Miguel was still concerned with what the children ate, when they slept, and that they took showers. Now, however, he would occasionally hit Daniel, Stephanie, and Maria with his belt. In addition, he instructed Lavonne when and how to hit the children. She believed that if she did as she was told, the children would suffer less than if he hit the children.

At one of their houses, Lavonne would take the children next door after Miguel went to work in the evenings. Her neighbor, who had been abused in her first marriage, reported seeing Lavonne with black eyes, cuts, and bruises. She understood the situation, though Lavonne was too fearful to talk to her about it. She never saw similar bruises on the children but knew Lavonne was not allowed to go out. In February 2002, after a beating, Lavonne ran to the neighbor's house at 11:30 p.m. and banged on the door. But Miguel "tackled" her on the lawn, and Lavonne left the children with her neighbor while they "talked it out." Neighbors had already complained to DCF, and Miguel threatened that the state would take her children if she left him because she would be seen as "unstable." He also threatened to hurt her family and friends as well as to take the children himself. Lavonne lived in fear for her life. But she was also afraid that he might kill her or her children if she left.

When Lavonne was five months pregnant with his child, Miguel told her to report David to the police for making harassing phone calls. When Lavonne was talking to the detective, she mentioned David's name. Because of this, when she hung up, Miguel beat her with a wooden board that had metal brackets attached. She still bears the scars on her back from this assault.

Miguel played games with Lavonne's mind. He would wake her up whenever he pleased, sometimes by initiating sex while she slept or by placing his hand over her face and mouth so that she would awaken gasping for air. Then he feigned sleep so that she would think she was sick or crazy. Or he would just slap her suddenly in her sleep. She would only pretend to sleep. As a result, she was chronically fatigued.

When Lavonne was seven months pregnant, in August, they moved again, Lavonne doing almost all of the physical work. The family that rented the house described finding filth everywhere, faucets broken, walls with holes—this from a family whose mother had prided herself in her homemaking skills.

Shortly after they moved, Miguel beat Lavonne so severely she went into premature labor. At the hospital, they gave her medication to control the contractions. She was "covered with bruises," but no one said anything about them. Despite the contractions, he continued to push and hit her.

In August, Lavonne called a DCF caseworker and asked about foster care, explaining that she wanted to report someone for abuse. Two weeks later, she called the caseworker again, this time saying she wanted to place Candy in foster care because she needed medical help. The caseworker gave Lavonne the number of a foster placement agency but offered no assistance. In the summer of 1992, when Lavonne drove Miguel to his night shift, he insisted the children be left behind, so she would return home. She knew Danny was too young to watch his sisters, but told herself this was better than their watching her get beaten or being slapped in the car.

Miguel would call frequently from work, sometimes several times an hour. Or he would come home suddenly to check on her. If a meal didn't please Miguel, he would throw the food in Lavonne's face. On other occasions, he put hot chili peppers and lots of salt on the food and forced Lavonne to eat it. Miguel wanted sex when he came home from work in the morning. Lavonne would lie down with him and the children would "nap" or play in their bedrooms. To ensure the children didn't disturb Miguel's sleep, Lavonne sometimes had the children play in the basement while she was drying clothes. She was particularly worried he would hurt Candy, whom he regarded as "David's child." So she made sure that Candy was with her when she went to the basement.

When Lavonne was eight months pregnant, Miguel tied her hands together and raped her. At this point, he was having her shower the children two to three times a day. He insisted the house be spotless when he returned from work, almost impossible given Lavonne's exhaustion and the children. Lavonne's attitude toward her abuse changed. Instead of crying, protesting, or resisting his abuse, she told Miguel, "I don't care what you do to me. Just get it over with." This infuriated him even more, she believed, because he wanted a "reaction."

When contractions were four minutes apart with Miguel's child, he demanded sex; she protested and he raped her. When contractions intensified, Miguel refused to take her to the hospital, apparently wanting to make sure the children stayed with him. Lavonne wanted the children to stay with her mother, but Miguel knew this might give her an opportunity to escape. He said, "Let them stay here. I'll know where they are. I'll know where you are." She finally prevailed. But, as he had done previously, he accompanied her to the hospital and never let her out of his sight, even going to the bathroom with her. Lavonne's extensive bruises were obvious.

STARK: Let me ask you this. If when you were in the hospital, a nurse had said to you, "you shouldn't be taking this," or had asked you questions about what was going on at home, do you think you could have heard this?

LAVONNE: I think I could have.

STARK: Because earlier. . . .

LAVONNE: At that point, I think I would have. If somebody had said, you know there's a way out, I would have.

No one at the hospital asked about abuse.

When Miguel told Lavonne he wanted yet more children ("three boys and three girls"), she asked to be "fixed." Miguel had long since stopped apologizing to Lavonne after he beat her. But he would apologize to the children after he struck them.

Miguel's excitement about having a son was short-lived. When she came home from the hospital, Lavonne realized something fundamental had changed in his attitude toward her and that her life was now in grave danger. The change was driven home when he beat her with the four-day-old baby in her arms. Something had also changed in the way he yelled at the children. She determined to get out but felt Miguel could read her mind.

The children tried to stay out of Miguel's way. Maria was particularly fearful and spent hours alone in her bedroom. This was when Lavonne laid the mattress in the basement for Candy. Initially, the idea was to make sure Candy didn't crawl on the cement floor while she was doing a wash. Later, however, Lavonne began putting Candy there when Miguel wanted her to, because he wanted her "out of his sight," for instance, or because he didn't want to be disturbed while he slept, and when she went to pick up Stephanie at the bus and Miguel was in the house. On one occasion, according to Danny, when Miguel had been playing with the children and Candy started crying, "Poppy hit her with the belt." Lavonne confronted Miguel, but he denied it, claiming, "you think I'm too rough with her because she's David's daughter." Lavonne believed Candy feared Miguel and tried to keep them apart. The fact that the basement wasn't accessible in the house minimized Candy's risk.

Just days after Lavonne returned from the hospital, she confronted Miguel about his treatment of the children. "They're not my kids," he told her. It was his day off. They had a fight and Miguel beat Lavonne. Overhearing the fight, Maria refused to come out of her room and had a bowel movement in her pants, though she had been potty trained for over a year. Miguel went into the room, yelled, "your bedroom smells," discovered the reason, and determined to "teach her a lesson." He told Lavonne to undress Maria, clean her up, and put her in the shower. Then, he turned the cold water on. Lavonne grabbed Maria out and screamed at Miguel, "Are you crazy?" Miguel wouldn't allow Lavonne to dress Maria and started snapping his belt, something he had previously done only with her. He hit Maria repeatedly with the belt, until she had large welts. But Maria said nothing, even when Miguel yelled at her to "say something." This was how Lavonne was responding to Miguel's assaults. At some point, Maria said, "Mommy, please make him stop. Tell Pappy I'm sorry." Miguel apologized to Maria; Lavonne and he argued, and he punched Lavonne.

This fight prompted a neighbor to call DCF and a worker came to the house to investigate. The DCF report noted that Lavonne was "overwhelmed." But the worker concluded that the children appeared cared for and that she has a "very supportive ally in her boyfriend." Several days later, a DCF worker who had visited earlier in the year made a follow-up visit, writing the report excerpted at the beginning of the chapter. Lavonne reported that she could not care properly for Candy, but the worker focused on Candy's wet diaper, the sour milk in her bottle, and the smell in Maria's room rather than Lavonne's condition. The police who arrived later in that day noted multiple bruises on Lavonne. But DCF never questioned her about these injuries, never interviewed her "supportive ally," and made no recommendations for services or support.

On a previous occasion, Danny had taken some scissors out of a drawer, and Miguel had beaten him with a belt. A neighbor observed bruises and marks on Danny's arms and legs and reported hearing the children "scream" at night. Danny had already been questioned by another neighbor, whom he told "Miguel gets upset when people ask questions." On one occasion, Danny had "accidentally" shot Miguel with the BB gun in the rear. When Miguel again caught Danny with the BB gun a few days later, he was furious. Lavonne simply wanted to make it to the weekend, hoping that her mother would give her the money to leave. To preempt a more serious beating by Miguel, Lavonne hit Danny twice in the back with a belt. Miguel took the belt from Lavonne and told her he would show her "the proper way to discipline." He hit Danny repeatedly in the back of the legs. When Lavonne protested and told Miguel to stop, Danny replied, "It's okay, Mommy. I deserve it." Miguel took Danny over near the stove. Then, he placed his hands on the electric burner.

Lavonne was terrified when Danny failed to return home on September 12. She called the school and the principal told her he would bring Danny home. Instead, the police arrived with the DCF worker who had visited most recently. Lavonne's first thought was that Danny had been in an accident. The social worker said they were taking her children, and she would see them Monday. When the police entered the house, Miguel stuck fast to Lavonne. While she was nursing Miguelito in the bedroom, with a police officer only yards away,

Miguel grabbed her hair and told her she had better say all the right things or she'd have worse problems when they were released. Although the officers heard Miguel's warning tone and observed the bruises on her body, they put her next to Miguel in the car. On the way to the station, Miguel reiterated his threats, telling her what to say and threatening her (in Spanish) if she did anything else.

At the station, the detective showed Lavonne pictures of the children's injuries and told her that she was a terrible mother and that, unless she cooperated, she would never see her children again. Observing bruises on Lavonne's face, arms, legs, and thighs, an officer drew the logical conclusion. The children had already told police that Miguel beat them. But instead of charging Miguel with these assaults, a detective pounded his fist on the desk and demanded that Lavonne admit Miguel had battered her. The detective then stood, started pacing, returned to the table, and again pounded on the desk. Just before he beat Lavonne, Miguel would also would pound on a table and yell. Lavonne went blank, numb with terror. She declared that it was she—and only she—who beat the children, that she alone was responsible for their discipline, that Miguel was "supportive," and that she had sustained the bruises during childbirth.

Lavonne's "confession" contradicted what the children and Miguel had told the police and what was obvious to detectives. But she was arrested along with Miguel and both were charged with multiple counts of risk of injury to the children. She was placed in a cell next to Miguel for seventy-two hours. During this time, he instructed her on how to behave and what to say and threatened to hurt her again if she didn't do as she was told. Then he was deported, and she was released on bail.

Since the experience of being battered unfolds "behind closed doors" and often with little or no documentation, a case study approach has the advantage of allowing varied audiences of jurors, service providers, students, and the like to "walk in the shoes" of a victim. Where children are harmed, case studies have the added advantage of highlighting the "battered mother's dilemma," posed when she must choose between protecting her children and her own safety.

Constructing a case, however detailed, presumes a selection process grounded in a theory of which events are key to abuse. For example, the victimization narrative illustrated by Walker's (1984) theory of "battered woman syndrome" uses a violence model to weave parallel strands of escalating violence (described as "cycles of violence") and psychological deterioration culminating in "learned helplessness," a depressive adaptation. Lavonne's history contained major elements of Walker's model, including repeated "cycles" of explosive violence and apology and the reluctance to seek help consistent with the "learned helplessness" theory of depression. In my report to the court and my testimony, I described the cycles of assault and apology and used Campbell's (1995) "dangerousness assessment" scale to show that Lavonne had experienced most of the factors that predict homicide in abuse cases, including serial violence, sexual assault, assaults with objects and weapons, alcohol abuse, threats to kill, violence in public, violence against children, and violence during pregnancy. Miguel assaulted Lavonne several hundred times in their two years together, and his violence was sufficiently severe to justify his claim that he could "do with [Lavonne] what [he] want[ed]," a threat Lavonne knew meant he could take her life. When she was arrested, Lavonne was suffering a slow death to which she might have eventually succumbed.

Although Lavonne had clearly suffered continued and severe violence, there was little evidence of Miguel's assaults apart from the visit to the doctor after he kicked her in the head and the observations by police. The children had not mentioned Miguel's abuse of Lavonne. Moreover, although she had suffered appalling violence, the image of Lavonne as a helpless victim failed to capture the complex interplay of romance, resistance, conciliation, and subjugation revealed by her history. Lavonne acknowledged making some bad choices. But she wanted the court to understand the calculations that went into her decisions to harm Danny, allow Miguel to hit Maria, or leave Candy in the basement. Lavonne had been depressed, had failed to frankly discuss her situation with the others, and had reached a point when she told Miguel, "I don't care what you do to me," all possible signs of "helplessness." There were proximate explanations for these symptoms, such as Lavonne's chronic exhaustion and her fear of losing the children. As important, she was largely asymptomatic when we met. The court recognized that Miguel had been abusive but did not connect his violence and the crimes for which Lavonne was charged.

Using Coercive Control to Reframe the Failure to Protect

In framing Lavonne's abuse, I faced two challenges: to show how an intelligent and psychologically normal mother might hurt her children or "allow" them to be hurt and to capture the range of Miguel's abusive tactics without eviscerating the rational kernel of Lavonne's personhood.

The coercive control model addresses these challenges in two steps. The first is to describe abuse as a comprehensive, multifaceted strategy of domination that constrains a partner's decisional autonomy within ever-narrower parameters. The second is to identify the protective logic underlying a victim's decision making within these constraints, an example of what I call "control in the context of no control." The proximate contexts in which this logic unfolded was the use of the children as a form of control over their mother ("child abuse as tangential spouse abuse") and the resulting "battered mother's dilemma," when the victim must weigh her own safety, autonomy, and dignity against their child's.

Elsewhere, I have reviewed the empirical evidence that a majority of the victimized women who seek outside assistance are suffering the interlocking violations to their rights to physical integrity ("domestic violence"), dignity (degradation), psychological security ("intimidation"), social connectedness and support ("isolation"), and autonomy ("control") that make up coercive control (Stark, 2007, 242–288). Control in this context involves tactics of appropriation, exploitation, and regulation that extend from denying victims the resources required for basic survival (such as food, money, and means of transport and communication) through the micromanagement of how they conduct themselves in everyday life. These tactics may be described as "structural" to the extent that they create an objective condition of subordination and dependency independently of the personalities involved or the proximate circumstances. Coercive control is what Dempsey (2010) terms "domestic violence in the strong sense," because it builds on and exacerbates sexual inequality. The most dramatic consequence of coercive control is an almost hostage-like condition of "entrapment," where the victim is forced to survive in a universe defined by the absence of rights, options, and resources. From this vantage point, because control disables a victim's capacity to effectively resist or escape, a victim's primary vulnerability to serious injury or death is a function of the level of control in the abusive relationship rather than of the level or frequency of physical violence (Glass, Manganello, and Campbell, 2004). Thus, battering has less to do with what abusive partners do *to* women than with what they keep women from doing for themselves. Women's agency is not eliminated but driven underground and must operate indirectly, by selecting the least harmful of available options, for example.

Violence and Control

Lavonne realized that Miguel's behavior early in the relationship set the stage for his total control later on. At first, she wrote, Miguel worked twelve hours a day and spent all of his free time with her and her children. She continued,

By mid-May, he and I had a complete relationship, friendship, intimacy; he was helping me with my children, he started making suggestions that he felt were beneficial to us, I shouldn't hang around the diner, keep the house cleaner, the ways I fed the kids and what I fed them, the times they went to bed. (I promised no contact with David since he was no good for me and the kids and only upset me.) I had never felt so loved and cared for as I did then.

Lavonne's dysfunctional family history undoubtedly predisposed her to confuse "love" with predictability, loyalty, and the expectation that she would play a stay-at-home housewife, mother, and caretaker, a real *señora*. At first, Miguel's jealousy, resentment of David, being taunted at work, and his difficulties with alcohol seemed plausible explanations for his "outbursts." But once Miguel abused Lavonne, she responded in a rational, measured, and strategic way, by eliciting an agreement that he would not drink in the house and putting him out when he broke his promise. To mitigate his "embarrassment" about her having "David's baby," she stopped going to the diner, proving her loyalty. Unfortunately, these compromises made Lavonne less visible, allowing Miguel to complement his almost daily outbursts with a routine of pushing, shoving, grabbing, and other relatively minor physical assaults, accompanied by dramatic acts of intimidation: Miguel smashed the car windshield and dashboard, removed and snapped his belt as a warning, beat his friend "bloody," and called from work at all hours to check up on her. He also destroyed objects that linked Lavonne to her past.

Once Lavonne became structurally isolated, Miguel took control over the rest of her life. AFDC and a small supplement from Maria's father had allowed Lavonne a certain independence. She also shared household expenses with her mother. Since Miguel knew "best" how to reorganize her life, he took her monthly check, dispensed only what he thought she needed, regularly questioned her about all expenditures, never allowed her to go shopping alone, and hit her if he thought she spent money frivolously. After the couple moved, they survived on Miguel's meager wages, minus his alcohol. Their desperate state was confirmed by tenants at one of their apartments, who noted there was no running water in the bathroom, no heat, broken windows, and little electric. A neighbor's report stated that they were stealing bottled water.

Miguel's microregulated Lavonne's default responsibilities as a woman, including how she cooked, dressed, and cleaned. Activities that had given her pride were now sources of shame. Miguel demanded she fix complete Mexican meals like a *señora,* something she initially enjoyed. But then he would throw the food on the floor or in Lavonne's face or make her eat it after adding hot spices. Later, he made her eat it first so she wouldn't poison him. Miguel dictated how she and the children dressed, forbidding her to wear pants, for instance, and how she could wear her hair. Miguel's control extended to basic bodily functions, including sleeping, sex, and when and how she went to the bathroom. In addition to waking her with a slap, by initiating sex, or by holding his hand over his mouth, he would call her from work throughout the night. Too fearful to sleep while Miguel was awake, she became chronically fatigued.

Cornell (1995) has emphasized the importance to personhood of an "imaginary domain," where persons devise their sexual identity. Miguel superimposed his "male imaginary" on hers, using rape and constant demands to eviscerate any individuality she might salvage as a gendered being by determining the where, when, how, or how often of sex. He demanded sex when it had been proscribed by the doctor, when she was four centimeters dilated, when she returned from the hospital after giving birth, when she began spotting, and regardless of whether the babies were present. His demand that they "nap" when he came home from work in the morning meant leaving the children unattended and made it impossible to properly prepare Danny or Stephanie for Head Start or school. Lavonne had two unwanted pregnancies, lost a baby, and felt so completely degraded that she attempted suicide. Miguel also dictated personal hygiene, by telling Lavonne when she should or could shower and insisting that the children take two or three baths or showers a day. Lavonne asked permission to go to the bathroom.

Isolation

We have already tracked how Miguel deprived Lavonne of social support, increasing her vulnerability and depriving her of alternative versions of reality to weigh against his. Miguel's friends and coworkers were aware of his abuse. As undocumented immigrants, however, they lacked any formal means of complaint, and Miguel effectively closed informal channels by his hyperviolent response when challenged. Lavonne initially accepted the "new order" at home. Only Lavonne's mother openly challenged Miguel for Lavonne's loyalty, a contest that peaked on Christmas Day, 1991, when they engaged in a tug-of-war. After he wrecked the car, he returned home and threatened suicide if Lavonne didn't return. Miguel may also have used less direct ways to undermine her family relations. For example, an anonymous caller told police he had molested a niece for whom she was baby sitting, causing a break with her sister. A male neighbor reported that Lavonne was forbidden to talk to men. She was also forbidden to drive her car except to transport him to work or the children to school, and she was forbidden to shop by herself. She was expected to remain in the house all day while Miguel was sleeping. Although none of this allayed Miguel's jealousy, she was completely entrapped by the time she recognized her confinement for what it was.

Even when Lavonne did talk to neighbors or let the children play in their yard, she and they were too frightened to talk about the abuse. If anyone offered to help, Lavonne's fears intensified because of the implied threat of discovery. Fearful of making a "mistake," she became a virtual shut-in, leaving the house only to get Stephanie at the bus or to drive Miguel to work. Lavonne's isolation became complete when the couple moved a second time. Although she had a car and there were often several at the house, she was not allowed to drive by herself. If she called DCF, Miguel warned, they would say she was crazy and take the children, a threat she and the children took seriously, particularly after Lavonne started leaving Danny home with the children when she drove Miguel to work.

The professionals Lavonne saw were well aware she was being abused, including the police, the physician, the nurses at the hospital, and the Head Start teacher. But they did nothing. One officer's report detailed the bruises he observed and concluded, "L . . . was being abused (beaten) by her boyfriend Sabastian." But instead of protecting her, police used Lavonne as an interpreter, put the couple together in the backseat and in adjacent cells, and accused her of being a "bad mother" when she failed to implicate Miguel. DCF's response was more complicated. Lavonne requested help with Candy and described herself as "overwhelmed," code language that should prompt an offer of services or respite. Not only did caseworkers who visited the house ignore physical and circumstantial evidence of battering and neglect to offer assistance, but they also chided Lavonne for inappropriate parenting and described Miguel as "supportive." If Lavonne failed to utilize outside assistance, this had less to do with "learned helplessness" than with the denial, minimization, and victim blaming that characterized the professional response and deepened Lavonne's dilemma, reinforcing Miguel's control.

Entrapment

One result of Lavonne's isolation was that Miguel's moral compass became her principal guide until, like him, she acted as if the children were "bad" and required correction if they disturbed Miguel's sleep or violated his rules. Obeying

Miguel's rules was impossible, however, since there were so many and they were always changing. They were designed to calm his anxiety about things being out of control that he had inherited from his own upbringing (and his sexual abuse as a child) and his rigid notions of masculinity. Illustrative was the "rule" that the children shower and change their clothes several times a day. Out of fear for herself and the children, Lavonne tried to get the children to comply. But there was just too much going on to make this work. Moreover, by continually degrading and abusing Lavonne, Miguel had undermined any authority she had with the children. Life at home quickly descended into chaos, sending Miguel into a panic and intensifying his abusive attempts to impose control. One result was that Lavonne's disciplinary repertoire became increasingly limited to physical punishment. Lavonne felt "trapped" after Candy's birth. She realized he might kill her, however, only just before Miguelito's birth. She prepared to escape with money from her uncle. Before she could do so, Miguel beat Maria with the belt and burned Danny's hand on the stove, and they were both arrested and charged.

The Battered Mother's Dilemma

In my testimony to the court, I explained that the behavior for which Lavonne was charged was a direct consequence of Miguel's regime of domination and of her being deprived of the rights, resources, and liberties she needed to make safe choices for herself and the children.

Like the police, DCF blamed Lavonne for the harm to the children, drawing connections between the sorry state of the house (symbolized by the odor of feces in Maria's room), the squalor with which Candy was surrounded in the basement, Lavonne's hesitancy to remove Candy, and Lavonne's parenting. The caseworker wrote, "Advised mother that child can't be left alone down here. . . . Mother said 'ok, I respect your opinion, if that's what you think, I'll take her out.' When the mother didn't move . . . I moved aside the bed frame and mattress and lifted the baby out." To the caseworker, Lavonne's sluggishness reflected her depression and low intelligence. In fact, Lavonne was "frozen" by a battered mother's dilemma. Bringing Candy upstairs put her at risk from Miguel. But if she refused or revealed Miguel's abuse, she risked having Candy removed. She decided on a dangerous gambit. She projected an image that converged with the preconceptions of the caseworker, that she was "unable to cope" and "overwhelmed," hoping this might get her and Candy the help they needed. This strategic use of her depression was an example of "control in the context of no control."

A similar dilemma was evoked when the detective demanded she implicate the man the police had allowed to threaten her in the squad car and an adjacent cell. But if was only when the detective insulted her, threatened she would "never see your children again," and pounded on the table that the association with Miguel was complete. Even here, Lavonne took the safest course of action, confessing to hurting the children rather than risk Miguel's abuse, and even assuming the "false self" of the "bad" mother they projected.

Conclusion

Because of its focus on harms to liberty and autonomy, the coercive control model of abuse addresses a key challenge to the defense of battered women in criminal, child welfare, or divorce proceedings where children have been harmed: how to convey the full extent of the abuse a victim and her children have experienced while still preserving the dignity, courage, and rationality of a mother's decision making. It does this by identifying a logic of maternal love, caring, and resistance behind even ostensibly abusive or self-destructive behaviors, "control in the context of no control." This model has helped us reframe Lavonne's decision to take Candy to a basement room that was inaccessible from the house as an attempt to protect her from Miguel, the safest choice given the constrained options she had. A similar logic guided Lavonne's use of the belt with Danny, her failure to intervene earlier when Miguel used a belt on Maria, and her acquiescence in Miguel's decision to let Danny watch the younger children. The importance of locating Lavonne's agency in this way is that it makes clear that the solution to Lavonne's dilemma lies in realistically expanding the options available rather than blaming her for acting as she did. This means walking in Lavonne's shoes to appreciate "the special reasonableness of battered women."*

References

Brownmiller, S. (1989). *Waverly place*. New York: Grove. Campbell, J. C. (1995). Prediction of homicide of and by battered women. In J. C. Campbell (Ed.),

*After the couple had been apart for some years and Lavonne had remarried, she ran into Miguel in a store, where she was shopping with her sister-in-law. She reported that he bowed to her and, for the first time, addressed her as *señora,* a term of respect. At that moment, she told me, she felt "vindicated." Danny has just finished his second tour of duty in Iraq. The girls and Miguelito are doing as well as can be expected.

Assessing dangerousness: Violence by sexual offenders, batterers and child abusers. Thousand Oaks, CA: Sage.

Cornell, D. (1995). *The imaginary domain: Abortion, pornography and sexual harassment.* Routledge: New York.

Dempsey, M. D. (2009). *Prosecuting domestic violence: A philosophical Analysis.* Cambridge: Oxford University Press.

Glass, N., Manganello, J., and Campbell, J. C. (2004). Risk for intimate partner femicide in violent relationships. *DV Report, 9*(2), 1, 2, 30–33.

Johnson, J. *What Lisa knew: The truths and lies of the Steinberg case.* New York: Putnam, 1990.

McFadden, R. D. 1987. Parents of girl 6, charged with murder after she dies. *New York Times,* November 6, B3.

Stark, E. (2002). The battered mother in the child protective service caseload: Developing an appropriate Response. *Women's Rights Law Reporter, 23*(2), 107–133.

Stark, E. (2007). *Coercive control.* Oxford: Oxford University Press.

Walker, L. (1984). *The Battered Woman Syndrome.* New York: Springer.

Commentary

Shuki J. Cohen and Chitra Raghavan

Systemic Revictimization

We began chapter 2 with attempts to define domestic/intimate partner violence, and we end this section of the book with a personalized glimpse on how survivors negotiate the legal system and try to end the violence, regain custody of their children, and, despite enormous hurdles, begin new lives. Two radically different expert voices are presented. Specifically, Stark approaches the issue of systemic control top down: he uses a case study to highlight the nuances of his theory of coercive control and how he uses his power to collaboratively bring justice for his abused client. Gentile, on the other hand, approaches the issue of systemic control and abuse bottom up.

In the preceding chapters we have seen domestic violence framed as a psychological problem best studied behaviorally, as a public health issue, as a sexual minority issue framed uniquely in this subculture, and as a feminist issue. In her chapter, Gentile frames domestic violence as a human rights issue. Thus, she argues that domestic violence is best analyzed historically using a postcolonial framework that explicitly takes into account the political nature of defining and interpreting domestic violence. Further, differently from most other authors in this book, she explicitly situates vulnerability at the crossroads of race, gender, and sexuality rather than prioritizing one over the other.

Consistent with her theoretical frame, Gentile uses mixed methodology. In the first section of the action research, the author and a group of survivors collaboratively design a survey and collect and analyze data. In conducting participatory action research, Gentile gives voices to a marginalized and vulnerable population—the survey questions include what is important to survivors and not what the researcher thinks is important. (While participatory action research shares many characteristics with focus groups—knowledge and information are defined and generated from stakeholders and knowledge is constructed interactively through discussion—the expert steps out of the center, whereas in focus groups the expert moderates the discussion and ultimately chooses what information is to be disseminated.) The survivors identify the complexity of their lives and refuse to take reductive approaches to limit questions. As a result, the survey focus is broad and interconnected rather than neatly focused, restricted, and bounded, as quantitative surveys frequently are. The descriptive results suggest that women are not adequately protected during their court appearances and are unsupported by the criminal-justice system and that money and gender may obstruct fair procedure when fighting for custody—consistent with other research findings from family courts.

Uniquely, Gentile bridges some of the original tenets of participatory action research (i.e., to create relational knowledge) using relational psychoanalytic theory. This theory, she argues, provides a platform for researchers to actively engage with participants and allows them to identify the self as inherently complex and contradictory, wherein contradictions provide meaning and should be considered seriously rather than smoothed away. Relational psychoanalysis also explicitly recognizes the intersubjective unconscious that emerges during communication (Bass, 2001). Gentile also argues that the unconscious is crucial when we study domestic violence because narrative-forming symbolization and mentalization are frequently hampered in the presence of trauma and oppression.

Finally, framed within relational psychoanalysis, a particularly interesting layer of power also arises from this unique methodology. In addition to the researchers' relationships of power to the participants, the participants in Gentile's study struggle with their roles as ad hoc researchers. Gentile finds that the survivors who functioned as researchers suffered during the process, something that few of our other authors did (or at least report). The survivors struggled with feeling more powerful than the women they were interviewing, their discomfort with the privilege of having survived, and, ironically, the boundaries that developed because they were now on the outside. The researcher-insider-outsider struggle further informs us about the difficulty of obtaining data in its closest form to the reality that was experienced and notes the ethics of interviewing survivors and the potential for retraumatization.

Many of these same issues (i.e., custody, safety, etc.) are raised by Stark in his case study. Thus both chapters highlight the dangers of potential injustice associated with a superficial and decontextualized judgment of battered women's words and actions. Stark's chapter shows how a woman held legally accountable for potential abuse and neglect of her children might in actuality be an innocent "normal" person acting reasonably under an abnormally coercive environment, to maximally protect her children within the constraints of the chronic mental and physical toll that the abusive relationship has taken on her. Sometimes the authors evoke similar points but develop them differently. For example, Stark offers a developmental account of Lavonne's susceptibility to internalizing systemic societal coercive control by presuming that "Lavonne's dysfunctional family history undoubtedly predisposed her to confuse 'love' with predictability, loyalty, and the expectation that she would play a stay-at-home housewife, mother, and caretaker, a real *señora*."

In contrast, Gentile offers a clinical-developmental account of the women's inability to break the cycle of coercive control. She suggests that early trauma might have interfered with their process of symbolization, which in turn hindered their internal sense of agency and personhood when clashing with the system. Thus, while Stark argues that external societal oppression can disempower battered women, Gentile argues that there exists primarily a need to understand the unconscious motives at play and in particular the erosion of the unconscious motives that underlie the ability to differentiate and take agentic control in the face of cumulative trauma. For Gentile, the focus groups also serve as therapy groups, allowing vow women to conceptualize their own stories through collective narration. According to psychoanalytic theory, with the (largely group facilitated) resumption of narrative coherence comes also a felt (or embodied) sense of agency and its concomitant rekindling of individualized motivation for change and self-preservation. While structural isolation is a crucial factor also in Stark's coercive control formulation of Lavonne's case, isolation is bridged externally, with Stark providing support and advocacy.

Another significant difference between the authors is that Gentile believes that the speaker is the ultimate accurate observer and that even well-meaning advocacy on their behalf can be disempowering. Gentile not only relinquishes authority but further discovers that her very concept of authority that she was determined to relinquish is a source of suspicion and discomfort to the battered women. In an ongoing quest to engage experientially with the group dynamics, the author continuously modifies her stance toward the group and in doing so is increasingly made aware of subtle authoritative biases that an external observer might not be privy to. Mistrust concerns—for not having been a battered woman herself, for coming from a different class and educational background—are paradoxically becoming verbalized and expressed when the participants begin to accept Gentile as a participant-activist. Conversely, Gentile finds herself drawing on other life experiences she happens to share with some of the participants, experiences that have long become suppressed as the researcher gradually honed her current professional and social persona.

Stark, in contrast, believes that everybody is fallible in representing reality—both in introspection and observation—and that situations of trauma and distress can further confound matters. In such vulnerable situations, it is the expert with experience and theoretical tools who can sift through the narratives of the client and ultimately empower her within the existing system. Although Stark is briefly challenged by his client, she quickly reverses her position and decides that the author is trustworthy because her therapist recommends him highly. The structure of authority in this case is therefore sufficient to credentialize the author, in contrast to the participatory action research paradigm, where Gentile is left to painstakingly make the case for her credibility. As the case progresses, Stark's expert role becomes crucial, whereas Gentile's expert role diminishes. Lavonne accepts all blame and admits to violence that she did not commit against her children. Stark challenges the client's internalized marginalization and represents the client more faithfully both to herself and to the court system and in doing so bridges the dual role of being a sensitive clinician but also an advocate.

In conclusion, while the methodologies of the two chapters are different, the writing and the flow of inquiry in both of them is intimate and introspective and uses rich description to convey the phenomenology of the situations. Ultimately, while using different theoretical frameworks, methodologies, and participants, both papers arrive at an ecologically solid understanding of the women's experiences in the court system. Lastly, both scholars use their understanding to advocate for the battered woman to the larger scientific and legal communities and in doing so balance the complex roles of scholars and bona fide agents of social justice activism.

Reference

Bass, A. (2001). It takes one to know one; Or, whose unconscious is it anyway? *Psychoanalytic Dialogues, 11,* 683–702.

Critical-Thinking Questions

1. Who is a better judge of what is domestic violence—the experts who study it or the people who have experienced it? Why?
2. Compare Stark's and Gentile's relationship to their own authority as researchers. How do they differ from each other?
3. How does participatory action research differ from focus groups? What are the advantages and shortcomings of each?
4. Compare the participant selection in the two studies. Provide a strength and a limitation of each their selection strategies.
5. How does research methodology and the subject matter (e.g., definition of domestic violence) influence each other in Gentile's work?
6. Which of these two studies is more replicable? Why or why not?
7. In which ways do Stark's elements of coercive control manifest in Gentile's focus group discussion?
8. Compare how Stark and Gentile explain the paradox of the seeming inability of battered women to leave their abusers. How are they similar? How are they different?
9. According to each of the authors, what is the solution for a victim of domestic violence to break the cycle of coercive control? Compare Stark's and Gentile's strategies and comment on the differences.
10. How does Gillum and DiFulvio's focus group differ in approach from Gentile's focus group?

Advanced Questions

1. Identify one finding in both the studies (chapters 9 and 10) that contradicts each other or are incompatible. Is this difference related to the measurement strategies used or the definition of domestic violence employed, or both? Defend your answer.
2. Allen (part 2, chapter 5) conceptualizes gender as an ecological variable.

How does this conceptualization manifest itself in Stark's and Gentile's work?

3. How would the gender parity findings in domestic violence changed had the researchers used Stark's coercive control theory rather than physical violence? In what way does it contribute to feminist scholarship on the subject?

4. In what ways does Gentile's study contain elements of feminist scholarship that have not been addressed so far?

CONCLUSION

Keith A. Markus, Jennifer E. Loveland, Daphne
T. Ha, and Chitra Raghavan, John Jay College of
Criminal Justice

10 | Publication Trends in Intimate Partner Violence

Bridging the Division in Qualitative and Quantitative Methods

Both qualitative and quantitative methods contribute to research on intimate partner violence (IPV). In this chapter we first report a tabular review of IPV research, focusing on the use of qualitative, quantitative, and mixed methods.* We then explore the conceptual basis for distinguishing between qualitative and quantitative methods and argue that in at least one important sense, all methods are mixed methods.

Tabular Review of Qualitative, Quantitative, and Mixed Methods in Intimate Partner Violence Research

To investigate methodological patterns in intimate partner violence research, we conducted a tabular review. We designed the review to answer three main research questions. First, in what proportions do IPV researchers use qualitative, quantitative, and mixed methods? Second, how do IPV studies vary in terms of research questions, data collection, and samples? Third, what association holds between these two sets of characteristics?

Sample

As a first step, a search of empirical articles using the term *intimate partner violence* as a keyword was conducted from 2003 to 2008 using the database Psyc-

---

*References for the articles that comprised the literature review for this chapter can be found on Dr. Markus' website at http://jjcweb.jjay.cuny.edu/kmarkus/info.html#Pubs, or by contacting Jennifer E. Loveland at jloveland@jjay.cuny.edu.

Info. This search resulted in 751 hits, from which we excluded 150 books, book chapters, or other types of reports; 50 articles not available within the university library system; and 46 unpublished dissertations and articles without statistical analyses. For example, we excluded literature reviews and theory papers but included meta-analyses because statistical analyses were redone. The final 2003–8 sample thus numbered 405 articles that were subsequently individually coded.

Method

The coding of the methodological approach proceeded in three passes. The first pass grouped each article into qualitative, quantitative, mixed-method, or borderline categories. The borderline category referred to studies that had both qualitative and quantitative methods but eventually chose to report on only one aspect of the data. Of the 405 studies, 42 (10.37 percent) fell into the borderline category. For example, Medina-Ariza and Barberet (2003) included both surveys and open-ended questions in their study; however, in their final paper they reported only percentages.

The second pass applied a more in-depth coding of actual data-analytic strategies. Quantitative analytic strategies were divided into five categories (descriptive univariate only, pairwise classical statistical tests, multivariate statistics with three or more variables but no latent variables, modern statistical methods with no latent variables but with fit tests, and latent variable models). Similarly, qualitative analyses were divided into seven categories (thematic analysis; narrative analysis; ethnographic descriptions; critical studies, or power relations between societal groups; grounded theory; other forms of qualitative analyses; and unspecified qualitative methods). The third pass then consolidated this detailed breakdown into four broad types.

We first examined the areas of the primary research question. Eventually, we generated four content codes as follows, each which had separate and more detailed subcodes. The four main codes were (1) exploratory or prevalence content, including the incidence and proportion of participants who reported IPV; (2) the examination of resource use, including hospitals, shelters, help-seeking behaviors, court involvement, and orders of protections; (3) measurements, including screening tools, reliability and validity of measures, and model testing; and (4) factors associated with IPV, which were further subdivided into mediating factors, risk factors, health consequences, and other factors.

Next, we examined the data-collection strategy, which we coded into four overarching categories: (1) interviews, which included face-to-face, telephone, and group; (2) surveys, which included mailed, Internet, in-person, or unspecified; (3) mixed strategies; and (4) archival or clinical data. One study did not specify data collection strategy and was thus coded as missing.

Third, we coded the sample with respect to gender (male, female, matched couples, mixed gender but unmatched, child, parent), race (white, African American, Hispanic, Asian, mixed, diverse, international, and other), and population type (shelter or clinical survivor, batterer, college sample, community or nonclinical, population-based survey, health service providers, religious or community leaders, and high risk or vulnerable populations).

Results

The results for the methodology type appear in table 10.1. Of the total 405 articles, 58 were qualitative (14.32 percent; 95 percent CI [10.9 percent, 17.7 percent]); 17 were quantitative with only descriptive statistics and frequencies (4.20 percent; 95 percent CI [2.2 percent, 6.2 percent]) and 318 were quantitative with inferential statistics (78.52 percent; 95 percent CI [74.5 percent, 82.5 percent]), for a total of 335 quantitative studies; and 12 used mixed methods (2.96 percent; 95 percent CI [1.3 percent, 4.6 percent]). Although almost 14 percent of the studies had the capacity to provide mixed-methods results, less than 3 percent did so. The 2009–12 data mirror the pattern of the previous data with proportionately more quantitative than qualitative types.

Table 10.2 contains the frequencies for gender and sample characteristics, and tables 10.6 and 10.7, data collection methods and research questions. The results suggest a diversity of populations, data collection strategies, and research questions. As one might expect, there are few studies that focus on ethnic minorities and LGBTQ populations and fewer male-only studies compared to female only, although the total percentage of studies that included men in some fashion was about 40 percent.

The remaining results focus on differences between studies adopting different types of methodology. One of the most prominent differences involved gender. Of the 58 qualitative studies, almost 76 percent used *all* female samples, with about 16 percent using mixed samples and less than 4 percent male-only samples (table 10.3a). In contrast, studies of both quantitative types (descriptive and inferential) included female-only samples (53 and 56 percent) and male-only samples (6 and 10 percent), and about a third to just under half were mixed matched and unmatched samples (35 and 32 percent). Collapsing to a two (quantitative, qualitative) by three (female, male, mixed) table, the analyses were significant such that gender differed across methods $\chi^2(2, N = 393) = 8.46$, $p = .015$.

The pattern of ethnic minority and diversity in qualitative and mixed-methods studies differed from the quantitative studies (descriptive and inferential combined) in an interesting way (see table 10.4a); qualitative and mixed methods combined had more studies that targeted a particular ethnic minority sample (African American, Hispanic, or Asian compared to other race and ethnic groups, 24.3 percent) compared to quantitative (11.4 percent; OR = 2.50, 95 percent CI [1.32, 4.72]). Quantitative studies (descriptive and inferential) used more samples that had different or mixed-ethnic groups (63.17 percent [211/334]) compared to combined qualitative and mixed methods (35.71 percent [25/70]). OR = 0.32, 95 percent CI [0.19, 0.55]). Interestingly, despite a suggestive trend, the data do not support a conclusion that either type had more international studies (OR = 1.59, 95 percent CI [0.81, 3.11]).

More than half the qualitative studies focused on survivor populations (56.14 percent) compared to quantitative studies (descriptive and inferential, 28.36 percent; OR = 3.23, 95 percent CI [1.83, 5.72]; see table 10.5a). Qualitative studies also included more community samples (19.30 percent) compared to quantitative (descriptive and inferential, 6.27 percent; OR = 3.58, 95 percent CI [1.64, 7.80]). More than a quarter of quantitative studies focused on random or representative samples (25.37 percent) compared to one study in qualitative methods (1.75 percent; OR = 0.05; 95 percent CI [0.01, 0.27]). Qualitative and quantitative studies were equally likely to study batterer, college student, service provider, and high risk samples.

As one might expect, qualitative data collection strategies focused on interviews and discussions (95.71 percent [67/70]), comparing all interview methods: face-to-face interviews, telephone interviews, focus groups, unspecified interviews, mixed interviews, and mixed interviews and surveys. The quantitative strategies (46.87 percent [157/335]) included face-to-face interviews, telephone interviews, focus groups, unspecified interviews, mixed interview, and mixed interviews and surveys (OR = 25.32; 95 percent CI [8.47, 75.73]; see table 10.6). However, the main difference between qualitative studies and quantitative studies involved the use of focus groups (OR = 78.17, 95 percent CI [13.88, 440.23]). Descriptive quantitative studies used archival and clinical data sources much more than inferential studies (OR = 6.38, 95 percent CI [2.35, 17.29]).

Finally, almost a third of the qualitative research (qualitative and mixed) focused on the prevalence of victims (31.43 percent [22/70]) as compared to quantitative research (descriptive and inferential) (13.13 percent [44/335]; OR

= 3.03, 95 percent CI [1.68, 5.47]; see table 10.7). Qualitative research (qualitative and mixed) was also more likely to examine resources available, which included service providers' knowledge and attitudes) toward IPV (35.71 percent [25/70]), compared to quantitative research (descriptive and inferential) (60/335=17.91 percent; OR = 2.55, 95 percent CI [1.46, 4.45]). In contrast, quantitative research (descriptive and inferential) was not more likely to examine measurement issues (10.75 percent [36/335]) compared to qualitative research (qualitative and mixed methods) (5.71 percent [4/70]; OR = 1.99, 95 percent CI [0.72, 5.48]). Quantitative research (inferential and descriptive) was also more likely to examine health-related correlates of IPV (26.87 percent [90/335]) compared to qualitative research (qualitative and mixed) (11.43 percent [8/70]; OR = .35, 95 percent CI [0.16, 0.75]). No differences were found between qualitative and quantitative methods with respect to mediation effects or risk factors.

Finally, a subset of these analyses were replicated for the period 2009–12, using the same search criteria but narrowing the scope of coding, resulting in a review of 440 additional studies with fewer categories. Specifically, we examined the proportion of qualitative to quantitative and the gender breakdown (although we present data on race and population type for the interested reader). The tabular analysis suggests that while the overall proportion of qualitative, quantitative, and mixed studies remained, one interesting gender shift emerged: the number of qualitative studies focusing on female-only populations dropped from 76 to 61 percent, with a threefold increase in male-only studies and a fivefold increase in child-parent dyads. Proportionally, the number of studies focusing on survivors across all categories dropped from about a third to 15 percent (with a sharp drop in the number of quantitative studies on survivors; see tables 10.5a and 10.5b), possibly accounting for this trend.

Tabular Review Conclusions

This brief tabular review suggests that the field might benefit from more mixed methods and qualitative work overall. Further, more research using mixed and qualitative methods that examine violent men, service providers, high-risk populations, and the chronic health concerns that have been noted in survivors will add to our knowledge. Quantitative methods might include more survivor samples, nonrepresentative samples, unique populations, and larger representations of single ethnic groups. The qualitative-quantitative divide appears most strongly along gender lines and race lines, and the choice of populations may be what subsequently drives the questions that are researched.

A follow-up analysis from 2009 to 2012 suggest that, overall, the number of studies focused on female-only samples dropped from about 59 to 51 percent (see table 10.3b), while male-only samples increased from about 8 to 12 percent. Further, as shown in tables 5a and 5b, these differences are better explained by the trends in quantitative research—such research may be moving away from survivor-only populations to service providers and community populations. A more in-depth coding is required before coming to any firm conclusions on or implications of these trends.

Using just the term IPV instead of related terms such as family violence, intimate partner abuse, dating violence, and domestic violence may have excluded a few articles. Additionally, using only PsycInfo as the primary search engine likely excluded articles from other disciplines that are not cross-listed, including nursing, public health, legal studies, and criminology. However, including all of the search terms and databases was beyond the scope of this study, intended to give the reader a flavor for the patterns of research strategies in the field.

The Differences between Qualitative and Quantitative Research

Yin and Yang are interested in conducting research on intimate partner violence. Yin favors quantitative methods, whereas Yang favors qualitative research methods. Based on the patterns found in the literature, chances are that Yin and Yang will not only adopt different methods of data collection and data analysis but will also focus on different phenomena and ask different research questions. Yin is more likely to collect standardized data using an impersonal method, summarize the data in terms of numbers, test prespecified hypotheses, focus on objective characteristics of the participants, and ask questions about statistical associations or causal relationships between variables that summarize such objective characteristics. Yang, in contrast, is more likely to collect idiographic data using personal contact with the participants; summarize the data verbally; develop interpretations from the data; focus on the intersubjective *lifeworld* composed of shared meanings, understandings, and practices; and ask questions about the experience of certain types of individuals with certain aspects of intimate partner violence. In contrast to the lifeworld studied by Yang, Yin studies the objective world: magnitudes and qualities that exist independent of the observer, even if they are psychological properties of the people studied, and independent of how observers communicate about them.

Indeed, perhaps the most fundamental distinction between qualitative and quantitative methods, the distinction from which all the others follow, is between studying the lifeworld as opposed to the objective world. Quantitative methods are based on a physical science model in which the researcher measures physical magnitudes such as the weight or volume of a substance or the speed or force of an object's motion. This approach conceptualizes human phenomena as analogous to such physical measurements. Researchers measure attributes of people such as memory, understanding, personality, hostility, or control the same way that one might measure the length of a steel rod. This approach understands such variables as objective properties of people that describe them as a matter of scientific fact.

In contrast, most qualitative research instead focuses on the lifeworld: the world as it is created, shaped, and experienced from within the sociocultural framework of understanding common to the participants—and often to the researcher as well. For example, rather than taking it as an objective fact about the world that participant A remembers something about an event correctly, qualitative approaches tend to have more interest in understanding how the memory is experienced and shaped within the existing milieu of intersubjectively shared understandings. Kondo (1990) relates an event in which she attempted to order in Japanese at a restaurant counter in Japan and was unable to complete the order because the person there simply could not imagine that a nonnative could speak Japanese. Approached as a matter of objective fact, her Japanese may have been flawless, but in the context of the restaurant employee's lifeworld, such a possibility was inconceivable and certainly not a fact. When it came to obtaining the food order, the lifeworld carried the day and prevented successful communication, much to the author's frustration.

However, more common examples of the lifeworld concept involve successful communication. Garfinkle (1967) developed a method called ethnomethodology, designed to help bring the implicit structure of the lifeworld into view. Anyone who has ever had a sustained conversation with a three-year-old has a pretty good idea how ethnomethodology works. Yin asks Yang to return a book to the library for him. Yang asks why. Yin responds that it is almost due and he will be out of town for the weekend and that Yang had told him that she was headed to the library for other reasons. Yang asks why he wants to return the book. Yin replies that he borrowed it and so has to return it. Yang asks why borrowed things have to be returned. Yin replies that it is the difference between borrowing and taking. Yang asks if people could borrow something and then change their mind that they want to take it instead of borrow it? Yin replies, no.

Yang notes that you can borrow a DVD from the campus DVD rental shop and then decide that you want to keep it. Yin replies that the two cases are different because the DVD shop has this policy, but the library does not sell books. Yang asks if the librarian hands her a book and she walks away intending to borrow it, would it still not count as borrowing unless the library staff also understood themselves as lending the book to her? Yin replies that he supposes so. Yang asks how it is possible for her to return a book that she did not borrow when the lender does not know about the intention for her to return it for Yin. She wants to know if she is borrowing the book from Yin to return it to the library? Yin replies that he'll take the book to the library himself.

One disadvantage to ethnomethodology is that it can be somewhat annoying for study participants. However, Yang's point in the exercise was not to get out of returning the book but rather to uncover the rich pattern of presupposed understanding necessary for Yin and Yang to successfully communicate about the returning of the book and also to successfully complete the action of returning the book (one way or the other). This pattern of intersubjectively shared understandings constitutes the lifeworld that serves as the object of inquiry for much qualitative research, in contrast to the physical location of the book or Yin's ability to recall the due date as recorded in the library's electronic database as objective facts about the world. In one view of the matter, natural sciences study facts about the objective world, whereas social sciences study shared understandings about the lifeworld. Quantitative methods have often been viewed as natural science methods, whereas qualitative methods have been viewed as social science methods—or at least the methods of interpretive social science.

Bridging the Divide

Habermas (2005) has presented a subtle but important argument that bridges the traditional divide between our understanding of the objective world and the lifeworld. This argument applies quite directly to the understanding of the relationship between qualitative and quantitative methods. Habermas does not discuss methodology in the social and behavioral sciences, so the remainder of this chapter first explains the relevant aspects of Habermas's argument and then applies the argument to the use of qualitative and quantitative methods in research on intimate partner violence.

Habermas (2005) summarizes his argument as follows: "Because (a) the concept of experience is understood pragmatically, (b) knowledge is seen as a function of learning processes, which (c) are enriched by the entire spectrum of lifeworld practices; (d) this gives rise to an architectonic of lifeworld and objective world, which (e) corresponds to a methodological dualism of understanding [*Verstehen*] and observation" (12). After reading that summary twice, Yang wishes that she had taken Yin's book to the library instead of going back to her dorm room to read Habermas. So, what does it mean? Let's take it one step at a time.

To understand what Habermas means by understanding experience pragmatically, one needs to have something with which to contrast that point. Kant (1878/2003) argued very influentially that experience involves both the objective world that one experiences and also the structuring properties built into the minds with which one experiences the world. Kant understood certain features of how one experiences things, such as time, space, and causation, as hardwired into people from the start and thus transcending all experience. One might learn through experience that trees generally come in larger sizes than bushes, but the experience of trees and bushes in terms of size reflects a property of how all people experience things that transcends all experience, because it reflects the cognitive structure of how people experience the world.

When Habermas describes experience as pragmatic, he means that one cannot sustain the view that personal introspective access to experience provides a foundation for understanding. Yang cannot look at Yin's library book and trust that she has a complete understanding of how she experiences that book in light of the fixed forms of human perception. Instead, her experience of the book takes place within the context of efforts to accomplish tasks, such as Yin's effort to return to the book to the library and the more stable social practices that develop around them. These social structures of the lifeworld do not determine experience. The book will not return itself to the library even if Yin comes to believe this as the result of a social milieu that supports this belief. Likewise, some imaginable norms cannot attain socially sustainability (Harre and Gillett, 1994) because they defy the flow of information (e.g., requiring borrowers to return books before someone else asks to borrow them) or because they are too complex (books due as many minutes before sundown as the square root of the number of days since the last solstice or equinox times pi rounded to the nearest 693 milliseconds except on Fridays, when due times follow the Fourier sequence described on the library web page). However, neither does the structure of experience represent a fixed and immutable part of the human condition unaffected by context and history. Failures, like library fines, serve to shape the lifeworld through the efforts of individuals to cope with the objective environment from within that shared lifeworld.

This shift in perspective from how Kant understood perception to the understanding of it available today shifts with it the understanding of the objects of perception. Instead of simply understanding why people perceive the cover of the library book as red or the weight of the book as heavy, one also needs to understand how people experience transactions involving the library book within social practices that support lending, borrowing, using, returning, and so on. These are normative practices that extend beyond the mere description of behaviors to include mutual understandings of what counts as successful completion of a task and what people should do under various circumstances. Such norms and understandings make up an important part of the shared lifeworld.

So, it appears that the objective world shapes the lifeworld, because people develop norms and practices to cope with the contingencies of the objective world. At the same time, the lifeworld shapes every perception and interaction with the objective world because humans have no experience outside of the social context of shared norms and understandings that shape all experience. Knowledge always involves a three-way relationship between the objective world, the knower, and the people with whom the knower communicates that knowledge. For example, for Yin to succeed in asking Yang to return the library book, Yin needs to communicate to Yang the objective identity of the book in question so that Yang can recognize and return the correct book. This involves both the perception of the objective word, for instance, perceiving the cover as red, but also the pattern of norms and shared understandings by which people communicate about such matters. A change in either the color of the book or the shared practices by which Yin and Yang communicate about color could foil Yin's efforts to ask Yang to return the book.

As such, one cannot understand the properties perceived as redness nor the norms and practices surrounding color talk, or library talk, as basic and fundamental to the other. Instead, the fundamental interaction between the two forms the primary basis for knowledge. One can understand the perception of the objective world only within the guiding structures of the lifeworld and one can understand the norms and practices of the lifeworld only in relation to people's interactions with the objective world. The two are interwoven and mutually sustaining. Consequently, Yin cannot successfully measure and study the objective aspects of human life without understanding how the norms and practices of the lifeworld shape those objective aspects. Likewise, Yang cannot successfully investigate and describe the norms and practices of the lifeworld without understanding how the objective aspects of the world shape these aspects of the lifeworld.

Qualitative and Quantitative Methods in Intimate Partner Violence Research

Suppose that Yin and Yang share an interest in decisions by female victims of intimate partner violence about whether or not to leave the abusive relationship. Yin might gather data on a handful of predictive variables and one or more outcome variables for many more women than variables and use a logistic regression model to predict which women tend to leave relationships and which do not. For instance, women with an alternative support system may be more likely to leave an abusive relationship. On this approach, leaving a relationship and the various predictors are objective characteristics of the women whom Yin can measure. Likewise, the relationships between the various predictors and the outcomes are objective characteristics of social reality that can be studied and recorded objectively.

Yang might instead interview thirty or forty women in depth about their decisions, beginning the interviews with some standard questions or topics but allowing each interview to develop in a direction influenced by the participant and the unique aspects of the participant's decision. As a first pass at the data, Yang might go through verbatim transcriptions of the interviews to look for themes that repeat across questions and across participants. A more theoretical analysis might then begin with looking for broader narrative forms on which the women draw in organizing their answers and describing their situation. Yang might then explore specific points of content found in the common themes in relation to which types of narratives emphasize or minimize which kinds of content. Next, Yang might look at elements of the discourse of the women that appear to borrow from or be shaped by their partner's discourse (e.g., rationalizing abusive behavior). Finally, Yang might consider the social norms of question-answer exchanges and how they influence her interaction with the participants and their constraints within which they form and justify their answers to her questions. In various ways, each of these analyses get at characteristics of the shared lifeworld, articulating norms and shared understandings and relating them to how women understand and enact their choices about leaving an abusive relationship.

Given the traditional bifurcation between qualitative and quantitative research, Yin and Yang might not review any of the same literature, publish their research in the same outlet, or even know about each other's work. Yang might seek moral support in commiserating with fellow qualitative researchers about being excluded from publication outlets dominated by quantitative research, while Yin might feel exasperated with having his work dismissed as positivist by disdainful qualitative researchers. However, the argument canvassed earlier suggests that this traditional separation rests on antiquated philosophical premises. Let's look a little more closely at Yin's and Yang's research projects.

Yin wants to measure, as one outcome, choices to leave an abusive relationship, and he collects this information using a survey. This research procedure involves two sets of interactions regarding the characteristics that he seeks to measure. First, he interacts, albeit remotely, with the participants by asking them questions through the survey. As such, the psychometric aspects of the survey involve a form of question-and-answer dialogue between the researcher and the respondent. Part of the psychometric qualities of the survey involves the process through which Yin and the respondents achieve sufficiently shared understandings that Yin can confidently interpret the results of the survey. For example, Yin needs to establish through his survey a common frame of reference regarding what counts as leaving a relationship. If different respondents understand this phrase differently and apply it differently in reporting their own situations, then this lack of shared understanding translates into measurement error that reduces the accuracy of quantitative research findings. The second interaction involves Yin's interaction with his audience of readers and reviewers as he reports the results of his research and has to justify his knowledge claims to his audience in a way that they will accept. Yin needs to demonstrate that he collected the data appropriately to minimize sources of bias and rule out rival interpretations of the data and that he analyzed the data in a way that appropriately provides support for the substantive conclusions. These practices of communication and justification all involve social norms that govern the lifeworld shared by the behavioral science community. So, Yin's research doubly rests on the shared cognition of leaving relationships, shared first as his respondents communicate to him through the norms and understandings of the survey process, and shared again as he communicates to his readers through the norms and understandings of quantitative research reporting.

Yang wants to gather data that offers insight into the lifeworld of women making decisions about whether or not to leave an abusive relationship. So, her emphasis already lies with the lifeworld of norms and practices that shape the women's lives and options. However, her research also involves the threefold relation described by Habermas. The use of language between she and her participants, both to convey information and accomplish tasks, never amounts to a purely formal exercise of symbol manipulation within the norms of the lifeworld. Instead, the norms are put to use to communicate things about the objective world and to accomplish things in the objective world. When a participant reports that she has left an abusive relationship, she wants Yang to believe that she has left the relationship and not merely understand that she believes this. The respondent wants to communicate to Yang an objective fact about the world and also wants to accomplish the task of informing Yang about this fact. One cannot properly understand either the communication or the performative action as entirely internal to the norms and practices that constitute the lifeworld. Each makes use of those norms and practices to interact with the objective world.

Both Yin's and Yang's research, then, involves the threefold relationship between individuals communicating with one another and the world about which they communicate. Both Yin's survey and Yang's interviews involve communication with the participants about their decisions. Both draw on the communicative resources of the shared lifeworld to structure and facilitate that communication. Both involve norms of asking and answering. Both make use of shared cultural and linguistic resources to effectively communicate questions and interpret answers. Both make use of answers to gain knowledge about women's decisions regarding leaving or remaining in abusive relationships. Both will report their research in a way that seeks to convey this knowledge to others.

Yin's research adviser might object to this characterization of Yin's research. She might object that the variables all have operational definitions and that the rules of scientific method and reporting all have reasons behind them; they are not arbitrary conventions. Yin's adviser might express concern that this characterization undermines the objective basis of behavioral science research or characterizes the conclusions as arbitrary or a matter of preference. Yang's research adviser might also object to the characterization of Yang's research. He might object that the nature of leaving a relationship constitutes a social construct that can mean entirely different things depending on the discourses in play. A victim could truthfully claim that they had left a relationship while their abusive partner denies it, and both could make these contradictory claims in good faith and with good justification based on their understanding of what it means to leave a relationship. Yang's adviser may express concern that to assert that some overriding truth of the matter exists that can be known or measured mischaracterizes the nature of socially constructed phenomena.

Yin and Yang would do well to acknowledge an element of legitimate concern in their advisers' objections. However, these stem from the traditional separation of qualitative and quantitative methods and its effects. After reading Habermas together, Yin and Yang are in a good position to allay their advisers' concerns. The key point for both Yin and Yang boils down to the idea that social construction does not impugn the reality of the product of social construction (Hacking, 2000). Yin might emphasize that the social processes involved in cognition and justification of knowledge claims provide the means to learning about the objective world, not an impediment to it. Yang might emphasize that the viability of different sets of norms governing different discourses and different social constructions depends on the use of those norms, discourses, and social constructions to successfully talk about things, communicate, and complete actions using language. Without the referential function of language, different discourses would collapse into one undifferentiated hollow language game with no semantic underpinning. In the process, both underline the threefold relationship between the speaker, the objective reality communicated about, and the listener.

One can multiply examples with little difficulty. Archival data represents facts about the history of the research participant (perhaps without active participation), but social norms of the lifeworld play a role in the generation of the archival records and the processes of coding them into data, interpreting the data, and reporting research findings. Studies that rely on life-history data to capture and investigate the lived experience of intimate partner violence victims seek to communicate findings to their readership that they want readers to take as veridical and not just as reports of beliefs. Moreover, they use methodologies to collect, analyze, and report life histories that remain open to professional criticism and justification by other researchers knowledgeable in life-history methods, and such critique would have no grounding without some connection to objective reality beyond the lifeworld. Randomized controlled trials aimed at estimating the causal effect of treatment interventions for victims of intimate partner violence seek to estimate those objective effects on the basis of socially developed and maintained norms for such practices. Qualitative methods that explore meanings and norms involved in the process of recovery presuppose factual causal effects that the mechanisms create. Evaluation of various means of reaching intimate partner violence victims rests on an assumption that as a matter of fact some methods work better than others but also that they work through the existing norms and practices of the shared lifeworld. If those norms and practices changed, they might change the criteria of effectiveness, the effectiveness itself, or both. In every case, the threefold relationship between the learner, objective reality, and the interlocutor appears in various forms. The traditionally quantitative emphasis on measuring objective reality and the traditionally qualitative emphasis on understanding the lifeworld both rest on this threefold relation in which both objective reality and the lifeworld play an essential role. Like Yin and Yang, all quantitative research depends on a qualitative element and all qualitative research depends on a quantitative element.

Conclusion

A review of the literature on intimate partner violence and domestic violence demonstrates some interesting patterns. For example, the lion's share of research on IPV uses quantitative methods, followed by qualitative methods. Mixed methods remain relatively rare. Quantitative methods break into distinct categories, with those using descriptive statistics sharing only some characteristics more in common with qualitative research than inferential quantitative research.

The literature on intimate partner violence and domestic violence displays a division between qualitative and quantitative methods characteristic of many areas of research. Consideration of an argument from Habermas (2005) undermines the bases for this radical division between the two types of methods. The basis for the underlying unity between them rests with the threefold relationship between the cognizer, objective reality, and the interlocutor. Access to objective reality comes only through the intersubjective lifeworld, and understanding of the intersubjective lifeworld comes only through mutual cognition of objective reality. As such, qualitative and quantitative mechanisms each drink from the same trough. Rather than emphasizing their differences, emphasis on this underlying unity between the two types of methods can help bridge the divide between the two schools of research. That can result, in turn, in a more unified and productive research literature.

Appendix

Table 10.1 Methodological approach

Method of inquiry	2008–12 total (%, n)	2009–12 total (%, n)
Qualitative	14.32 (58)	17.95 (79)
Descriptive	4.20 (17)	—
Inferential	78.52 (318)	—
Quantitative	82.72 (335)	80.00 (352)
Mixed	2.96 (12)	2.05 (9)
Total	100.00 (405)	100.00 (440)

Note: Different categories were used for the 2003–8 and 2009–12 databases. The categories for the years 2003–8 were qualitative, descriptive, inferential, and mixed, and those for 2009–12 were qualitative, quantitative, mixed, and borderline.

Table 10.2 Sample and study characteristics

Variable Characteristics	2003–8 total (%, n)	2009–12 total (%, n)
Female	59.01 (239)	51.14 (225)
Male	8.40 (34)	12.04 (53)
Matched	5.68 (23)	8.64 (38)
Unmatched	23.95 (97)	13.18 (58)
Child/Parent	1.98 (8)	10.68 (47)
Child/Unknown	0.99 (4)	4.32 (19)
Population type		
Survivor	32.18 (130)	15.23 (67)
Batterer	9.90 (40)	3.64 (16)
College student	4.95 (20)	6.14 (27)
Random/Representative	21.29 (86)	4.77 (21)
Service provider	17.57 (71)	21.82 (96)
Community	8.42 (34)	22.27 (98)
High risk/Vulnerable	5.69 (23)	4.55 (20)
Mentally ill	0.0 (0)	6.14 (27)
Multiple	0.0 (0)	6.59 (29)
Unknown	0.0 (0)	1.59 (7)
Other	0.0 (0)	7.27 (32)

Note: The categories for the years 2003–8 initially included mentally ill, multiple, unknown, and other.

Table 10.3a Sample gender (2003–2008 data)

Gender	Qualitative (%, n)	Descriptive (%, n)	Inferential (%, n)	Mixed methods (%, n)	Total (%, n)
Female	75.86 (44)	52.94 (9)	55.98 (178)	66.67 (8)	59.01 (239)
Male	3.45 (2)	5.88 (1)	9.75 (31)	0.00 (0)	8.40 (34)
Matched	1.72 (1)	0.00 (0)	6.60 (21)	8.33 (1)	5.68 (23)
Unmatched	13.79 (8)	35.30 (6)	25.16 (80)	25.00 (3)	23.95 (97)
Child/Parent	0.00 (0)	5.88 (1)	2.20 (7)	0.00 (0)	1.98 (8)
Child/Unknown	5.17 (3)	0.00 (0)	0.31 (1)	0.00 (0)	0.99 (4)
Total	100.00 (58)	100.00 (17)	100.00 (318)	100.00 (12)	100.00 (405)

Table 10.3b Sample gender (2009–2012 data)

Gender	Qualitative (%, n)	Quantitative (%, n)	Mixed methods (%, n)	Total (%, n)
Female	60.76 (48)	48.58 (171)	66.67 (6)	51.14 (225)
Male	11.39 (9)	11.65 (41)	33.33 (3)	12.05 (53)
Matched	2.53 (2)	10.23 (36)	0.00 (0)	8.64 (38)
Unmatched	8.86 (7)	14.49 (51)	0.00 (0)	13.18 (58)
Child/Parent	5.06 (4)	12.22 (43)	0.00 (0)	10.68 (47)
Child/Unknown	11.39 (9)	2.84 (10)	0.00 (0)	4.32
Total	100.00 (79)	100.00 (352)	100.00 (9)	100.00 (440)

Table 10.4a Sample race (2003–2008 data)

Race	Qualitative (%, n)	Descriptive (%, n)	Inferential (%, n)	Mixed methods (%, n)	Total (%, n)
White	8.62 (5)	5.88 (1)	2.21 (7)	8.33 (1)	3.47 (14)
African American	8.62 (5)	5.88 (1)	5.99 (19)	16.67 (2)	6.68 (27)
Hispanic	10.34 (6)	5.88 (1)	3.47 (11)	0.00 (0)	4.46 (18)
Asian	1.72 (1)	0.00 (0)	1.89 (6)	25.00 (3)	2.48 (10)
Mixed race	39.66 (23)	70.59 (12)	62.78 (199)	16.67 (2)	58.42 (236)
Other	3.45 (2)	0.00 (0)	0.63 (2)	0.00 (0)	0.99 (4)
International	18.97 (11)	5.88 (1)	12.93 (41)	16.67 (2)	13.61 (55)
Unspecified/ Unknown	8.62 (5)	5.88 (1)	10.09 (32)	16.67 (2)	9.90 (40)
Total	100.00 (58)	100.00 (17)	100.00 (317)	100.00 (12)	100.00 (404)

Table 10.4b Sample race (2009–2012 data)

Race	Qualitative (%, n)	Quantitative (%, n)	Mixed methods (%, n)	Total (%, n)
White	5.06 (4)	4.83 (17)	0.00 (0)	4.77 (21)
African American	3.80 (3)	6.25 (22)	11.11 (1)	5.91 (26)
Hispanic	8.86 (7)	5.11 (18)	22.22 (2)	6.14 (27)
Asian	5.06 (4)	3.41 (12)	0.00 (0)	3.64 (16)
Mixed	21.52 (17)	48.86 (172)	11.11 (1)	43.18 (190)
Other	3.80 (3)	2.56 (9)	0.00 (0)	2.73 (12)
International	20.25 (16)	15.06 (53)	22.22 (2)	16.14 (71)
Unspecified/ Unknown	31.65 (25)	13.92 (49)	33.33 (3)	17.50 (77)
Total	100.00 (79)	100.00 (352)	100.00 (9)	100.00 (440)

Table 10.5a Sample population type (2003–2008 data)

Population type	Qualitative (%, n)	Descriptive (%, n)	Inferential (%, n)	Mixed methods (%, n)	Total (%, n)
Survivor	56.1	58.83 (10)	26.73 (85)	25.00 (3)	32.18 (130)
Batterer	4 (32)	5.88 (1)	11.32 (36)	8.33 (1)	9.90 (40)
College student	3.51 (2)	0.00 (0)	6.29 (20)	0.00 (0)	4.95 (20)
Random/ Representative	0.00 (0)	23.53 (4)	25.47 (81)	0.00 (0)	21.29 (86)
Service provider	1.75 (1)	5.88 (1)	17.61 (56)	33.33 (4)	17.57 (71)
Community	17.54 (10)	5.88 (1)	6.29 (20)	16.67 (2)	8.42 (34)
High risk/ Vulnerable	19.30 (11) 1.75 (1)	0.00 (0)	6.29 (20)	16.67 (2)	5.69 (23)
Total	100.00 (57)	100.00 (17)	100.00 (318)	100.00 (12)	100.00 (404)

Table 10.5b Sample population type (2009–2012 data)

Population type	Qualitative (%, n)	Quantitative (%, n)	Mixed methods (%, n)	Total (%, n)
Survivor	26.58 (21)	12.50 (44)	22.22 (2)	15.23 (67)
Batterer	5.06 (4)	3.41 (12)	0.00 (0)	3.64 (16)
College student	2.53 (2)	7.10 (25)	0.00 (0)	6.14 (27)
Random/ Representative	0.00 (0)	5.97 (21)	0.00 (0)	4.77 (21)
Service provider	32.91 (26)	19.60 (69)	11.11 (1)	21.82 (96)
Community	12.66 (10)	24.43 (86)	22.22 (2)	22.27 (98)
High risk/Vulnerable	2.53 (2)	4.83 (17)	11.11 (1)	4.55 (20)
Mentally ill	6.33 (5)	5.97 (21)	11.11 (1)	6.14 (27)
Multiple	5.06 (4)	6.82 (24)	11.11 (1)	6.59 (29)
Unknown	3.80 (3)	1.14 (4)	0.00 (0)	1.59 (7)
Unique communities	1.27 (1)	2.84 (10)	0.00 (0)	2.50 (11)
Other	1.27 (1)	5.40 (19)	11.11 (1)	4.77 (21)
Total	100.00 (79)	100.00 (352)	100.00 (9)	100.00 (440)

Table 10.6 Data collection strategies

Data collection	Qualitative (%, n)	Descriptive (%, n)	Inferential (%, n)	Mixed methods (%, n)	Total (%, n)
Face-to-face interview	31.03 (18)	5.88 (1)	26.10 (83)	8.33 (1)	25.43 (103)
Telephone interview	0.00 (0)	5.88 (1)	6.60 (21)	0.00 (0)	5.43 (22)
Focus group or group discussion	18.97 (11)	0.00 (0)	0.31 (1)	8.33 (1)	3.21 (13)
Unspecified interview	34.48 (20)	5.88 (1)	2.20 (7)	8.33 (1)	7.16 (29)
Self-report survey	0.00 (0)	5.88 (1)	17.61 (56)	8.33 (1)	14.32 (58)
Mail or Internet survey	0.00 (0)	0.00 (0)	2.52 (8)	0.00 (0)	1.98 (8)
Unspecified survey	0.00 (0)	5.88 (1)	7.55 (24)	0.00 (0)	6.17 (25)
Mixed interview	13.79 (8)	0.00 (0)	1.57 (5)	8.33 (1)	3.46 (14)
Mixed survey	0.00 (0)	0.00 (0)	1.57 (5)	0.00 (0)	1.23 (5)
Mixed interview and survey	0.00 (0)	5.88 (1)	11.32 (36)	50.00 (6)	10.62 (43)
Archival	1.72 (1)	47.06 (8)	19.50 (62)	8.33 (1)	17.78 (72)
Clinical data	0.00 (0)	17.65 (3)	2.83 (9)	0.00 (0)	2.96 (12)
Unknown	0.00 (0)	0.00 (0)	0.31 (1)	0.00 (0)	0.25 (1)
Total	100.00 (58)	100.00 (17)	100.00 (318)	100.00 (12)	100.00 (405)

Table 10.7 Type of research question (2003–2008 data)

Research question	Qualitative (%, n)	Descriptive (%, n)	Inferential (%, n)	Mixed methods (%, n)	Total (%, n)
Prevalence	34.48 (20)	29.41 (5)	12.26 (39)	16.67 (2)	16.30 (66)
Resource	39.66 (23)	35.29 (6)	16.98 (54)	16.67 (2)	20.99 (85)
Measurement	1.72 (1)	5.88 (1)	11.01 (35)	25.00 (3)	9.88 (40)
Mediating	6.90 (4)	0.00 (0)	3.46 (11)	8.33 (1)	3.95 (16)
Risk	3.45 (2)	0.00 (0)	11.95 (38)	0.00 (0)	9.88 (40)
Health	6.90 (4)	5.88 (1)	27.99 (89)	33.33 (4)	24.20 (98)
Other	6.90 (4)	23.53 (4)	16.35 (52)	0.00 (0)	14.81 (60)
Total	100.00 (58)	100.00 (17)	100.00 (318)	100.00 (12)	100.00 (405)

References

Garfinkel, H. (1967). *Studies in ethnomethodology.* Upper Saddle River, NJ: Prentice Hall.

Habermas, J. (2005). *Truth and justification.* Cambridge, MA: MIT Press.

Hacking, I. (2000). *The social construction of what?* Cambridge, MA: Harvard University Press.

Harré, R., and Gillett, G. (1994). *The discursive mind.* Thousand Oaks, CA: Sage.

Kant, I. (1878/2003). *Critique of pure reason* (N. Kemp Smith, Trans.). Hampshire, UK: Palgrave Macmillan. (Original text published 1878).

Kondo, D. (1990). *Crafting selves: Power, gender, and discourses of identity in a Japanese workplace.* Chicago: University of Chicago Press.

Shuki J. Cohen

Domestic Violence Methodologies
Closing Comments

Thus far, the modus operandi of this book has been to present the reader with individual studies and generalize their findings to better understand the phenomenon of intimate partner violence. To take a larger perspective, the commentaries following each chapter contrasted studies that touched on the same phenomenon using different methods. This last chapter takes the perspective angle a notch wider, to rigorously examine the methodological and publication trends, preferences, and biases as they manifest in the "real world" of available data to researchers. This bibliometric approach to intimate partner violence research is uniquely capable of tapping hidden biases that cannot be gleaned from individual studies.

For example, one hidden bias that can be tapped using bibliometric analysis is the phenomenon known in cognitive science as "experimenter bias," or searching-for-the-penny-under-the-lamppost bias. Thus, Markus and others find a tendency for qualitative studies to preferentially study minority populations, whereas quantitative studies included both groups. One reason for this is perhaps because quantitative studies assume that we share core universal values and properties and any difference between groups can be explained by variations in these universals. However, qualitative research seeks to understand why this is the case and what it means to the stakeholder. If two bodies of research have such different research and foci, can we ever adequately align or reconcile this qualitative body of literature with the findings of quantitative studies, even if the research questions are similar? Can the two bodies of literature ever cohabit our understanding of intimate partner violence?

Contrary to adversarial views that see the quantitative and qualitative approaches to intimate partner violence as opposing each other, Markus and others advocate embracing the use of contradictory data as the strategy of choice for building a richer understanding of intimate partner violence—rather than privileging one or the other. In supporting this position, Markus and others provide both empirical and theoretical rationales. Empirically, they show that independent coding of the methodology as used in a large representative sample of published studies reveals that most of them use both qualitative and quantitative methods implicitly but mostly report results that conform to one approach. Philosophically, Markus and others point out that postmodern approaches to knowledge no longer accept observations independently of their observers—on their stance and assumptions. In this sense, postmodern approaches to scientific data seem to have rediscovered the moral of the ancient Indian allegory of six blind men who mistake their particular experience of different parts of an elephant for the definitive representation of an elephant. Markus and others remind us that this state of affairs is hardly confined to intimate partner violence research. Rather, studies across the social sciences, and especially those that use ethnomethodology and linguistics to tap the dual implicit and explicit aspects of cognition and experience, usually report low to no correlations between their measures (Bosson et al., 2000; Gawronski and De Houwer, in press)—with few exceptions (e.g., Cohen, 2011, 2012).

Markus and others' findings can further demonstrate the utility of the perspective afforded by bibliometric analysis in pointing to a potential rift between the circles of readerships that may be accessing quantitative and qualitative data. Thus, they show that even though many studies use de facto mixed methods, quantitative studies are not likely to publish qualitative data in their report, and qualitative studies are not likely to publish quantitative data—not even on a descriptive statistics level. This makes for a state of affairs in which the two approaches may be publishing for different readerships and hence would likely appear in different journals. In doing so, this publication pattern may inadvertently contribute to the exacerbation of the metaphorical blindness of the six men in the ancient Indian allegory mentioned above. Consequently, even the enlightened researcher who wishes to integrate findings from various sources would be hard-pressed to find a common denominator between them to do so.

How might future research shrink this chasm? One possibility would be for authors to present both quantitative and qualitative data, however potentially contradictory, in their manuscripts. Another complementary possibility would be for scientific journals to become more inclusive and inter- or transdisciplinary in their publication pattern and err on the side of educating their readership and "nudging" them to branch outside their disciplinary comfort zone rather than cater to said readership's niche bubble.

However, not all the reasons for this chasm within the discipline of intimate partner violence research are rational, and we would be remiss not to remind the reader of the myriad ways in which quantitative research has been (and, unfortunately, sometime is still) used to marginalize women and minorities. Taking these politico-emotional considerations into account may render Markus and others' findings crucially instructive to the field. Thus, the partiality of qualitative studies toward marginalized communities can be seen as an attempt to bring to light their experience in their own voice rather than foist on them potentially prejudicial assumptions that originated in the hegemonic scientific community. Similarly, the partiality of quantitative studies toward neat study designs that simplify measurement schemes and use relatively homogenous population samples in the name of boosting their impartiality, reliability, and reproducibility has become increasingly suspect due to its potential (and, sadly, track record) in marginalizing women and minorities.

In the future of intimate partner violence research, employing Markus and others' two main points—that most studies use de facto mixed method schemes and that contradictory results from qualitative and quantitative designs can only boost our understanding rather than detract from it—may provide us with a template not only for a better research in intimate partner violence but arguably also for a better world.

References

Bosson, J. K., Swann, W.B., and Pennebaker, J. W. (2000). Stalking the perfect measure of implicit self-esteem: The blind men and the elephant revisited? *Journal of Personality and Social Psychology, 79,* 631–643.

Cohen, S. J. (2011). Measurement of negativity bias in personal narratives using corpus-based emotion dictionaries. *Journal of Psycholinguistics Research, 40*(2), 119–135.

Cohen, S. J. (2012). Construction and preliminary validation of a dictionary for cognitive rigidity: Linguistic markers of overconfidence and overgeneralization and their concomitant psychological distress. *Journal of Psycholinguistic Research, 41,* 347–370.

Gawronski, B., and De Houwer, J. (in press). Implicit measures in social and personality psychology. In H. T. Reis, and C. M. Judd (Eds.), *Handbook of research methods in social and personality psychology* (2nd ed.). New York: Cambridge University Press.

Index

ACS (Administration for Children's Services), New York City, 176

action research, 171–95; advantages and pitfalls of, 172–73, 179, 188, 193–95; commentary on, 224–27; contextual versus individualized view of domestic violence, 171–72; human rights violation, treating domestic violence as, 171–72, 173, 224; mixed methodology, use of, 224–25; relationship between researcher and participants, 183–86, 226–27; retraumatization resulting from, 173, 179, 186–92, 225; symbolization and ability to construct narrative, impact of trauma on, 181–83; theoretical foundations of, 173–74, 178–81, 225; trust in fellow survivors, 192–93; VOW family court research project, 173, 174–78, 194

Administration for Children's Services (ACS), New York City, 176

Adorno, Theodor, 48

advanced questions: criminal justice system and domestic violence, 228–29; defining and measuring domestic violence, 50; gender and domestic violence, 125; same-sex domestic violence, 167; survivors of domestic violence, 228–29

AFDC (Aid to Families with Dependent Children), 207, 218

African Americans and domestic violence, 107–8, 112–13, 121–22, 131. *See also* culture and ethnicity

Aid to Families with Dependent Children (AFDC), 207, 218

Alarcón, N., 182–83

Allen, Nicole E., 45, 102, 117, 121–22, 124

Amnesty International, 171

analysis of variance (ANOVA), 21

Anderson, Edward R., 43, 53, 117, 124

Anderson, K. L., 104, 105, 106, 121

ANOVA (analysis of variance), 21

antisocial personality disorder, 28

Archer, J., 85

Asian cultures, domestic violence in, 12, 131. *See also* culture and ethnicity

athletes, gender, and violence, 113

Atkinson, M. P., 109

authority subscale, Dominance Scale study, 17*t*, 19, 21, 22–23

automated telephonic data collection, 11

Balsam, K. F., 154

Baraitser, L., 181

Barberet, R., 234

battered mothers and their children: child custody issues, 54, 55, 56, 61, 63, 74, 80, 118, 176, 177, 189, 200, 224, 225; child support issues, 80, 176; family court decisions endangering children, 176; foster care, 176, 201, 202, 211–12; parental alienation, 177. See also *State of Connecticut v. Lavonne L.* case study

battered woman syndrome, 215–16

Battered Women's Resource Center (BWRC), New York City, 173, 174

Beck, Connie J. A., 43, 53, 117, 124

Benedict, J., 113

Bhabha, H., 182–83

bibliometric (tabular) review of methodologies, 233–38, 247–53*t*, 254–55

Bion, W. R., 192

bisexuals. *See* same-sex domestic violence

Blay, E., 29

Bonferroni approach, 135

Brazil, perceptions of domestic violence in, 26–37; commentary on, 43–48; cultural and ethnic issues, 36–37, 45–46; gender aspects of, 28, 29, 35–36, 124–25; government recognition of domestic violence as problem, 26–28; methodology of study, 31–32, 162; participants in study, 31–32, 31*t*; preliminary categories and working definitions, 32–33; results and discussion, 33–37, 34*t*; statistics and data, 26, 28–31

British Object Relations, 179

BWRC (Battered Women's Resource Center), New York City, 173, 174

Campbell, J. C., 216

Canadian National Survey, 111

Castel, R., 27

Centers for Disease Control and Prevention (CDC), 142

children of battered mothers. *See* battered mothers and their children; *State of Connecticut v. Lavonne L.* case study

Coercive Control (Stark, 2007), 93

coercive control model of abuse: as alternative to violence paradigm, 81–84, 91–94, 97; in divorcing couples study, 60–61, 63, 64; in *State of Connecticut v. Lavonne L.* case study, 201–2, 216–21, 222

coercive controlling violence: in divorcing couples study, 60, 61, 63, 66–67*t*, 67–73, 69*f*, 70–71*t*, 72*f*; in *State of Connecticut v. Lavonne L.* case study, 217–19

Cohen, Shuki J., xi, 41, 117, 119*, 158, 224, 254

collateral report, 10

collective efficacy, 129–30

college students, urban, and same-sex dating violence. *See* neighborhood violence and same-sex dating abuse

common couple violence, 80–81

compensatory masculinity, violence as, 109

computerized data collection, 11

Conflict Tactics Scales (CTS), 9, 54, 58, 60–61

Connecticut Department of Children and Families (DCF), 200–201, 203, 210, 211–12, 214, 220, 221. See also *State of Connecticut v. Lavonne L.* case study

Connell, R. W., 96

construct, concept of, ix*, 4, 41

construct validity, 3, 16, 18

contextual view: of gender as ecological variable (*see* ecological variable, gender viewed as); of survivors and perpetrators of domestic violence, 171–72

convergent validity, 17

Cook, Sarah L., 3, 41–43, 46, 47, 49, 124

Cornell, D., 219

couple-level data, 54, 55

criminal justice system and domestic violence, viii; acts outside violence paradigm, 89–90; advanced questions, 228–29; commentary on, 224–29; critical-thinking questions, 228; episode-specific response, 90, 121; human rights violation, treating domestic violence as, 171–72, 173, 224; learning objectives, 169; "violence paradigm" of domestic violence and, 88. *See also* action research; battered mothers and their children; *State of Connecticut v. Lavonne L.* case study

critical-thinking questions: criminal justice system and domestic violence, 228; defining and measuring domestic violence, 49; gender and domestic violence, 124–25; same-sex domestic violence, 166–67; survivors of domestic violence, 228

Cronbach's alpha, 58, 64, 65*t*

CTS (Conflict Tactics Scales), 9, 54, 58, 60–61

CTS2 (Revised Conflict Tactics Scale), 134

culture and ethnicity: in Brazil, 36–37, 45–46; in contextual view of gender, 107–8; in defining and measuring domestic violence, 11–13, 26, 45–47; race and domestic violence, 107–8, 112–13, 121–22, 131; relationship to domestic violence, 29; in *State of Connecticut v. Lavonne L.* case study, 204, 205

"Culture of Violence," 60

"dangerousness assessment" scale, 216

Daniel L. *See State of Connecticut v. Lavonne L.* case study

DataSenado, 30

dating violence. *See* domestic violence

Davies, J. M., 188

Davis, Shara, 102, 117, 124

DCF (Connecticut Department of Children and Families), 200–201, 203, 210, 211–12, 214, 220, 221. See also *State of Connecticut v. Lavonne L.* case study

De Oliveira Gaioli, C. C. L., 30

deficit model, 118

defining and measuring domestic violence, viii, 3–24; advanced questions, 50; "coercive control" paradigm for, 91–93; commentary on, 41–48; constructs, variables, and operational definitions, 4–8, 41–42; critical-thinking questions, 49; culture and ethnicity, role of, 11–13, 26, 45–47; incidence, prevalence, and frequency rates, 8; IPV (interpersonal violence) generally, embedding of domestic violence within, 34–35, 43–46; lack of consensus regarding definition, 88; learning objectives, 1; modes of measurement, 10–11; neighborhood violence, network violence and same-sex

dating violence, measures of, 133–34; scales of measurement, 8–10; scope of measurement, 13–14; violence, defined, 26, 27; "violence paradigm" for, 82–84, 87–90. *See also* Brazil, perceptions of domestic violence in; Dominance Scale study

DeKeseredy, Walter S., 112

Dempsey, Michele, 84, 217

Deslandes, S. F., 30

dichotomous scales of partner violence, 8–9

differential validity, 21

DiFulvio, Gloria T., 122, 142, 159, 160, 161–64, 167

disparagement subscale, Dominance Scale study, 17*t*, 18, 20, 21, 23

divorcing couples studies, 53–75; broad range of abuse behaviors, 54, 60–73, 65–67*t*, 68–69*f*, 70–71*t*, 72*f*; commentary on, 117–21; couple-level data, 54, 55; court-mandated divorce mediation, participants involved in, 55–56, 58; lower-level acts of physical abuse, 53, 54–60, 57*t*, 59*f*; measures of violence (broad range of abuse behaviors, typology of, 60–64; lower-level acts of physical abuse, 58); methodology and participants (broad range of abuse behaviors, 64, 65*t*; lower-level acts of physical abuse, 56–58, 57*t*); patterns of domestic violence in, 72*f*, 74; results and discussion, 73–75 (broad range of abuse behaviors, 65–67*t*, 65–73, 68–69*f*, 70–71*t*, 72*f*; lower-level acts of physical abuse, 58–60, 59*f*)

Domestic Abuse Intervention Project, Duluth, Minnesota, 93

domestic violence, vii–xi; criminal justice system and, viii (*see also* criminal justice system and domestic violence); debates regarding, viii–ix; defining and measuring, viii, 3–24(*see also* defining and measuring domestic violence); epistemologies informing views of,

45–46; gender and, viii, 79–98 (*see also* gender and domestic violence); methodological approaches to, vii–viii, 233–53 (*see also* quantitative, qualitative, and mixed methodologies); same-sex, viii (*see also* same-sex domestic violence); survivors of, viii (*see also* survivors of domestic violence; terms for, vii*)

Domestic Violence-Focused Couples Treatment (DVFCT) study, 15, 16, 21

dominance: in definition of domestic violence as coercive control, 91–92; as variable in studying domestic violence, 6

Dominance Scale study: administration, 23; authority subscale, 17t, 19, 21, 22–23; commentary on, 41–43, 46; disparagement subscale, 17t, 18, 20, 21, 23; jealousy in, 17t, 18; language issues, 13–14; marital satisfaction in, 17t, 18; negotiation tactics, 15, 18, 19t, 20t, 21–22; participants in study, 15–16; patterns of dominance between spouses, 21; pilot study, 14; psychometrics properties of, 15–18; relationship between dominance, violence perpetration, and victimization, 18–21, 19t, 20t; reliability and internal consistency, 16; reporting load management, 14; restrictiveness subscale, 17t, 18, 19, 20, 21, 22, 23; scoring, 23–24; summary of data, 21–22; validity of, 16–17, 17t, 21; variable, dominance as, 6

DVFCT (Domestic Violence-Focused Couples Treatment) study, 15, 16, 21

ecological variable, gender viewed as, 102–14; commentary on, 117, 121–22; individual-level versus ecological view of gender as variable, 104–7; interactionist and structuralist approaches, 104–7; intersection of gender with other social factors, 107–10; peer context, 109–13; social construction of gender and, 104; in survivor studies, 227, 228–29

Ellis, D., 61

Ellis, R., 60

Emerge (program for abusive men), Boston, 93

emotional abuse. *See* psychological abuse

entrapment, 82, 91, 95, 108, 121, 220–21

epistemologies informing views of domestic violence, x, 45–46

Equal Rights Amendment, US, 95

ethnicity. *See* culture and ethnicity

ethnomethdology, 239–40

experts and professionals: failure of professionals to address domestic violence in *State of Connecticut v. Lavonne L.* case study, 209–10, 211–13, 214, 215–16, 220, 222; relationship between researcher and participants in action research, 183–86, 226–27; role of domestic violence expert in *State of Connecticut v. Lavonne L.* case study, 227

external validity, 21

feminist theory: action research and, 173, 178–79, 180; on autonomous subject, 171, 172; coercive control and, 81; contextual view of gender in, 107; on gender and domestic violence generally, x, x–xi, 84*; positivism and, 167; on sexual inequality, gender, and domestic violence, 83–84, 95–98

Fine, M., 179

Fischer, K., 60

focus groups: action research and, 173, 174–75, 183, 187, 195, 225, 226, 228; chapter index of methodologies, xiii; defining and measuring domestic violence and, 14, 31; gender and domestic violence, studying, 122; as methodology, 161, 162; same-sex domestic violence and, 144–45, 159, 161, 162, 164, 166, 167; in tabular (bibliometric) review of methodologies, 252t

foster care for children of battered mothers, 176, 201, 202, 211–12

fraternity-validated gender norms, 111–12

intersection of gender with other social factors, 107–10

intimate partner abuse (IPA). *See* domestic violence

"intimate terrorism," 60, 80–81

IPA (intimate partner abuse). *See* domestic violence

IPV (interpersonal violence) generally, embedding of domestic violence within, 34–35, 43–46

Javdani, Shabnam, 102, 117, 124

jealousy, in Dominance Scale study, 17*t*, 18

Johnson, Michael P., 60, 61, 80–81, 94

Jones, A., 93

Jones, Cassandra A., 121, 129, 131, 138, 159–61, 163, 164, 166, 167

"Justice Denied: How Family Courts in NYC Endanger Battered Women and Children" (VOW and Human Rights Project of the Urban Justice Center), 175

Kant, Immanuel, 241

Kaplan, C., 182–83

Kim (action research participant), 188, 189, 190, 191, 193, 194

Kondo, D., 239

Lacan, J., 181

Lang, M. M., 109

Langhinrichsen-Rohling, J., 54, 97

latent class analysis, 65–66, 70–71*t*, 72*f*, 74, 119–20, 125

Lather, P., 180

Lavonne L. *See State of Connecticut v. Lavonne L.* case study

Lazenbatt, A., 30

"learned helplessness" theory of depression, 216

learning objectives: criminal justice system and domestic violence, 169; defining and measuring domestic violence, 1; gender and domestic violence, 51; same-sex

domestic violence, 127; survivors of domestic violence, 169

Lehrner, Amy, 102, 117, 124

lesbians. *See* same-sex domestic violence

Lewin, Jurt, 178

"liberty crime," coercive control as, 94

Likert scales, 10, 12, 13

Lob, Susan, 173, 183, 188, 191

Loveland, Jennifer E., 233

lower-level acts of physical abuse in divorcing couples, 53, 54–60, 57*t*, 59*f*

Maguire, P., 185

male peer support theory, 130–31

Mann-Whitney tests, 135

marital satisfaction in Dominance Scale study, 17*t*, 18

Markus, Keith A., 233, 254–56

Massachusetts Youth Risk Behavior Survey, 142

Massumi, B., 183

McCollum, Eric, 3, 41

McKay, H. D., 129

measuring domestic violence. *See* defining and measuring domestic violence

Medina-Ariza, J., 234

Mehne, Tasha, 3, 41, 49

men as perpetrators and victims. *See* gender and domestic violence

metasynthesis, xiii, 117, 125

methodologies. *See* quantitative, qualitative, and mixed methodologies

Miguel S. *See State of Connecticut v. Lavonne L.* case study

military, domestic violence in, 110–11

Miller, J., 112–13

Minayo, M. C. S., 28

minorities, racial, and domestic violence, 107–8, 112–13, 121–22, 131

minorities, sexual. *See* same-sex domestic violence

"minority stress," 154, 163–64

mixed methodologies. *See* quantitative, qualitative, and mixed methodologies

Moallem, M., 182–83

moral aggression, 33, 34*t,* 35, 47, 48

mothers and children. *See* battered mothers and their children; *State of Connecticut v. Lavonne L.* case study

Multi-Country Study on Women's Health and Domestic Violence against Women, 30

mutual violent control, 63

My Exposure to Violence Scale, 133

narrative, impact of trauma on ability to construct, 181–83

Nasio, J., 181

National Data and Statistics on the Family and Domestic Violence against Women, Brazil, 26

National Family Violence Surveys (NFVS), 84–85, 93–94

National Survey of Families and Households, 109

National Violence against Women Survey (NVAWS), 85, 86*

negotiation tactics, Dominance Scale study, 15, 18, 19*t,* 20*t,* 21–22

neighborhood violence and same-sex dating abuse, 129–39; commentary on, 159–61, 163, 164; effects of witnessing neighborhood violence, 129–31; literature review, 129–31; male peer support theory and, 130–31; measuring neighborhood violence, network violence, and dating violence, 133–34; methodology and participants, 132–34; proposed relationship between witnessing violence, network violence, and dating violence, 131–32, 132*f;* results and discussion, 134–39, 135*t,* 136*t,* 137*t*

network violence: male peer support theory and, 130–31; measuring, 133–34; proposed relationship between witnessing violence, network violence, and dating violence, 131–32, 132*f,* 138–39

NFVS (National Family Violence Surveys), 84–85, 93–94

nonpositivism, 42, 47

Nussbaum, Hedda, 201

NVAWS (National Violence against Women Survey), 85, 86*

Okun, D., 92

Oliver, K., 173, 186

operational definitions, 4, 41

Ortega, Ramona, 173, 175

Pan-American Health Organization (PAHO), 27

parental alienation, 177

participatory action research. *See* action research

Partner Abuse Scales, 58

partner violence. *See* domestic violence

patriarchy and patriarchal norms, 17, 21, 22, 110, 111, 112, 172, 174, 191

Patrice (action research participant), 188, 189, 193

peers and peer networks: gender, violence, and peer context, 109–13; male peer support theory, 130–31

Pence, Ellen, 93

personality disorders and domestic violence, 28

physical violence: in Brazilian study, 32–33, 37; in divorced couples studies, 66*t,* 67*t,* 68*f,* 70–71*t,* 72*f;* as domestic violence variable, 6–7; gender and. *See* gender and domestic violence; same-sex. *See* same-sex domestic violence; survivors of. *See* survivors of domestic violence

positivism, x, 41, 47, 166, 167, 243

postpositivism, x–xi, 46, 159

Power and Control Wheel, 81, 93

prevalence, incidence, and frequency rates, 8

professionals. *See* experts and professionals

psychoanalytic theory and action research, 173–74, 179–81, 225

psychological abuse: in Brazilian study, 32–33, 37; "coercive control" distinguished, 93; in divorced couples studies, 66*t,* 67*t,*

teenagers and same-sex dating violence. *See* youth same-sex dating violence

Tehee, Melissa, 43, 53, 117, 118–20, 121, 124, 167

Thereasa (action research participant), 189, 194

Thompson-Cree, M. E., 30

typologies of domestic violence, 60–64, 80–82, 119

unconscious, 173, 180–83

United Kingdom, domestic violence in, 79, 80*, 90

urban college students and same-sex dating violence. *See* neighborhood violence and same-sex dating abuse

Urban Justice Center, 175

variables, 4–8, 41–42. *See also* ecological variable, gender viewed as

VAWA (Violence against Women Act), US, 80

victims. *See* survivors of domestic violence

Vidmar, N., 60

Violence against Women Act (VAWA), US, 80

violence variables, 6–7

Voices of Women Organizing Project (VOW), New York City, 173, 174–78, 194

Volpp, L., 46

VOW (Voices of Women Organizing Project), New York City, 173, 174–78, 194

vulnerability, Castel's model of, 28

Walker, L., 215

WHO. *See* World Health Organization

Wilcox, P., 172, 194

women as perpetrators and victims. *See* gender and domestic violence

World Health Organization (WHO): Brazil, statistics and data on domestic violence in, 28, 30; first World Report on Violence and Health, 27

Yale Child Study Center, 203

Youth Risk Behavior Survey (YRBS), 142

youth same-sex dating violence, 142–55; assumed female connection and, 151–52, 154–55; commentary on, 159, 160, 161–64; definition of sexual minority youth, 144; effects of, 142–44; homophobia, societal and internalized, 143, 146–50, 153–54, 163; methodology and participants, 144–45; prevalence of, 142, 145–46, 153; relationship tensions and, 152; results and discussion, 145–55; socially prescribed gender roles and, 150–51, 153; societal discrimination and, 155

YRBS (Youth Risk Behavior Survey), 142